WHAT DO YOU PACK?
IF YOU'RE NEVER COMING BACK...

Fifteen True Stories of
Those Who Left Their Past Behind

Roberto Di Marco

Orchid Press

Roberto Di Marco
WHAT DO YOU PACK? IF YOU'RE NEVER COMING BACK…
Fifteen True Stories of Those Who Left Their Past Behind

First published in Italian, as *Cosa ti porti dietro se sai di non tornare più?*,
Milano 2007

First English edition, copyright © Roberto Di Marco, 2014

ORCHID PRESS
P.O. Box 1046,
Silom Post Office,
Bangkok 10504, Thailand

www.orchidbooks.com

Protected by copyright under the terms of the International Copyright Union: all rights reserved. Except for fair use in book reviews, no part of this publication may be reproduced in any form or by any means, electronic or mechanical, including photocopying, recording, or by any information storage or retrieval system without prior permission in writing from the copyright holder.

Disclaimer: While the accounts contained within are based on true life stories, some of the names of places and individuals have been changed or supressed to protect the identities of those involved.

ISBN 978-974-524-152-7

Contents

Preface — vii

1 From Italy to Indonesia — 1
   Once upon a time in Bali

2 From Spain to the Philippines — 21
   'Have You Seen This Man?'

3 From France to Brazil — 41
   I've done it all for my wife

4 From Italy to Cambodia — 59
   Screwed by The System

5 From Romania to America — 85
   I met a man with a secret

6 From America to Japan — 99
   The geisho

7 From Italy to India — 113
   A life, a hundred lives

8 From Denmark to Thailand — 136
   I got a discount because she'd been in jail.

9 From Italy to South Africa — 150
   I felt at home nowhere

10 From Sweden to Yemen — 159
   Goodbye to the Mommy State

11 From Germany to Thailand — 169
   Smiling all the way to the crematory

12 From England to Ethiopia — 186
   Escaping from my own mind

13	From Italy to Laos *Only a communist really appreciates capitalism*	209
14	From Russia to China and Switzerland *The world is my home*	221
15	From Italy to Siberia *A second chance at life*	236

About the Author 259

Praise for the Italian edition of*
What Do You Pack? If You're Never Coming Back...

Today on the Internet you can invent a second life, another yourself, but between virtual and real life there is a big difference. Roberto Di Marco went to investigate those who have chosen to reinvent themselves in distant lands. **Marina Roscani**, Corriere Adriatico.

This book invites us to look inside of ourselves. It's an honest, engaging testimony in which we can recognize our own states of mind and gain a clear view of the adopted countries, from the inside as well as from the outside... but sometimes with a hint of nostalgia for our roots. It gives us an awareness of being the masters of our own fate and not just victims of the System. **Anna Maspero**, Acomeavventura, March 2008.

Extreme but interesting stories. Il Tirreno.

The wanderer above the sea of mists painted by Caspar David Friedrich shows us man facing the great expanse of nature, seeking answers. It's an image that makes you think, that is emblematic of romantic feeling: escape, infinity, freedom from earthly trifles. The latest book by Roberto Di Marco manages to capture the same feelings that reverberate throughout humanity. **Francesca Del Grande**. Latina Oggi, August 2007.

The expatriate hovers on the edge of two worlds and enjoys the feeling of foreignness and spontaneity, free of role-playing and formality. **Claudio Visentin**, Sole 24 Ore, November 2007.

The stories recount real introspective journeys through new worlds and unknown landscapes, in which one must question the certainties accumulated during an entire lifetime. An engaging, dramatic and passionate text that tells of the real conditions of life in foreign countries, known otherwise only by the clichés of the media. **Melina Chiapparino**, ROMA, September 2007.

The discovery of new countries evolves into revelations about yourself, as your involvement in new surroundings reveals unknown sides of your consciousness. Nuovo Rieti Oggi, September 2007.

The book is a fascinating mix of adventure... We live the daily life of foreign countries and understand the mechanisms that have allowed some of the characters to fit into a new culture. **Patrizia Andriola**, CulturaSpettacolo.it, July 2007.

There are those who, one day, made the big leap, who chose to invent another life. La Repubblica, July 2007.

Romantic but interesting stories. **Claudio Paglieri**, Il Secolo XIX.

* review excerpts translated from the original Italian

PREFACE

We all know them, or at least know of them—the ones who escaped, who left their lives behind and never returned.
What were they running from—or to?
Was it for escape, for adventure, or just to improve their lives?
How did they do it? How did they cope?
Did they reconstruct their lives abroad? Are they better off?
What are their real stories?

In the following pages all of these questions, and many more, will be answered. The reader will meet fifteen individuals who left friends, family, jobs, entire lives behind and set out to start again. You will hear their stories firsthand, in their own voices, telling you who and what they are, describing their own situations and motives. Some will be more likeable than others. Some you may consider to be brave, others perhaps cowards. One or two seem slightly mad while most others seem just like the fellow in the next office, the girl down the road, or even you or me.

At first the journeys might seem easy—getting away may be the easiest part. But how does one really adapt to total separation from one's roots?

During any travel, even extreme journeys, we usually remain anchored to our culture, and on returning home we are welcomed back by the familiar—places and objects, people and customs. But how do we react if, by choice or otherwise, we're transplanted into an environment totally alien to what we know? To what extent can you bring your past with you, and to what degree will you compromise it?

While some of the stories tell of a migration to a richer country, several describe what it's like to adapt to a place far less developed than the 'home' they left behind. Regardless of the choice, the reader will breathe the real air of the faraway destinations that these permanent expats chose, will learn from these firsthand accounts of the ups and downs of the change and to what degree the traveller eventually managed to integrate into his or her new environment.

The stories in this book are a rich mix of adventure, information and yes, even practical advice for those who are considering just such a change.

The book has been organized on the basis of each individual's motive to make the change. The first division is between those who escaped—the fugitives—and those who deliberately chose to live in a foreign country. A further subdivision among the voluntary expats separates those who leave for adventure and improvement and those who are escaping from an unhappy present life. All of these subdivisions, of course, are only constructs—in reality every one of us has a unique set of personal dissatisfactions and complex motives of our own.

"One day I will escape!" Did it ever cross your mind? Escape from what? From bureaucracy, from sleepy suburbs, from the same faces at the bar, from your partner, from politics, from the cold, from evenings in front of the TV? The fallacy that life is eternal makes us put off indefinitely everything that seems most difficult. The fears of such a move provide a handy alibi. Better leave it to the adventurers! Those who have no ties, who have no mortgage. One day perhaps—if I win the Lottery.

But it's not necessary to be stressed or chased to want to flee. It's a latent thought that lurks in every one of us.

In an appendix to every story, a brief summary of the psychological motivations of the characters aims to provide the reader some food for further thought, without pretending to give a definitive interpretation.

1

From Italy to Indonesia
Once upon a time in Bali

A man from Calabria, age 38:

Here everyone calls me Jo. I changed my name—you never know. I used to have an optician's shop doing discreetly well; I was married for 15 years, with a 13 year old daughter.

We had our little house with a garden and orchard, and I did not expect much more than what I already had from life, apart from a little more money, which never hurts. I had travelled abroad only once, with my wife, to Paris on our honeymoon and for some years we had dreamed of taking a cruise; we had our passports ready.

But there was always a little obstacle—like the mother-in-law who didn't feel well or the daughter who needed a little mountain air—and so the cruise was postponed to the next year.

At that time there were small-time extortionists around, who didn't give you a hard time if you weren't afraid of them. You could sense the presence of the police and of the state authorities, albeit at alternating times.

Then there had been a period of apparent calm, and I didn't realize that a strong mafia group had been established in my little city, so when a guy came by to ask for a 'favour', I kicked him out of my store. Unfortunately I am allergic to bully boys; I can't control myself. I end up completely losing my head and I may become more violent than them.

Nobody had died—I thought the matter was over; I'd sent a petty criminal off to lick his wounds somewhere. One morning I went to drive the car out my garage, as usual. I press the button of the remote control and I notice that the garage door does not roll down.

I think perhaps it could be that batteries in the remote control are dead. I get out of the car, go inside the garage, and pull down the door manually from the inside. Soon I realize that someone had forced it; sneaked in during the night to tamper with something. In fact, as soon as I lowered the rolling door, the car exploded. The garage door saved my life, because closing it from the inside shielded me from the blast. The door didn't collapse but it was ruined. That's why I survived virtually unhurt.

Of course, for the perpetrators, I should have been inside the car, or better, between the car and the sheet metal door. It wasn't a warning, or otherwise they would just have damaged my shop when there was no one there. They wanted to murder me in a spectacular way, to make me an example, to intimidate, to let everyone understand that they meant business. The message was clear—at that moment they were the only game in town and anyone who dared to oppose them would come to a bad end. At that point, in both a panic and a fury, I grabbed all the cash I had at home, tossed a few essentials into a backpack and ran out, without even waiting for my wife to come back from the market.

I quickly wrote a few notes on a piece of paper which I left on the kitchen table: "Honey, I'm fine; don't worry. I'll call you as soon as possible." As soon as I left my home, I called the bank saying that I had to withdraw a big amount of cash and I took the first available bus leaving town. Then, as soon as I could, I phoned my wife, trying to calm her down and to convince her to join me quickly in Rome, at a house there that my brother rented and used occasionally, but which, fortunately, was unoccupied just then. She was in shock; the house was swarming with cops. She couldn't completely come to terms with what had happened, nor could she make a decision. She was thinking about moving to her sister's house just a few kilometers away from our home. Imagine how easy it would be for them to find her there!

One morning in Rome, I left my brother's apartment and went to take the lift to the ground floor. When the lift door opened I was confronted with a face that I instantly recognized. I did not give him the time to act or to pull out a gun. I had an alertness, a speed of movement, that even surprised myself, since I hadn't trained in a gym for a long time.

I grabbed him by the throat until he almost lost consciousness, and I banged his head repeatedly against the glass wall of the lift. Maybe it was fear or the strength of my despair that suddenly turned me into a sort of Rambo character. Then I quickly ran out, guessing that his accomplice was waiting outside. In fact, outside of the main door, I saw a fellow on a motorcycle, who, strangely, didn't notice me.

At that moment a lot of people were coming and going so I tried to mingle in with the crowd and disappear without leaving a trace. They had been able to find out my brother's address. At that point they would have chased me to the moon! Obviously I should have complied with their requests in the first place! Then I learned that the fellow I had thrashed in the first encounter was a powerful member of the local mafia—the son of the boss—and I had fractured several of his ribs and put him in hospital.

At that point it was also difficult for me to rejoin my wife. She was in danger as well. I was calling her all the time, pleading with her to lock up the house and the shop and run away somewhere. We could keep in contact by phone or through our relatives and friends and then we could meet somewhere more secret and safe. She insisted that I had to go to the police, but I didn't trust anyone any more. I was shocked by the ease with which they had found me. I felt that I had to disappear, to evaporate, get away as far as possible from those criminals.

I decided then to transfer some money from my account to Switzerland. I could have sent money from my account in Italy but if the bank knew where to send the money, the police and maybe the mafia as well could find out, considering that they have informers everywhere. I had fallen into such a state of paranoia that I saw informers, persecutors and mafia messengers everywhere. Better to use the utmost caution and carry the cash in hand, even if you risk the border police confiscating cash in excess of the twenty thousand euro duty-free allowance.

Meanwhile I had to wait for a couple of days before a branch office of my bank in Rome could deliver the money to me. I slept in a boarding house for immigrants near the terminal station and, early in the morning, I showed up at the bank at opening time.

I withdrew the cash, took a bus and a train and got to Chiasso. From there, thanks to the advice of an old schoolmate living in Milan, I crossed over into Switzerland by foot via Mt. Generoso, at Val d'Intelvi, close to Como. You reach the top after a two hour walk along an uphill road until you see a line and a sign on the ground which says 'Italy–Switzerland'. Nothing more. There are no customs; there is absolutely nothing around—just a small restaurant and the little train station, probably located there on purpose.

My wife, meanwhile, was at a loss as to what to do; she hesitated and had not yet decided to join me. She gave the ridiculous excuse that our daughter had to attend a school play. Then I was unable to contact her anymore. I was told by a relative that both women had entered into a protection system—that's all. But I had no idea about the details of this protection system. For a while, they could not give me any more news. At that moment it was better not to expose myself. I contacted a friend of mine by phone, who had some links with the underworld. He suggested to me to change my location frequently to avoid being found by them, as even the phone lines could be monitored.

From Switzerland, via various flights and connections not even clear to me now, somehow I ended up in Jakarta. I had abandoned the idea of staying in Europe because the cost of living was higher, and there was a greater probability of being traced. Indonesia is one of the most densely populated nations in the world with over two hundred million people and about twelve thousand islands. Jakarta itself is a city of about ten million inhabitants.

Meanwhile, from the fragmentary news I could obtain by calling relatives and friends, I learned that my wife and daughter had moved to some locality in the States where one of our relatives was living, and where, as soon as possible, we could meet up again. From what I understood, it seems that there are bilateral agreements between Italy and the USA to deal with such situations.

The city of Jakarta seems to be entirely cast in concrete and divided evenly between more-or-less decent houses and slums. Pollution and traffic are everywhere. The subway is awful: it has no lights, so when you enter a tunnel, you are in total darkness. Some people climb onto the roof of the coaches to avoid paying the ticket, despite the presence of electric cables and notices warning that it's dangerous. Some coaches have no doors. A beggar passes through another one: children come through with portable karaoke music, singing songs. Blind and crippled men with no arms or legs. It's worse than the subway in Rome.

There is a neighbourhood with very few tourists around—Jalan Jacsa—which has cheap guest houses. It's nothing but a crossroad with four internet cafes. There is the sea, but it's filthy. There are islands in view; those look beautiful!

A few days later I moved to Bogor, 80 kilometers from Jakarta: a 'small town' of 800,000 inhabitants—at least that's considered small for Indonesia, where cities are far more crowded than in Europe.

I could move easier now, by foot or motor scooter. I did nothing much; just went to a bank, opened a bank account and asked for a safety deposit box. Afterwards I rented a quiet room with cooking facilities, in a guest house, at a very low rate. At night it was pitch dark. Apart from Jakarta and tourist spots, in Indonesia there is no street illumination. One has to go out with a flashlight or had better come back before dark. Until night-time the market is open and is full of life. Then, with the flashlight, you can see people sleeping, with only cardboard boxes for shelter.

Considering that there was no news from my wife, I started to think that I could stop for awhile in Bogor. As good a place as any there, where you could shop for essentials for just a few Rupiahs, come back to your room, eat and survive. Yet even there, after a short while, I became restless again.

Some tourists and I met in a restaurant; together we rented a minibus with a driver and set out to cross the island of Java from its north to its south coast.

I introduced myself with the name of Jo, trying to look like one more tourist among many. I smiled distractedly and pretended to participate, listening to their small talk. We climbed to over a thousand meters in altitude. We visited tea and pepper plantations and reached the halfway point between the north and south Java coasts, to a village called Garut, which featured spas with natural hot springs coming from a nearby volcano. Here I spoke to everyone.

But I really didn't feel like sharing in the company of holiday-makers. I felt uncomfortable, like a fish out of water. Some of their questions gave me trouble as well, such as: "How many days are you staying?" What I can't stand, when you are abroad, is that the minute you say you're Italian, they think of the Mafia. And every time that happened, it reminded me of my own painful involvement with those thugs.

I stopped in Garut for about a month. I soaked all day in the hot springs, men on one side and women on the other. I had not realized before that in Indonesia almost all of the population are Muslims. In the evening I could take a hot bath in my room—in each guest house the rooms had hot mineral water piped in from the volcano right to your tub. All for five dollars a night.

Of course I was still concerned about the cost because I had no idea how long I would have to remain in hiding. My little room was not exactly luxurious—it was completely bare and even lacked a mosquito net.

So I decided to bide my time there for at least a month, to see if things would cool down, and then I would try by all means to rejoin my wife. I had not yet recovered from the shock of being twelve thousand kilometers away from home. For hours I remained in the tub, half dazed. It relaxed me, helped to loosen my tension. I was still in shock from the unpredictability of my fate, and how my life had changed overnight.

I was also taking long walks, to try to calm my nerves and get rid of the stress that had accumulated since the day of my escape. The landscape, too, seemed designed to induce relaxation. Everywhere crops of rice, with the volcano mirrored in the marshes. The only contacts with my wife were through mutual friends, but often a different one each time.

I kept hearing from her that she didn't want to stay far from home much longer. Then, in an act of boldness or irresponsibility, she returned home with our daughter. After all, she didn't think that these thugs would attack her for an offense that I had perpetrated. It was not a matter of betrayal or slight—it was a personal matter between me and the boss's son, who couldn't accept being beaten by me. The police had, however, guaranteed to protect her and to post a patrol car in front of the house. But, despite that, just down the street from our home, she was approached by a boy who was playing nearby who warned her that "their account with me" was still not settled. Clearly some Mafioso had approached the boy and had given him a present in return for warning my wife with those words, that the boy probably didn't even comprehend. Understandably, my wife did not want to face the difficulties and consequences of being away from home. But by this move she had compromised our chance to get back together somewhere.

What to do at this point? Should I go back too and live under constant surveillance? If I had done so it would have put both her and my daughter's life at risk—we would have had to live with the nightmare possibility of the three of us being blown up.

The only choice I had was to wait, but I didn't even know what for and for how long. It was a matter of allowing time to pass in the hope that a solution might develop. But, for now, all was pitch dark! The separation from my family, without any idea of when we would meet again, disheartened me to the point that I fell into a severe depression. I began to feel an impotent rage. I had to surrender to the necessity of continuing to live in this absurd situation. And who knew for how much longer!

Of course I gave no one a forwarding address—I would have exposed the fact that I was thousands of kilometers away. Would my wife wait until my return? Or would she perhaps find a new love? It was a concrete possibility as my wife was still an attractive woman.

I tormented myself thinking which one would be the suitor. I speculated on various acquaintances, who might be the more likely, in my opinion, to take advantage of this situation. At the end I concluded that everyone would have been interested to console her, since I had been forced into exile. I was not even sure if I would ever be able to return home, as it's well known that the mafia never forgets and never forgives.

Cut off from your home environment and living in isolation, you end up in a frustrated rage that hurts yourself. The brain goes off on its own tangents, with thousands of paranoid ideas, and you start creating all sorts of nightmare scenarios: "My wife will hate me," I thought, "She will curse me for what I have done."

I imagined a series of catastrophic consequences about which I still feel guilty. My daughter will definitely be traumatized. If I had just bowed my head like everyone else, now I'd be at home to help her with her homework. The "protection money" would just have been the price of family serenity, a tax just like any other tax you have to pay for living in peace.

I spent whole days isolated, locked in my hotel room, without seeing or hearing anyone. Once, I even thought I heard the voices of my wife and daughter chatting in the room next to mine. I almost began to hallucinate! My mind kept returning to the start of that fateful day, trying to block out all that had happened since—pretending that all was still normal and that nothing had interfered with our lives. For me it was as if time had stopped at the moment of that explosion. As if in a slow motion movie, I returned back to that instant just before my normal life had stopped, to that morning when, oblivious of everything, I left the garage to go to work, just a few seconds before the explosion, while I was thinking that perhaps my wife should go on a little diet... My whole horizon was enclosed in that short stretch of road from home to shop. From there I had fled, and back there I wanted to return. I did not give a damn for Indonesia, or eternal summer, the sea, its islands, its volcanoes, its natural beauty...

I knew that the police had decided to withdraw the surveillance car that had been assigned to my wife, because, according to them, as long as I didn't return she was in no further danger.

There was, moreover, the problem of how to spend the time, the unlimited time on my hands. The days seemed to pass in slow motion. Sometimes I joined a few occasional tourists but surely they felt something strange about me. I didn't have the typical energy that a tourist might have, visiting a great place and living life intensely. Luckily reading helped me a little to fill the days. Sometimes I read but I found it difficult to concentrate because other thoughts were swirling around in my head. I had managed to pick up some books in Italian and more in English left behind by tourists passing through. I consulted a little dictionary when reading English and took two weeks to finish a book, sometimes without understanding a thing.

I do not want to drag the reader through every place I went. I did visit Malaysia several times. I always carried a large sum of money with me, which would allow me to leave the country suddenly, if needed. Often I wandered aimlessly—I was a forced tourist. But then you have also to live life as it happens to you, otherwise you fall into such a state of apathy that you might not be able to recover from it. You need to get a life where you are, create relations, interests, leisure pursuits, even if it makes you suffer when you think you are separating yourself more and more from your home environment, from your family. And your wife could be doing the same, building a new life without you. While I was plagued with jealousy, on the other hand I was starting to feel the lack of a woman in flesh and bones, of her physical presence.

In Malaysia it was useless to think about it. The religious police are constantly looking for anyone who indulges in casual affairs, especially married women who betray their husbands. There are even suicides to escape the religious police. I was in a place with swimming pools, artificial waves and water slides. There were mostly all males and the few women present were covered in black, jumping into the water with all of their clothes on. Meanwhile some women tourists, feeling uncomfortable, put towels around their waists.

The place where I spent more time was Pandagaran, on Java's south coast. The place is quiet; they make a little money from local tourism. The beaches are decent, the sea is clean and there are inexpensive places where you can sleep and eat—only three dollars for half board. I gave my passport to an agency and they returned it a few days later, with the visa renewed for another two months. It is not supposed to be possible to do this, but because of my European nationality, they didn't exercise too much control. It is just assumed that you are a tourist—and besides I was paying too! I used to fish in the bays and journeyed into the forest by river boat. Occasionally I encountered some rare visitors.

There are places where you can have a couple of beers but there are no discos or anything like that. I slept like crazy. Apart from the beaches, there was nothing. I was watching the seagulls fly, hour after hour. Sometimes I slept in a boat anchored in the bay. In the morning I was woken up by the jarring sound of the gulls and watched the sun peeping out over the side of the boat.

There you can appreciate such things because there is nothing else. The pleasure of seeing the sun rise! I would go out to fish on my own; sometimes I gave the fish to a restaurant as a gift, and in return I ate for free. I ate rice and fish every day. It's better not to talk about pork... But there was something in the air that I can't explain. I almost lost the sense of time passing. Eventually I began to learn the Indonesian language, because it's quite easy. It is also spoken in Malaysia. You speak it as it's written, as in Italian. Their grammar is very simple too, it has no future or past tense—past is indicated by using their word for 'before' and future with their word for 'after'. It's kind of like Esperanto. They've created an easy common language for a country where the people spoke fifty different languages. The locals treated me well—I was invited to their parties and weddings. During their festivals they become elated, they told jokes, bursting with joy and a zest for life that made me feel a little uncomfortable. I understood that I was a foreigner, having arrived from a strange country where people are increasingly distrustful and unable to express their simple emotions, to be excited by little things. Where I was then, on the contrary, you could feel a simple, naive trust in the world and in others, perhaps something that we have lost.

They also did everything to integrate me into the group. They brought me trays with fried bananas and a dessert they made, with eggs, grated coconut and cinnamon, a sort of stuffed pancake. And they asked me questions continuously, just so that I was not left alone. The hotel where I stayed looked like something out of Disneyland—a fanciful garden with buildings of all different colors. From my room I could enter directly into the pool area, a spa built of stone, with glass lanterns in the shape of a butterfly and a stone dragon as a shower. The bathroom toilet was a liberty-style chair. At the beginning I did not recognize what it was! I was sitting in the garden under a pergola, reading, when the waitress came to ask me what I wished to eat—it was the restaurant!

In this hotel I secretly met a Muslim widow, 34 year old, who had no children and worked at the reception desk. Being a widow, she could speak with other men. Of course, we could not afford to take a walk on the beach hand in hand in front of everybody, but I was contented. She dressed in jeans, long shirt sleeves and wore sandals on her feet. She was slender, a little taller than average, with two large black eyes that made her seem almost Indian, elegant in her movements, like all Orientals. But she always wore a veil on her head and a scarf around her neck that sometimes covered half of her face.

Speaking with other tourists, when I told them that I had been there for months, they must have thought I was crazy, because usually tourists would get bored after two or three days in the place.

But I was not that kind of tourist, who could splash out money for a few weeks. I had to deal with my economic realities and staying in Pandagaran, not being a popular tourist destination, allowed me to live on the bare essentials. Nevertheless, I can't say that I was uncomfortable. It's hard to explain. Catapulted into this remote place, distant from the family that, until that moment, had been my only reason for living, there were times I felt alright, but at the same time, for some reason, I also felt a strange anxiety.

There was an Australian tourist who scandalized the local people because she would drop by the minimarket dressed in her swimming costume. They demanded that she cover herself. If a female tourist walks around alone, she is often stopped and if she is not married, they ask her why. For them, a woman traveling alone is unbecoming. Imagine if she enters into a minimarket in a swimming costume! For this reason the Australian wanted me to accompany her all the while she was in Pandagaran. She did not feel free to walk around alone.

Then, like lightning, I had to escape again, this time not from the mafia, but from Pandagaran.

The widow came to me very upset and told me to leave Pandagaran immediately. Someone had discovered our relationship. She had had a violent argument with her deceased husband's brother, so we ran the risk of being arrested. I understood immediately that I was sticking my neck out. I was a Christian, an infidel. My word was worth nothing in the face of their law.

I would have preferred to have escaped alone. We had had brief, fleeting encounters, without having the time to get to know each other. And then we never had too much to say. Sometimes she gave me a massage, or cut my toenails. But she was desperate, in tears, begging me to take her away with me. She feared the vengeance of the Muslim community. The brother-in-law would probably have killed her or have had her imprisoned, so in the end I could not help but take her with me. It was a big risk, however, because I was becoming responsible, an accomplice to her escape. It would be a cruel twist of fate to escape from the mafia and end up being knocked off by a Muslim!

We fled quickly in the night, in the direction of Yogyakarta, which is 200 kilometers away. To reach it takes a day trip by bus, three hours by boat on a river and then another bus ride. Yogyakarta is a fairly lively tourist destination but aside from a couple of tourist enclaves it was still very much a Muslim country. In the evening we went to eat at the base of the temple of Borobudur, a unique and spectacular place protected by UNESCO, where every night a play was staged.

My companion always wore a contrite and afflicted expression, while I pondered abandoning her, although I would have felt myself a worm if I had. I understood her predicament very well—like me, she had suddenly been thrown out of her world, her home, her environment. I should have felt a sense of communion with her. Instead, at times, I hated her because I felt she was a chain around my neck, the cause of my umpteenth flight. And then I linked her to the Muslim world, to a closed mentality that had once again forced me to flee. I could barely stand the sight of her.

She was obviously aware of my feelings, and knew that I had risked, and was still risking, my neck for her. So she tried to humour me, to be as little a burden as possible. But behind her passivity, I sensed a character that was neither easy nor malleable. If I criticised a little, telling her to lighten up, try to appear less Muslim, take off, for example, her veil and wear shorts, so as to blend in more easily among the tourists, she seemed to take offense and clam up. I hated her stupidity. Any other woman, realizing I had saved her, would have softened her behaviour.

Our dialogue was mostly silent, like the dumb, made up of glances and gestures, because, as I said, conversation with her was not the most brilliant. Once we were safe, I would dump her—I waited for the right moment. I would give her a sum of money and thereafter she would have to fend for herself. I had to think of myself. I could not be saddled with yet another problem.

One night in the guest house, while we were in bed, we heard loud noises coming from the reception desk. She immediately recognized the voice of her brother-in-law and I broke out in a cold sweat. How the hell had he found us? Fortunately, the manager of the hotel did not allow him to come up. I said to her, "Let's talk with him. Perhaps if you give up voluntarily, he would feel compassionate and stop persecuting us." I saw her crestfallen face, on the verge of tears. It was useless. I was involved and I could not leave her at the mercy of a furious madman.

With the help of the receptionist, we arranged for an unmarked taxi to wait for us in an alley behind the hotel at 2AM. From the second floor we went out onto the roof of the garage and from there, risking broken bones, we jumped down to the street. Fortunately, we escaped with just a few slight bruises. We decided to go to Bali—at least it was Hindu, without many restrictions. In Indonesia there are only two non-Muslim areas. One is Bali and the other one the infamous Christian East Timor. In a crowded tourist spot it would be harder to find us. And in an international environment, we would definitely feel more safe and secure.

By the following evening we arrived on the island of Bali and from there, on a bus, travelled up to Kuta, the most famous area of the island. The bus, from ferry to hotel, took five hours to travel only 120 km, due to our constant stops to pick up passengers! After a full night and day of travel we arrived completely exhausted and we took the first hotel we came across without even knowing where we were.

In the morning we went to breakfast. Not even a waiter approached. We wanted to go out but they stopped us. Everything was closed! Even the kitchen was closed; we were forbidden to go swimming. There was no traffic on the roads; nothing but an eerie silence. The police had the task of ensuring that no one came out from hotels and houses. Even the international airport was closed. All of this because once a year there are evil spirits who return to Bali, and to ensure that they leave they must be convinced that the island is uninhabited. I was shocked. An employee of the hotel, moved to pity, served us white rice.

I had stumbled into a world of fairy tales, a primitive, enchanted world. The next day was the resurrection! Great animation all around. There were many kites in the air, all tied to stakes—in Bali there is a constant breeze—look up and you always see kites. Bali is a continuous celebration; there is nothing like it anywhere else in the world.

That evening we saw a crowd of people who watched the sunset from the beach at Kuta. I have seen people climbing up the trees to watch the sunset. Foreigners arriving here are fascinated by this festive atmosphere, this curious symbiosis of nature, magic and people. It is the Hindu religion, which considers that every member of the living world, including plants, has a soul. And everything is ruled by spirits: the spirit of the rain, the spirit of the birds, of the sea, of the wind, of the woods. And, as a result, every day is a celebration.

In the morning you can see the hotel girl rolling banana leaves into small baskets, filling these with little sweets, then preparing drinks, garnishing it all with flowers and then leaving them as offerings at a little nearby shrine. In this way she draws away the evil spirits—and summons the rats, attracted to the food. There are ceremonies for all occasions. The Balinese are afraid of everything because there are spirits everywhere, ready to ambush them. Discipline is imposed on Hindu society by means of the caste system—the upper caste Brahmins use the bogeyman of the spirits to control the other castes.

My companion had created a new identity for herself by buying a driver's licence under another name, even though she did not know how to drive a bike; the cost was only $20. In hotels she registered under her new name, Ni—thus she became Balinese.

She spoke little, as usual. She was like a shadow, still disoriented and uncomfortable, partially because it was the first time she had ever been outside of Muslim society. But I almost did not recognize her when she wore shorts, to better blend in with tourists when we strolled past the shops and stalls selling local crafts (I had finally been able to convince her!) It's strange to say but I had never really noticed her beautiful, slender legs, her grace, her delicate manners and her almost aristocratic demeanour. I saw her with new eyes, more casual and relaxed, more beautiful, and I felt pleasure having her by my side.

It was as I had seen her in Bali for the first time. I just could not believe her miraculous metamorphosis. Evidently, in her home environment, I had lumped her in with other Muslim women in general. However, she had a strange sort of character, almost like two personalities, one totally in contrast with the other. On one side she had the rudeness of which I spoke earlier, a kind of armour, a closed disposition, and on the other side she was extremely sensitive. She could become excited or grow sad at the slightest thing. I began to accept her hardness that, in reality, seemed to be a form of defense, a type of pride and reserve. Sometimes, living together, I almost confused her with my wife, especially in the morning when, half asleep, I felt her body next to mine. And then I was racked with guilt. We had become a couple like many around us. In Bali there are many Muslim girls—out of their environment, they have escaped restrictions and behave more freely. They have no problem getting together with Western tourists. They often become quite sophisticated.

One evening, on a beach, just a few meters away from us, there was another couple. She was slender, about 50, and was accompanied by a boy who could have been her son's age. They started to kiss each other with such passion that they seemed to be very close to the sexual act. Ni was visibly annoyed and uncomfortable, but did not dare protest. She indicated to me that we had better get up and leave immediately. But up until then, I had adapted myself to Islamic customs—now it was up to her to adapt. For me, the scene was something poetic, with the background of the sea at sunset, and an almost deserted beach. Then we started chatting with the couple and, after less than half an hour, they invited us to their villa in Ubud, a unique artists' colony on the island.

There are courses offered there, of all types, such as wood

carving, sculpture and painting. You can learn how to make kites, and to bless them. One sleeps in guest houses that look like temples, surrounded by rice fields and you can also gaze out at a landscape of rice fields sitting at a bar, with tables built onto trees!

This French couple lived in a Balinese style villa with swimming pool, a large covered patio without walls and a huge oversized bed with mosquito net. It resembled a house scattered throughout a garden—one room here, one kitchen there. There was also a small artificial watercourse that passed by all the rooms. They used a model boat to send messages from room to room down the stream. At the end of the garden, there was a terraced slope, with lighting, by night, coming from underwater in a patch of growing rice! In a corner of the house I found nine women who sewed. The woman had designed an article consisting of a veil and two flowers; she paid $40 a month to the dressmakers and exported all of the finished product to France. For the price of a single dressmaker in Paris she was able to pay for the villa and all of her staff in Bali. She, Susette, was a fashion designer. She went around dressed in a simple sarong that left part of her breast uncovered. She looked like a woman used to the respect of others. Despite her mature age, she still exuded a certain sex appeal. The man, Pierre, with long brown hair tied in a ponytail, baggy silk pants, open shirt, broad shoulders, had a big dragon tattooed on his shoulder. Every morning he practiced the Chinese art of *tai chi* for an hour.

We were guests in their house; we joked like kids and told each other everything—even the sort of nonsense that usually you only think about, but don't voice. Pierre was a brilliant cook—he was a well qualified chef. His specialty was cakes made with carrots. He served up carrot cakes to us at all hours. In the evening we went to the disco. Ni was the only one who was a little out of tune with the rest of us, because she never let herself go completely. One evening, perhaps because she felt particularly close with us and did not want to feel excluded or perhaps because we were terribly insistent and she just could not say no, she agreed to try a drink of whiskey.

She had only a few drinks and her head began to spin; she was in high spirits and split her sides with laughter at Pierre's erotic tales of when he worked as a waiter on a cruise ship.

A little alcohol was enough to demolish her defenses.

Pierre's stories were like something out of *The Thousand and One Nights*. Perhaps he exaggerated a little as well—from the homosexual who waited for him in his room with the bed strewn with hundred dollar bills, to the lady who he found half-naked in bed while her husband was hiding in the closet. Pierre was very self-centered, but he could really tell a good story.

We talked, we laughed, we drank. We had tea with carrot cake at two in the morning. And lots of music! There, on that terrace, with the background of the pool, the four of us were dancing. Individually, we had nothing in common: a Muslim bigot, closed and reserved; a fashion designer, snobby, authoritarian and sensual; a narcissistic young man and a fugitive, a former family man, all home and work. On any other occasion we would barely have looked at or greeted each other.

Outside of your usual environment, you can become attuned to people who, in your country, you would never dream of having anything to do with. Away from home many formalities and roles fall away. Maybe it is because these are people you might know for only ten days, but they are more intense days.

Pierre had all of Fred Bongusto's CDs, but he had never been to Italy. That night, Ni also let herself go—her dancing had a very composed style, focused on slight movements of her hips, which enchanted me. Susette was a volcano, but Pierre especially was an irresistible dancer. He danced to the loud music like a belly dancer, in an incredibly fluid way. Then Pierre and Susette began a strange dance, which I had never seen before, made up of body touches. Susette had a black blouse with holes and shorts jeans covering half of her buttocks. Pierre was dressed simply in a pink singlet, bathing suit and baseball cap. The dance became more and more violent and intense. Susette's face was angry and she began to pull furiously at Pierre's singlet, to the point where the situation seemed to be degenerating. Previously there had been a jealous scene because Pierre had received a call from his ex-lover. In reality the whole scene just became part of the dance and had the sense of a game. They liked to play—they were masters of melodrama. Even a fight, for them, was nothing but a game, a way to perform a theater piece in which Ni and I were the only spectators. Then they let that anger pass, and begun kissing furiously.

Ni seemed relaxed and amused. In reality we had her drugged with alcohol; we had not been loyal. But at least she was quiet, her eyes were charmed, amused, rather than wearing that tough expression of detachment and unease. Surely the context, the situation of being far from home, helped her to feel more loose. Who knows why, but sometimes I thought that we might all go to bed together, as a natural consequence of the place, the unique atmosphere of living a life without schedule, beyond the 'normal' world. Perhaps our resistances would crumble as we cast aside our education, personal and cultural differences. Of course, it was one of those weird ideas that pass through the mind, without actually thinking, even remotely, of putting it into practice. The intercourse between Pierre and Susette that, initially, seemed to be turning into a 'red light' show, changed once again into something poetic: a long, endless scene of cuddles and kisses by the pool. Pierre held Susette, who basked in his arms and whispered to him in a voice like a little child's.

We rented two motorbikes and went on a trip to the island of Lembongan, known as "the island of turtles." Occasionally we spotted a pickup carrying turtles, of 50- perhaps even 80 kilos, with their legs tied with wire, probably intended for some restaurant.

Following the pickup, we saw a lot of bamboo canes planted in the sea—these were farms with hundreds of turtles. In Bali there is a tribe of ancient natives who don't have contact with anyone, either with Hindus, or with Muslims. They don't bury or cremate their dead, but instead take them out onto a little island in a lake, far away from their village, bind them to a tree and abandon them. After the vultures will come and nibble at the corpses. We went to see the hanging bodies, the shreds of human flesh at the mercy of the vultures—a ritual worthy of Alfred Hitchcock and Dario Argento combined. But for this tribe, evidently, it's not a horror scene. They see that the corpses of animals come to that end and they submit themselves to the same laws of nature.

Along the way you meet people who bathe in little rivers, women in the paddies who collect rice and smile at you. They wear batik fabrics and little caps and cut the rice with bare breast. They have always been so—they are Hindus. Then the Arabs arrived: a clash of civilizations between a serene, bare-breasted people full of song and the Muslims with all of their prohibitions and restrictions.

We went fishing. We watched the boats arrive, carrying baskets of fish, each with two colourful outriggers and a dragon's head painted on the bow, the same as it was a hundred years ago. Then the black frigate birds came swooping down to peck at thousands of fish leaping out of the water, all chased by a huge tuna with jaws open. It seemed that they were all staging a show in this wonderful sea with its colourful boats.

And I was drowning! I had been enchanted as I swam and watched the show all around me—and suddenly there was no more shore. I am a good swimmer but I had underestimated the waves. And what waves they were! They scooped you up and then dropped you down 20 meters. I could not get back. Then I felt my hands burning—they were covered with blood. The bottom was not sand but corals and I had washed up on the reef. Then Pierre came out with fins and a mask. He shouted, "Stop, come back, I will check." I had started to go further out to sea to avoid the sharp corals. Pierre found a field of algae under the water where there were no corals, perhaps two meters deep. "Follow me here." He gave me a fin and I followed him.

When I arrived on shore I embraced him. He had saved my life. Swimming here is not recommended—the waves can easily carry you away and suck you under. You have to be clever to get back out. You can try swimming in some little bay, but there are turtles, sharks and stone fish that have a powerful poison in a spine. They dig into the sand and lie in wait there—I've seen several with the spines already pointing up. Each wave brings in possible new prey. But, in the meantime, if you step on it wearing flip flops, it is like being struck by a cobra; you do not know if you will survive.

I have to admit that sometimes I forgot that I had a family in Italy, even though I would have a sudden mental flash to shake me up. And these were like open wounds. My wife and my daughter seemed so far away that I was almost afraid they had forgotten me.

I realized that I had left too many days without calling! But I didn't want to call them from Bali. Usually after I called I travelled at least 200 km. But every time I ended up hearing the same news and not even directly from my wife. I promised myself I would go to Singapore, not far from Bali, and phone my wife directly from there.

Between Ni and Susette, seemingly from two different planets, a strange bond was growing, a sort of magical complicity. They cooked and shopped together. Ni even began to abandon herself to the senses. She was much more at ease, yet still maintaining a slightly aloof attitude, a reserve which did not disturb me any more.

She was, however, definitely shaking off some of that stiffness, excessive modesty and shame due to the education she was receiving. Then these rooms without walls... you can imagine what the nights were like!

Now, she was fitting more and more into the role of wife. I was her man—perhaps something more than just a partner. I sensed in her an absolute dedication that went beyond a normal relationship. Since she had decided that I was her man, she lived according to me and all of my wishes. Out of her environment, she had only me in her world now and you could see that she was becoming tied more and more to me. After all I saved her life, kept her under my protection and provided her with an economic security. One evening, trying to defend me, she came between me and an Australian drunk who was lurching toward me with a bottle in his hand, after a stupid argument.

Once I went into a shop full of books. There was a table with two chairs: all very artistic as usual; gulls on a blank canvas as chandeliers. Suddenly a big man with a cleaver appeared. I felt trapped. That Muslim brother-in-law had found us. I was in panic!

But in fact, I had only entered a butcher shop. The owner was coming out of the refrigerator, a metal door with a big gong in bas relief. Bali is like this. You cannot be sure if you're at the restaurant or at the dentist. They are all artists. Here one feels realized when able to create something artistic, and not when one becomes rich or has a career as an engineer. In Italy, the cottage with a garden and the car had been my goal. Here the ability to decorate figurines or paint a picture means one has arrived. Everything is celebrated with a ritual. The rising of the sun is greeted with offerings.

I eventually resumed contact with my wife and daughter and soon we will embrace again. All three of us cried on the phone. The mafia gang that terrorized us in my little city is no more. They left behind a string of deaths and the police eventually made raids and arrested them all. Now there is another mafia group to replace them...

After all, I didn't kill anyone and I am not a witness under threat. My return will not mean that anyone else ends up in jail. So now my ordeal can finally be considered finished.

I lay on the bed, my eyes closed and hands behind my neck. I feel a tremendous sense of exhaustion; my legs tremble a little, as if all of the tension accumulated since the day of my escape comes down on me for the first time. Pretty soon I will begin my life again with my wife and daughter. I repeat this in my mind as a sort of mantra. But words float in the darkness, and I can barely absorb their real meaning. I will open a small kiosk, for Ni to sell pancakes. At least I will leave her with some good memories. Maybe—who knows—one day, I will return as a tourist, if my wife permits!

Postscript

A few days later, on October 12th, 2002, the now-infamous bomb attack at the Sari Club occurred, where Ni, Susette and Pierre all lost their lives and Jo barely escaped. There were 202 deaths in all. In October 2005 there was a second attack, resulting in 23 more deaths.

A Psychological Perspective

Throughout his life, Jo doggedly followed a traditional path without considering any other possibilities. Then, for the first time, he confronts a choice of two alternative ways of life. On one hand the family, the stability, the duty, the future preordained. On the other hand a life according to nature, more tied to the emotions, going beyond the norms, discovering the world. It is the eternal contradiction between our need for security and our desire for freedom, the choice between routine and adventure. In this case, the return to the family becomes for him a more deliberate, conscious and painful choice. Another person, having the ability to see a little farther beyond his nose, might make a different choice.

2

From Spain to the Philippines
'Have You Seen This Man?'

A Spanish man:

I was involved with several trading companies and was compelled to work hard just to make ends meet by the end of the month—not because of a lack of essentials but because of superfluous needs. My holiday cottage needs a new sofa; my daughter wants a new brand of handbag; my wife has to renew her cosmetics supply. Even when I was at home there was no escape—colleagues would chase me on my mobile phone. I was spending about two hours a day to commute to my office via the "ring road".

At home we had the typical problems of a Spanish family. Everybody needed money. My son's car needed repair. The water heater had to be serviced. I eliminated all expenditures on entertainment.

My wife was getting fatter and more petulant each year. We lived in her house, which previously had belonged to her father. I wasn't even able to get a normal home for my family. To be honest we did manage to buy a very tiny cottage close to the beach. In the off-chance that I had some spare time, I did not know what to do with it—I had even lost the ability to amuse myself. My daughter looked down on me because I was a clerk, while she socialized with high-class people. She blamed me because, although I had an engineering degree, I had not had a successful career; while I was an efficient clerk I was still just a subordinate. I had inherited a strip of land, but I had not built anything on it.

If my company were to have fired me I would have been jobless at forty-six. My daughter, being very beautiful, had a boyfriend, the son of a prominent lawyer, with a villa in Formigal. Both were students at the University.

For the past 17 years I had promised myself, "next year I'll spend a week on the ski slopes"—but of course that never materialized. Meanwhile my daughter was skiing regularly on my salary.

As a boy I had been active in sports. I am a former football player and had in past always kept in good shape, but now I was struggling to make it up two flights of stairs on foot. I was living only to bring money into the home and nothing more.

I found a job for my daughter but she was unable to keep it; she was fired and didn't tell me about it—I was not even consulted. A father should have some influence on the family; otherwise, what is a father for? My own father could command respect with just a glance.

And often, when I had to make a decision, my wife scolded me in front of our children. I asked myself, what kind of father am I? I'm a useless man; a mere spectre. My son reproached me, saying that once as a child I had beaten him and if I ever did it again, he would send me to the hospital. My daughter, at seventeen, decided to live alone and demanded that I pay the rent for her apartment. When I refused, she said that she would disown me as her father.

My sex life was reduced to four rapid moans; a Saturday evening quickie.

Then there was the beach house to put in order, where the boys never bothered to go.

One day I was admitted to a hospital for an emergency operation. I was given blood transfusions. My sons came to visit me only once, more or less "hit and run". And my wife, also beside me, was not the comfort I wished her to be. She seemed bloodless and treated me like a child.

We were married in 1975. My brother organized the bachelor party—a dinner with friends at Lloret, by the sea. He made me a present of eight million in postal savings bonds, which I kept hidden from my wife. In case of need I would have pulled it out as a nice surprise. Now the bonds were worth much more than sixty million.

Lying there in hospital I started thinking. What if I were to die? What have I accomplished in life? Working! Nothing but working!

And then I thought: "What if I were to give up everything and disappear?" At that moment the thought scared me. I tried to drive it out of my mind as ridiculous. I watched my family and I tried to imagine how they would react. I thought about it constantly for months—it became a fixation. I would wake up suddenly at night and I could not get back to sleep again. I looked at my wife, I wandered around the house, going to the bathroom, looking into the mirror. I said to myself: "Are you going crazy? What the hell do you have in your mind?"

Once, in the middle of the night, I started rummaging through a drawer of various atlases and geography books. While I was browsing, I looked up to see my wife just in front of me, in her nightgown, with her eyes wide open. It was like a horror movie. I felt caught in the act, even though she was miles away from imagining what was going through my mind.

Perhaps it was that very night that I made the decision to run away. And I must admit that the following days were the worst of my life. Sitting at the table with them, all totally unaware of what was about to happen, had become a sort of torture for me. But it was a decision which, by that point, I could not give up.

Of course I could have dealt with the situation in a civilized manner. I could have discussed it, dealt with the practical problems, the divorce, the separation of assets, the legal issues. But it would have been like twisting a knife in a wound. I needed a totally clean break, with no consequences to deal with. I did not understand why, but I had this raging urge to vanish without a trace. There was an element of revenge or malice, for which I felt guilty. The thought was like a seed that keeps swelling and then finally explodes.

On the one hand I did not wish to drag myself through the painful and distressing scenes of mutual accusation, lawyers, blackmail and revenge, and on the other hand there was a latent desire within me to reconstruct a new life, a new identity, to be born somewhere else as a totally new person.

After many years of family life, it seemed that they knew nothing about me, and had lost all interest and curiosity in who I was. What was I to them? In that house I had become anonymous, a decorative ornament, similar to a chair or a wardrobe.

I started thinking about how to disappear. I picked up the atlas and pointed my finger at a random location. I could move anywhere!

If you are Spanish, there is no registration of your departure at the Spanish border. One exits only by presenting one's passport. At the airport, however, the airlines record all departing passengers. The police can trace a departing individual merely by requesting airline records. To ensure that your departure is not recorded, it's better therefore to avoid the plane and instead take a train to France or Portugal. I did not think anyway that they would investigate me so thoroughly—after all I'm not a criminal. But the gravity of what I was about to do weighed heavily on me; I felt nevertheless like a criminal hunted by the international police.

I recalled the case of one guy, wanted for murder, who added a couple of letters to his name on his ID card, established a new residence in Crete and went to work at an airport car rental booth. A tourist recognized him because he had seen his picture on a TV program: "Have You Seen This Man?" And so the fugitive was arrested. Therefore I had to take precautions; I would avoid using my credit card and stay away from the Spanish embassy in my new, foreign home.

In addition, to disappear without a trace, I lacked the most important accessory—a fake ID! So I took my brother's passport surreptitiously, knowing that he would never use it. Afterwards I would warn him. I was sure he would understand. He has always been an unconventional person; someone who didn't care about others' opinions and we had always covered for one another.

Meanwhile I had already decided where to go: the Philippines. I had spoken to a colleague who had married a Filipina. There is the sea, the heat and life is cheap, so my money would last longer. There is also the advantage that everybody speaks English. Their language includes many Spanish terms, as they had been dominated by Spain in past, a history that had influenced their culture and converted them to Catholicism. Therefore their mentality is closer to our own, compared with other Asians.

There are 7,108 islands surrounded by coral reefs, some of the 'most beautiful islands in the world'; 60% were uninhabited. If you visited one island a day, it would take you nineteen years to visit all. So I was quite sure there would be a small island with room for me.

Furthermore, due to its more peripheral geographical position relative to other countries in Southeast Asia, the Philippines are less visited by tourists. So the chances of meeting some Spanish tourist who may recognize me would be minimized.

I imagined the curses of my boss while he tried to find a copy of that agreement with his client. And my office e-mail! No one knew my password, which I had recently changed. I thought of what a mess my absence would create! Surely they would miss me.

If they caught me, I would be guilty of the crime of abandonment of the marital home. And what if I let the dream go? Impossible. I already felt as though I was 'on the run'—and soon thereafter, I was. I withdrew the money from the postal savings; I sold the land for 17 million pesetas. I travelled to France, then to Basel in Switzerland, then to Austria and Slovenia. From there I entered Hungary by bus, then flew to Bangkok. From Bangkok to the Philippines—to Manila, the capital city.

In Manila I nearly wet my pants in fear. I was carrying a lot of cash. I ended up in an area that was terrifying, even though the place where I slept was decent. Posted on the wall of my room there were warnings such as, 'If someone approaches you with a newspaper, probably the newspaper is concealing a knife', 'Beware of those on the street who approach you as friends' and 'Do not accept drinks from strangers'.

I had rolled up 60 one thousand dollar notes in two tiny packets that I had sewn into my jeans. Then tiny rolls of 100 dollar notes everywhere, even inside a pen that I was always carrying with me.

At nightfall before going to sleep, I strolled around the hotel. The sidewalks were flooded with water. Abandoned, half constructed skyscrapers were concrete skeletons where people had camped out on different floors; they climbed up to their bedrolls on various levels using rope ladders. People were begging, strange faces staring, children sleeping on the wet pavement! All of this I saw on the small strip of road that I ventured along from the guest house to the nearby Center Point Hotel, which was a meeting place for foreigners.

That night I had a nightmare; I thought that someone had entered the room. There was the noise of the fan and voices emanated from the window panes; strange smells mixed with moist heat.

But my goal was not Manila. It was a small fishing village with a long beach, clear seawater and coconut palms. So from the Center Point Hotel, the next morning, I took a bus that ended up at a port outside Manila. It took more than two hours, passing through a good slice of Manila, past slums where naked children were playing with the garbage. They were kicking a ball made of rags into a basket hung on a twisted pole, very close to the double railway track that the trains sped past on. When a restaurant, shop or building appeared between the rubble I immediately noticed the presence of armed security guards.

The last stretch of road, about four miles, was not paved and the bus appeared to be engaged in a Camel Trophy run among deep potholes, puddles of mud, huts with tin roofs, until it finally reached its destination.

The boat was not more than five meters away from the bus stop, yet the conductress warned, "Be careful, there could be thieves about..." You think: "I am just five yards away! I do not have to cross the harbour." There's the boat, with the ladder ready. In fact, as soon as the doors open, a dozen Filipinos try to grab your bags. Some bags head off in the wrong direction and you must chase them. Eventually I gave a dollar to a Filipino who carried my bags five yards onto the boat, rather than stealing them.

Of course the average tourist doesn't experience these sorts of problems. He travels with an organized tour that picks him up at the hotel and deposits him on some lovely island. This is especially necessary for countries like the Philippines, if you do not want your vacation ruined. But this is not my situation. I have decided to live here, perhaps to stay forever. I can only pray to God for the best.

Finally aboard the boat, I take a deep breath. Luckily some of my fellow passengers are more educated Filipinos. I arrive at last in a small harbour, the sea water clear and emerald green, bordered by a fringe of luxurious palms along the shore. A typical tourist picture.

The first thing I saw was my wife's head drifting under the water among the corals! This hallucination lasted only a moment, perhaps brought on by fatigue and the stress accumulated on my long journey.

Standing nearby was a guy armed like someone out of the Wild West, complete with holster and gun, but this was not a hallucination. He was not even a policeman because cops here wear white shirts with the word "Police" across them, and they carry machineguns bigger than themselves. He was most probably just a wealthy man, armed to defend himself. In the Philippines you can buy weapons as easily as biscuits; they are even advertised in the newspapers.

I took a sort of shared taxi called a 'jeepney'—an American jeep originally belonging to NATO forces who still maintain some bases here. These jeeps are reconditioned; behind the driver there are two rows of seats facing each other. Scattered around the vehicle are a dozen assorted holy pictures and crucifixes. Pray and make the sign of the cross before departure...

All the jeeps are colourfully decorated, inside and out. There are jeeps roaming everywhere, carrying people to their destinations, passengers even perched on the roof. In the Philippines people often use jeeps and all-terrain vehicles because there are not so many paved roads.

I arrived at a village close to the sea. I avoided the local tourist resort "par excellence" and ended up in one of the most secluded corners of the island, home to a small community of about a hundred inhabitants. The first thing that struck me was a small beach, quite deserted; just a little jewel hidden from the eyes of the world, where, standing on the shore, you can look out over a coral reef.

I lodged as a paying guest in a family home where nobody requested my documents. All they asked was: "Do you want to eat with us tonight? One dollar!" They spoke English rather well. The English language is bantered about everywhere here. Filipinos of a certain class sometimes even speak English among friends and relatives, as a sign of class distinction.

Then I started looking around. The place was not bad—really a respite from the world of noise, civilization and bills. Electric light was available only in the evening, for 3 or 4 hours; thereafter it's candles, batteries and mosquito coils, as you please. As for noise, in our latitudes we are used to crowing roosters announcing the dawn. Not so in the Philippines, though; here there's a huge population of cocks raised for cockfighting, and that leaves them in a state of constant stress. Their crowing carries on all night, rotating from house to house, so that it seems eventually they are all perched on one's own roof! At that point, there aren't ear plugs that can withstand the racket, and you dream of them all roasting on a spit!

Then, just to give a little relief to my ears, neighbouring Filipinos are belting out tunes on the karaoke every night.

The sudden change in my life had resulted in my feeling a severe level of anxiety—I felt almost a sense of vertigo, of drunkenness and physical tension, especially in my legs. Doubtless it was going to end in disaster.

Going through the forest on foot, after about five hundred meters, one emerges onto another beach where there is not a soul in sight. Walking perhaps a kilometer and a half further along the beach, you are suddenly confronted by a magnificent dream-like resort; very expensive, comprised of small bungalows which you can walk into even without being a guest of the hotel. For them, we

Westerners all look the same. You may also sit in the bar, chat with some tourists and inhale the international atmosphere.

Another kilometer farther along from the resort, among forests and small creeks, I met a young American who had just opened a crate full of axes and nails and was starting to build a house. He was a student from Illinois, an odd kind of person, of few words, already fleeing a failed marriage.

There are missions and U.S. associations that send young Americans here for two or three months, each with clear objectives. For example, one has been assigned the task of teaching the villagers to draw safe drinking water from a well and another one to instruct them in the principles of basic hygiene.

About three weeks later I found myself in the middle of a typhoon, barricaded at home. Immediately I thought of that American who was building his house. But I learned later that he had cut and run in time to avoid disaster.

"Nail the windows closed and lie down in the hallway! Do not worry," they said. No lights—these must all be disconnected to prevent further damage from possible explosions or fire. Secure everything with boards and nails. Lying on the floor, at the mercy of the typhoon, everything is vibrating around me. The Filipinos are all praying and hoping that their homes would not blow away. There is no contact with the outside world. The inhabitants of these lost islands are warned, but not evacuated. There isn't any organization to protect civilians. Here comes the hurricane and.. amen! You must be quiet, with bated breath, waiting for the return of peace. You cannot take a helicopter and run. Regularly once a year we spend four days in such seclusion, hoping that not too many of our belongings will be carried off in the storm.

I had to arrange my finances. The closest bank was in the same harbour where I had arrived by boat. It is not open every day and it provided limited services, so this option did not inspire much confidence. To tourists they advise, "If you want to exchange travelers checks, better to do so in a restaurant." The restaurant owners will then cash them in Manila. Maybe one day, coming back to that bank, I might find it completely empty with the sign, "For Rent." Bye-bye millions.

I kept the bulk of cash in U.S. dollars and the rest in this bank, turned into a savings account. I buried three packages of cash. One was walled up in my room and two in iron boxes, wrapped in plastic bags, and in specific places in the forest. To find a safe deposit box in a decent bank, I would have had to go back to Manila.

It is better not to be registered in a computerized database. I've got a passport, but it's not mine. I could find myself in a situation of not being able to withdraw the money. After all, I'm on the run!

Of course, I led the owners of the guest house to believe that I received into my account a fixed monthly remittance from back home. They have to know in which way I get the money. And if they believe that I receive a monthly income, they are motivated to keep me alive, in good health, served, fed and revered—in the event that I die, my money supply dies with me. But if they knew about my buried money, perhaps it would be more convenient to bump me off, steal the loot and bury me in place of the cash.

Some negative aspects of the Philippines play in my favour. It seems that the local police tend to resolve things on their own. Maybe at times no trace remains of a case in their archives. The police stations or military bases are small centers of power.

I send my brother an email anonymously, saying not to worry and not to renew his passport! I did not say where I was. In my message I recounted a classic episode that only the two of us knew, so that he did not think it was a hoax.

One of the first things that I had to learn was how to deal with doctors. Here people blindly believe in the doctor, who is just as likely to dose you with medicine meant to treat elephants.

In Spain I fretted over side effects, read the drug leaflets religiously and sometimes even sought a second opinion. Here the relationship with the doctor is like going to a garage mechanic. You change the brakes and things slow down again. The doctor puts tablets in a sachet, inscribes it with your name and hands it to you. And for them it's the best they can manage—most often they do not have the money to stock medicines. Frequently they make use of herbs.

I contracted a minor infestation of lice. The doctor gave me a cream and said "Apply this for one week." Then I discovered on the Internet that it was Lindane, a pesticide that, among other side effects, resulted in "convulsions, usually followed by death". At first I was paranoid. There is malaria. You must be careful not to be stung by mosquitoes. There is cholera. You must get a vaccination. There is typhus. The water is not drinkable. You must only use sealed bottles. In my country I used to open the fridge and drink mineral water. Now I have to check if the bottles have been refilled and sealed fraudulently.

For more than a month I have been plagued by an absurd diarrhoea. I went through all of the tests in the best hospital in Manila. And finally a witch from Siquijor Island cured me with a concoction of herbs of a disgusting taste.

The Island of Siquijor is considered an almost bewitched place generally. It has a mountainous area inhabited by healers. Their powers in preparing herbal potions are known everywhere. People arrive here for treatment even from abroad.

There is also another spell linked with this island. Just sit yourself still under a native tree some dark and silent night... Gradually you have the feeling that all the stars are dancing around you, and are nothing but a myriad of fireflies! For this reason, the Spanish Conquistadors gave it the nickname "Isla de fuego."

Of course, on that island I took the opportunity to visit their limestone caves. It is better to do this accompanied by an experienced guide. You must be spiritually prepared to face the humidity and other difficulties that might discourage even the most adventurous people.

I prepared myself to minimize discomfort. I was equipped with water-repellent clothing and an anti-bat helmet, ready to overcome the many fords on the trail. But maybe I lacked enough of that adventurous spirit, as I gave up after awhile and returned to the resort at San Juan

I had arranged everything quite nicely for myself. Beside the sea, a boat at hand, a natural life. A satellite TV link meant that I missed almost nothing, including the football games, the news on International Spanish TV and even my favourite program about disappeared people—"Have you seen this man?"

Yet, at times, I felt a tightness in my chest, almost a shortness of breath. Thinking back to my family, I wished to see them again, or at least to observe them, spy on them. "Surely," I thought, "their life has not changed. My wife meets her usual friends. They stroll in the center of town and play canasta and bridge in the evenings. My son and daughter must, as usual, be consumed by their possessions, the motorbike, music, piercings, movies, weekends. Growing more and more arrogant, and at the same time more insecure, like many kids today."

I regretted not being able to speak with them confidentially. For certain they will have had to roll up their sleeves, tighten their belts a little, maybe get a job, because now there is no more dad to slog for them.

Perhaps they are beginning to miss me!

But then, ultimately, I could also picture them going about their normal lives as if nothing had happened. Maybe I had already been relegated to a back shelf in their mental archives.

It's one thing to come to a place like this on holiday, and quite another thing to take up permanent life on a small island.

After awhile you know all the fish by name. The tropics are not perfect. There are mosquitoes, the crazy heat that forces you to stand still, draped in a wet blanket, in front of the fan. If anything serious happens to me, I would not know which way to turn. Just to get to a hospital in Manila takes one entire day. If I crack up here, then it's good-bye... Who knows if some day in future someone will discover packets of my buried money!

On this island, many villages are isolated. The roads are few and far between, so we go by boat—often a small, unstable bamboo boat—to reach our destination. Sometimes I traveled in the back of a truck, sitting on boxes with other improvised passengers. My bottom ended up flattened by the journey. Other times I traveled by bus with no glass in the windows, overflowing with people, even in the space between the driver and the door. One can imagine passing through a demonstration with people attacking the bus from all sides....

There was an American, a certain Fred, who took tourists on jaunts in a seaplane. A former Vietnam vet, of a whimsical, sometimes unpredictable nature, a great utterer of curses and too fond of the drink.

He lived in a house with a maid, a dog and two armed guards with alternating shifts to provide him with 24 hour protection. It is quite normal to have private security guards in the Philippines, even if you are not particularly rich. The maid cost, perhaps, $50 a month plus board and lodging, while the guards received a salary of $120 per month.

Among his friends there were former politicians and public officials. He introduced to me a Spanish diver who had to renew his passport. On the pretext of helping him to prepare the papers, I borrowed his passport, photocopied it, and had stamps made up, identical to those of the embassy—if necessary, I will renew my own passport myself when the time comes. Perhaps I will have further problems at the Spanish Embassy as a result of this, but at least I will not end up in a Philippine prison. Compared with them, Spanish prisons are five-star hotels.

I travelled with Fred to Manila by seaplane.

When you live in a village by the sea, sometimes you feel a vital need for city life, a craving for a dose of nightlife, losing yourself in the mass of humanity. On Friday evening, the best nightlife is on Nakplin Street; rave music outdoors and dancing until dawn.

There are also shopping malls offering expensive and precious goods.

On the road I was touched by scenes of extreme poverty everywhere, by the chaos, the traffic, the gas fumes, the beggars. But with Fred or someone else to accompany you, it can be fun to visit Manila. I prefer not to be alone in that city—as a non-Asian, you are easily targeted and sometimes harassed. The surrounding stream of poverty forces you into a state of constant alert and discomfort.

Yet I've never been in any serious danger. Of course, if you flaunt wealth or expose a wallet stuffed with money, it's a different kettle of fish…

Anyway my salvation was the shopping mall, one of those huge shopping centers, with many floors, where you feel like you've magically stepped into another world. The contrast with the street is absurd—well-dressed people, elegant coffee-shops, luxury shopping, international restaurants.

Fred knew Manila like the back of his hand and also knew the right people to trust for any need. Some protection is necessary if you want to get around in a city like Manila and he was well enough protected to afford things that others could not.

He always had the look of a gentleman and at the same time that of a depraved old retiree. He was outspoken and could be very shameless. You would never think that such a guy had a passion for philosophy and eloquent speech. You don't have to ask him twice about Plato or Nietzsche. But I forgot to mention that besides being a past-master of blasphemy, he was also the sworn enemy of the priests.

Sometimes Fred and I climbed into his little plane and roamed around, aimlessly. His comings and goings were utterly spontaneous, as though he were seized with a fit. I tended to imitate him in everything, to make his habits mine and to assume a similar, slightly crazy and improvised lifestyle.

Once I spent the night with a singer and the next morning, as she packed her things, I decided to go with her. A few hours later we were on a flight to Puerto Princesa on the island of Palawan. She had two large suitcase filled up with gifts for her family, which was comprised of ten people; mother, father, brothers and sisters. It was an interlude out of this world, sufficient for me to forget even my escape from Spain. We traveled on a rather dilapidated bus for 8 hours along dirt roads and river crossings to arrive at a stunningly beautiful place called El Nido. There her luggage was unloaded from the bus onto a makeshift cart pulled by a buffalo.

Then, on the return trip, we took the bus and stopped at Sabang, a small village with beautiful beaches and... not a soul in sight!! In the place where we lodged, there were five bungalows but no tourists. Going out to eat we had to walk about a half kilometer along a path that meandered under the palm trees or along the beach.

From there we moved on to the island of Cebu where she had some friends. We travelled on to Mactam Island, to the city of Lapu Lapu.

Lapu Lapu, the namesake, was a fellow in local history who had rebelled against the Spaniards and killed Magellan. I visited the spot where Magellan was slain and where stood a monument to Lapu Lapu, who is considered a national hero.

There were three-wheeled taxis, to ride in which one should ensure that his tetanus shots are up to date. Once, returning from a beach, the taxis had disappeared and we had to hike half a mile, trying to avoid a nearby bull.

Fred and I once landed on an island full of American veterans. There seemed to be more of a sense of order there—American communities have, I think, a strong influence on a place. There were also some local politicians there on holiday and one of them— once he learned that I was Spanish and a former football player now permanently based in the Philippines—asked me to coach a football team that his son had joined. I gave them some free lessons. In return for the help I gave these 'upper crust' children and their Manila football team, I found the right place to renew my visa with no questions asked. A classic exchange of favours and typical of the mentality of Filipinos in politics.

Most of the people living on that island seemed to be politicians. The town was the only one I had seen that had all municipal services working, properly paved roads, houses hidden in lush greenery, tennis courts and playgrounds for children. It looked just like a place back home, where one could happily ride around on a bicycle.

The first time that I traveled by seaplane, the air pockets and the lack of any toilet on the plane combined to make me feel quite ill.

The manner in which Fred darted through the clouds, all the while sipping on a bottle of San Miguel beer, gave me gooseflesh. Suddenly he did not seem so bright. He kept increasing altitude to get over the higher cloud banks and my head started spinning. I felt sick. Up and down, between air pockets and lack of oxygen. I poured a bottle of water down my back then laid down between the seats, until Fred shouted out that we had landed. I had not even noticed. It took two to carry me off the plane. Then Fred gave me a massage on back of my neck for thirty minutes and I slowly began to recover. He said, "I didn't know what to do to help you. I've seen monkeys give each other this massage—since you're a hairy fellow, I thought it might work on you as well..." I'm still not sure if he was joking or not.

On the advice and insistence of Fred, I tried to get over my initial fear of flight. This was a new experience for me and to conquer it you need to develop great mental control. I took flying lessons from him. We skimmed among the islands by seaplane. Sometimes he even let me fly solo before taking my pilot's license test, which I managed to pass in less than a year.

I discovered a passion that I was previously unaware of! There is an almost frightening feeling of physical power when flying, with the freedom to move in any direction in space. The seaplane landing and taking off from the water... the panoramic views of the islands from above... Slaloming down those high and swollen clouds that look like whipped cream, then skimming the next lot with the wings; it's as though one is flying among mountains. You experience a wonderful sense of speed, of constantly shifting proportions and dimensions, above and below the clouds. On a straight path along a street there are many obstacles; carts, people, potholes. In the plane, however, there is nothing in your path and in a place like the Philippines where movement can be restricted, you get up in the air and in few minutes you are free to go anywhere. Soon I was willing to spend almost all of my money to buy a flying machine.

Fred sold me his plane at a discounted price that included a special arrangement: to let him use it occasionally. At sixty years of age he was beginning to lose his desire to fly.

It's a 1970 Cessna A185E, a four-seater repainted blue, with the engine rebuilt in 1995. For $100,000 he handed it over to me, with all the accessories and even his regular clients, who contracted him for flying assignments.

Now I swan around for aerial photography and boat research; I also make some emergency flights. I meet all types of unusual characters. More than once I took up a chemistry professor from New Zealand, who was trying desperately to find a woman he had loved twenty years ago. But he didn't have the slightest clue where to look—a madman who threw a lot of money my way.

Another time, I flew the seaplane looking for a fourteen-year girl who had disappeared. I accompanied her distraught mother among islands and villages and at the same time I relived my own escape, imagining my family in the same state of mind as that mother. I said to myself: "You've done it."

This sort of search without a seaplane would have been impossible. You could spend days just to get from one island to the next, from one village to the next, because there are no easily travelled roads. This mother suspected that her daughter had been abducted by some gang of criminals who specialized in kidnapping girls and then forcing them into prostitution in the brothels of Pasay or Kalookan. Someone even mentioned the possibility that she had been brought to Angeles, a complete brothel-city north of Manila, near to a U.S. forces base. This town is made up of bars full of prostitutes, restaurants and various shows, all there for the amusement of the U.S. troops. The American base is no longer there, but remaining behind are hundreds of sex bars, massage parlours, and thousands of mixed Eurasian children.

I do not know how many villages we sifted through, but this girl truly seemed to have vanished. We received tip-offs but these all led to dead ends. You are never sure what role anyone is playing in a situation like this. Everything is corruptible and everything negotiable in the Philippines—from red tape to romantic encounters, to all things illicit.

Once, passing through brush, we heard shots and out popped a big shirtless guy screaming in broken English with a Spanish accent, while behind him stood a Filipina saying something in Spanish. We had stumbled onto someone's private domain in the middle of nowhere. To find a compatriot in the Philippines is not so easy... I apologized and said that we were lost; that I was Spanish.

I thought that might be enough to calm him down, but he continued to point the gun and scream at us to get out immediately. Of course we didn't wait for him to repeat himself.

We received another tip-off that seemed to be on the right track. The girl had apparently been kidnapped and taken to a deserted island. Her mother offered me an astronomical sum of money to help to negotiate with the kidnappers. I asked her why she had not called the police but she was evasive. We landed on the coast of that island, near a ruined house on a small hill; it appeared to be abandoned. We stood on the beach, near the plane. It was rocky with a nearby cliff rising from the sea. Because I felt sorry for her I plucked up the courage and climbed up to the house. I risked my neck doing so, because there was no path to follow.

I knocked on the door of the house and two boys appeared with rifle in hand and a bullying expression. I said that I had come to pick up a girl and they replied, with ugly expressions, that there were no girls there, all the while pointing the rifle at me.

Promptly I said, "if that is the case I will leave," and turned on my heels. But at that moment they caught sight of the mother and beckoned her to come up. They only wanted to speak with her.

After more than an hour I saw mother and daughter coming back down. The daughter was lean, with only a hint of breasts under a green blouse; barely fourteen years of age.

I was immediately struck by her relaxed look. It seemed as if the kidnapping had not been an unpleasant experience. She certainly didn't have the look of one who had been kidnapped and isolated. The mother, on the other hand, was still tense, as though something had gone wrong. At my suggestion to report the incident to the police she was reluctant, saying that any complaint would be useless. Perhaps she was afraid of retaliation by the kidnappers.

Before landing at the village, she wanted to pay me and so I knew that she had been paid handsomely by the kidnappers. In fact, besides the money that she had brought with her, gathered in a scarf, she brought out of her pocket a bag bulging with dollars which she handled with both feigned nonchalance and extreme delicacy. The envelope contained a lot more money than she had to give me, so it was obvious that she had received this cash, shortly before, from the kidnappers.

At the village there was a merry procession of Filipinos who came by to visit the two women, to celebrate the return of the girl. The mother did not have the courage to speak the truth. She feared that her daughter would no longer find a husband, nor even anyone else to kidnap her and then enter into a shotgun marriage. She declared publicly that the daughter had run away after having an argument with her and all of the Filipinos pretended to believe this story.

In this country there are still arranged marriages, the 'repair' of highly valued virginity, kidnapping and elopement followed by the presentation to the family of a *fait accompli*. They even turn a blind eye to rape, as long as it's followed by marriage. As the saying goes, "who breaks it, pays for it, and the shards belong to him."

Inside of me I suspected that the girl was in league with the kidnappers. I had this confirmed when a boy of about twenty years of age, with the typical arrogant expression of the 'high society' Filipino kid—probably the son of some big shot—asked me for a flight on the seaplane. We landed in a deserted cove, sheltered by a forest, next to an abandoned cabin. I asked no questions—my job was merely transport. I saw the 'kidnapped' girl emerge from the forest. They ducked into the cabin and left me on my own, as a lookout, for nearly two hours. In return for this and a promise of silence he revealed that he was the famous—or rather the fake—kidnapper. He devised a fake kidnapping to enjoy a holiday in peace, away from prying eyes. If they were discovered, the 'kidnapping' and rape would exonerate her from any responsibility or of the stigma of being an "easy girl". However, they were deeply in love. By marrying her, of course, he would have solved the problem... but he was already married to a woman of his own social rank, the daughter of some other rich guy.

In this place, often it's the community rather than the family that establishes public morality. It even acts as judge and jury in cases of dispute and litigation—community opinion is more frightening than the courts of law. For a Filipino to lose the respect of the community and end up exposed to public contempt is the worst possible disgrace and it usually results in the target fleeing the scene. In the Philippines, the key issues are related to the respect that you give and that which you receive. One thing is for certain: Filipinos do not tend to live in isolation.

They also do not have the unflappable detachment for which Asians are known. Despite an upbringing which stresses the control of emotions, Filipinos are the most passionate and aggressive people of Asia. Fred explained to me their great tendency to become agitated. According to his theory, it resulted from their Christian education, which taught forbearance and forgiveness. You swallow bitter pills one after another until you explode and resort to mayhem. Here perhaps the Spanish domination has left its mark, nevertheless without affecting that other Asian attribute of putting the community before oneself.

Matchmaking is their favourite sport after basketball; it's a kind of mania. Just glance at a girl and there is a broker immediately ready to arrange a meeting. They introduced me to a woman that I had eyed, who was working at the port authority. On the very first meeting, she arrived with a dozen family members who had organized dinner at a restaurant—at my expense, of course. Here it's always assumed that anyone who has a lot of money will pay for the whole group. It's a rule that applies almost universally throughout the Philippines.

If you are a foreigner, they are always of the opinion that you have money to burn. So wherever you go you have no chance—you will always be expected to fork out the money without complaint!

At the dinner table the conversation revolved around the woman's homemaking skills, my financial resources and the wedding date. I quickly realized that if I pursued this course I would have to escape a second time.

Now I live in another village as a matter of convenience; here I am closer to the markets and I do not always have to make a journey to buy what I want. I found another family who rents me a room. The husband works in Belgium and sends back money to the family, as do all Filipinos living abroad. A lot of people here survive on the remittances of over three million Filipinos working abroad. Thanks to his support, they have built this house, which nevertheless lacks some finishing touches. And nearby, they have an improvised restaurant under a gazebo, consisting of 4 tables and 8 chairs. They also cook Australian specialties. Australian food is nothing special—meat, pasta or rice in portions so abundant that you can't finish it. The occasional backpacker or a few Australian tourists arrive for a meal from time to time.

I also tried Filipino cuisine, but apart from a few dishes, it's not for me. Filipino dishes can be disgusting for us Westerners—but better to smile regardless, if you try. There are boiled duck eggs with the chick embryo inside, or a salty mixture of microscopic shrimp. The stewed vegetables are edible and the rice with chicken is even good. Also they cook very small fish, almost larvae, which they eat whole without cleaning them. Fortunately, even in a remote village, Western cuisine is known and appreciated.

The mistress of the house has become my secretary, now that I operate the private plane business. But I've learned to handle her with kid gloves. She is very sensitive to criticism, as indeed are most Filipinos. If you have to make some critical remarks, it's better one-on-one and never in front of an audience. Sometimes you are forced to beat around the bush so as to avoid offending them.

To collect annual taxes, a little man comes by who takes some amount of money from everybody. Who knows if the money ever arrives in Manila?

There is a veranda attached to my room. It's my lookout point, and there I go to relax when I want to be alone. I lie on the deck and listen to the geckos, those small lizards with their characteristic sound. There is the beach and seaplane in view, and in the background the landscape of the islands. During the monsoon season you can watch the lightning and rain showers in the distance, and every evening the clouds arrange a different sunset.

I often say to myself: this is your refuge. You are a fugitive, a wanted man, even if of little account. Two years have already passed and I have changed. I challenged fate, a life that had been predetermined. Before I worked hard for the family and in the process gave meaning to my life. Now I have nobody to care about. I am the center of my own universe. Now I live for adventure, I fly, I live on nothing. I recklessly seek excitement and out-of-the-ordinary situations, far removed from the normal life that I once led.

The Filipinos would judge me with contempt if they knew that I had abandoned my family and escaped from family obligations. Here a man who keeps two families, wife and lover each with their children, enjoys the highest esteem.

Especially when I'm alone at night, I remember my former life—it feels all so far away and out of focus now, as if the past had melted into the sea. I'd like to browse through a family album, see photos of my marriage, or of times when we were all happy. But I no longer have any photos to look at.

At times the urge to call is strong. I no longer have the fear of being discovered. At these moments I could even go back—I imagine myself passing by everyone at the bar, the doorman, the tenants of my old building. I would calmly ring the doorbell; I would appear in front of my family, as though it were the most natural thing in the world.

Of course, I wish to see my home, even the old office. Colleagues would shower me with questions and I had so much to tell. There are moments when I wish deeply that I could do these things, but of course I do not, because going back I would be even more despised than when I left. The defeat would become bigger. And then I would not have my little plane to play with.

Was I was a coward to run away or I would have been more of a coward to have stayed? I wonder sometimes...

A Psychological Perspective

The protagonist's unconscious defence mechanisms are almost perfect. He allowed himself to be humiliated by his wife and children and it seems that he wanted to lose all remaining dignity, in order to provide him with a valid and legitimate reason to abandon his family without guilt. He tells himself that he had no choice. The underlying cause of his situation seems to be a relationship with his wife that has come unravelled—but why flee instead of trying to reach a peaceful resolution?

It is not resentment towards the family that pushed him to flee but rather his lack of self-esteem. He feels that he is a failure within his family and in the larger community. In this case the flight provides an opportunity to rebuild a new life, a new identity. The past, however, refuses to disappear entirely, resurfacing in his mind and leaving him with a subtle sense of guilt.

3

From France to Brazil
I've done it all for my wife

Michel, from France:

I had a beautiful wife and I was afraid of not being good enough for her, that someone, sooner or later would take her away from me. I was a little shorter than her and had a big nose—I look like Georges Brassens. I was jealous also because she dressed provocatively, to attract attention. I often got into fights with people because of the many compliments she received. Let's face it, she liked to tease men. And because of my jealousy, we often fought badly.

Everywhere we went, I always had the feeling that she was being ogled by someone. She did not go unnoticed, not just for her beauty, but also for the attractive sensuality that she emanated. More than once, in the midst of a party, I dragged her away from friends and acquaintances. Then we solved it all in bed. An uncontrollable urge took me and I had to make love at all costs as soon as we entered the house, to feel her again as mine, to seek confirmation that she did not belong to anyone but me. But I felt that she didn't hold me in high regard, perhaps because sometimes she implied that she had deserved someone better than me.

There were many men, much richer and more handsome than me, ready to take my place. That's why I wanted to earn more. By becoming rich, I would acquire more power, more strength, more security and more right over her. Everything I have done, even getting into trouble, I have done only to feel worthy of her. I loved her too much and I was afraid of losing her. I was in heaven just holding her hand. And when you love at that level, you are lost, in the sense that you're willing to do anything. But she, too, loved me. She married me against the wishes of her parents, who wanted their daughter to have a wealthy, professional husband. They viewed a pauper like me, the son of a grocer, like smoke in their eyes.

Ours has been a great love. I recall the time we were engaged and the first years of marriage, and when our son was born. We were happy! It may seem like a big word. But then some friction started. Sometimes I came home and she had not prepared dinner. Sometimes I even beat her.

I come from a southern family and the woman, in my opinion, must be able to take care of the house. She, however, was the classic middle class woman, sophisticated and lazy. And sometimes I had to cook, because, among many other things, I am also an excellent cook. The money, however, was never enough. We were always nervous about this issue and we constantly quarrelled over trivialities. I always worked hard. I worked as an upholsterer, as a carpenter, a painter, an electrician and at the same time even more jobs. I tried to set up companies. The thing that I most wanted was to see my wife and my son happy. That's all. They had to have everything, even things they didn't need. Just a fetish in my head and perhaps also compensation for what I had not had in my life.

Also I became involved in the gambling world. Once I came to blows with a guy twice my size, who proceeded to give me a sound thrashing. A boy intervened, defending me, and put the bully out of action with a couple of quick moves; a normal, simple guy. One of those people you trust blindly. We became friends. He lent me some money without interest, maybe for a little special gift for my wife or my son. I have always lived beyond my means. I always wanted more than I could have. And this man was the right person to urge me, encourage me, energize me. I felt a sincere affection for him and some gratitude. More than once I saw him put someone in their place and teach him a hard lesson because they had tried to be too clever and arrogant with his friends. He kept order in the gambling den, and commanded everybody's respect. He was a sort of judge, although he was physically completely normal.

I needed to pay him back a large sum of money but I didn't have enough available. Then, with the sympathetic tone of someone who wants to come to your aid, he said that it would be enough for me to do a simple errand for him—deliver cocaine to various customers. In return I would have paid off the debt. The customers were all good people, well-known football players. I didn't think the work was too risky or bad. And then he didn't seem like a criminal. In fact I viewed him as a great man, a benefactor, because he was the guy who took care of everyone and everyone was a little in awe of him. Perhaps this is the tactic of the real Mafioso, appearing to be the most generous person around and at the same time taking you under his protection. I am convinced that this is the *modus operandi* of the boss, of the godfather, who has other criminals under him willing to do anything. He's the one who extends a hand to you, can understand you, takes care of your problems, follows you step by step like a father and leads you slowly, elegantly, down the path to crime, without you realizing it. Whatever he had asked me to do, I would have done with my eyes closed. Even when he became violent, I did not pay attention because I always thought that he was doing things the right way.

I was constantly in debt. I always had to earn more, invest more, spend more. I closed a company to open another, to silence the creditors and gain new trust at a new bank. My friend acted as a financial adviser and I learned to work together with him. Sometimes his customers gave me sums that I returned with high interest. So I gained confidence and they gave me more and more money. Together with him I invested in various things with the money they lent to us, and even played the horses. I was his right arm and partner in business.

Sometimes he came to dinner at my house. My wife had become more friendly and caring and I had a new, smart look: always neat, in well-cut suits. I no longer came back home exhausted, smelly from work and I had the impression that my wife treated me with more respect. Further clouding my mind was all that money I handled. I learned to juggle money between Switzerland and the banks in Luxembourg. One day I found myself with a lot of money that wasn't mine, part of which had to be delivered to my friend.

One afternoon I returned to my house unexpectedly. I found my wife with a red face, wearing only her bathrobe. My friend was in the bathroom. My blood froze. I felt my legs shake as if I had been stabbed in the belly. It felt like I had some sort of fever. I ran into the bedroom and I found myself facing a mess of sheets and pillows. I did not have the strength to react, to do anything. The next day I learned from the porter that my friend was often at my home whenever I was not there. This had been going on for some months.

What I can never forgive my wife for is that she had ridiculed and humiliated me in front of a friend who was regularly at lunch and dinner in my house. I should have known that he had his eyes on my wife from many little clues. But I was too enthralled by his protective attitude, by his false, sugary generosity.

At that point I found myself faced with a terrible choice. He had taken my wife to bed; I had to react. In the face of someone who does not bow even in front of the Almighty, what should I do? Either I kill him right away or I become his bootblack. There would have to be a violent confrontation—I had to extinguish him. He was not the kind of man you can just kick in the pants. I spent a night walking through the town like a madman, thinking about how to get rid of him. Then I thought: "What if I end up in jail?" All this for a worthless woman. Even if I had stayed with her, our life would have been hell. I would have ended up beating her all the time and I don't know what consequences that would have led to. On the one hand I had to suffer the arrogance of a thug, becoming the laughing stock of him and of the whole neighbourhood; on the other hand I had to spend my life in jail. Then I thought of the third solution—to sneak away with the money. I was holding a mountain of money to be returned to half of the city, including that asshole. My fear was that he could take it out on my son, but my wife was also involved in a love affair with him. And then I knew things about him that he would not have liked me to blab around.

My wife had understood that I knew everything, and she feared my violent reaction. But I had nothing more to say. When the woman you love is on your side, you're ready to kill a dinosaur in order not to lose her, you're willing to do anything to save your relationship and those moments that only she can give you. But when she goes with another man, when she has no more respect for you, it is like she is breaking your legs. You only have one desire—to make her pay.

I left home with a bag stuffed with money, without saying a word. I took the first plane available. I remember the day and the year: October 10th, 1984. I started flying around like a crazy bird. I went to the airport, looked at the airline counters and decided just on the spur of that moment where to go. I arrived in Paris, from there to Honolulu. I was also in Sri Lanka and the Bahamas. My wife would certainly not sue me for abandoning the marital home. My creditors? If they went to the police, what would that have solved? It is not an offense that would put you to jail. I had borrowed money on a personal basis—rounds of grants to private accounts. I wasn't a finance company. In the end, on the advice of a Frenchman I had met in a casino in the Bahamas, I chose Brazil, Rio, the place to numb your thoughts, to forget, to drown your sorrows.

In Rio, you're always in the middle of chaos, music, euphoria. You hear music all day, everywhere. In every corner there is a radio, a stereo, someone who plays an instrument. Here I experienced a new feeling, living without plans, without any future. Today you're dancing, laughing, joking, surrounded by beautiful women, tomorrow perhaps you have nothing. At every corner you see the other side of the coin. Why torment yourself about what may happen tomorrow? You are only living in the present moment.

There is a sentiment typical of Brazilians, which they call *saudade*. It's a hard word to translate—a sort of nostalgia for somebody and a sadness that they drown in euphoria, in fun, in chaos. They use this word a lot. I also felt a lot of saudade. I missed my wife. I would have strangled her, buried her, let her be eaten by worms, but I was always in love with her. I distracted myself with amusements. Like many Brazilians, I threw myself into the midst of a sea of bodies and danced. I went everywhere: casinos, brothels, dance halls, living for nothing important, only for music and revelry.

The typical seaside Brazilian, born and raised on the coast, possibly of mixed race, is just like that. If he has some black rice and beans, cooked vegetables, all is ok. He lives day by day. But do not touch his dancing. It's not like at home, where we go to the disco on Saturday night, kick our legs for three hours like madmen and then we've had enough for the whole week. Here it is sufficient to have a box of matches in hand, and they'll begin to beat with their fingers and dance: on the road, on the beach, it happens everywhere, and any time is good.

The most beautiful dances and music have been born from improvisation, on the street. Masterpieces have come from the *favelas*, the shanty towns. The music of the samba has come out of some of the places with the worst reputation. You may see someone who is a real artist and then at night he is a fugitive from the police. These are the *carioca*, the natives of the *favela*.

I wandered without valuables, without a watch, without chains, to avoid being targeted by some poor schmuck; I dressed in jeans, a pair of sandals, a faded shirt. From the outside I looked like many other Brazilians. Here whites, blacks and mulattos can all be Brazilian.

I spent hours sitting in a bar or on the beach at Ipanema or Copacabana, looking out to the sea. I lunched and dined alone despite the Brazilians' communicative nature. They don't keep you at a distance, even if they say we outsiders use them, and that it's our fault that they are in misery. They call us *gringos*. They envy us a little, I think.

I was born in a working class neighbourhood where you talk to everyone. And Rio is the same. In Rio the neighbourhood of

Santa Teresa still has an old tram system, without glass windows, wide open. Sometimes it rains—passengers get wet. Then it dries quickly. I also took the tram, the *bondigno*, a little tram all painted yellow with people hanging out the sides. Then there is the district which takes its name from Christ the Redeemer and where there is a statue of Christ; just below, there is a huge favela. I never strolled so much as in Rio. In France, who gave me all that free time? When I was twelve, I was already working with my father in the market. What I couldn't do in France I have made up for here.

At first I was seized by a sudden anxiety, as if there was someone stalking me. Then I realized that there was no one, that I had only the problem of killing time. Sometimes I ran to the phone and I called my mother-in-law, asking about news of my son. She replied that he was in the yard playing with friends. It seemed as if everyone lived peacefully without me. I was not, after all, so essential. It took a little time for me to figure out that I was accountable to no one. I had all the time in the world in front of me and I could be a tourist for at least another three years.

A dodgy-looking guy, with a small but pretentious office, said that he was the tour guide for the favela—probably he paid bribes to the underworld. I intended to contact the local underworld. I was ready to vent my bile on anyone; I had so much hatred and anger that I could not vent in France. I dreamed of meeting that bastard again and torturing him. I wanted to see him die slowly, tear him apart piece by piece, humiliate, destroy, render him impotent. But they were only fantasies. I would have paid an accomplice to take him out. I also had a Macumba made against him—that's a curse, a practice of sorcery, of African origin, popular in Brazil.

To demonstrate the exceptionality of the service he offered, the guide told me that even the police did not enter the favela. They are afraid. They only go when they are forced to, with bullet-proof protection, special helmets, guns in hand. As I wandered among the huts, I saw an imposing, huge villa, protected by boundary walls and guard towers, which stood out completely from everything else around there—the dirt, the kids playing in the trash. They were all traffickers, so they are not short of money. And they are very well armed.

The favelas are real schools of crime, from which different criminal talents have emerged. Lucio Flavio is famous. He gave the police a hard time but eventually they caught him. You know—betrayal, rivalry, envy... It was not even a favela; just a poor neighbourhood.

Even Pelé—Arantes do Nascimiento, a Portuguese surname—came from a poor neighbourhood. I know him personally. Then they made him minister of sport. Sympathetic, easy-going; he comes from the people. They have football as well as the samba. They say that if the government were to abolish football and the samba, there would be a revolution.

Every evening there are boys, teenagers, youths and grown-up men playing football on the beach. During the day the beach is occupied by tourists but in the evenings there is only football, all over the beach. Many poor boys grow up with the game of football; that is the only thing they can afford! They want to succeed in order to redeem themselves from economic misery. Many famous players came from poor families: Pelé, Ronaldo, Romario, Garrincha, Ronaldinho. They get famous, they make millions and actually stop working on themselves and gain weight.

They are a free and wild people—imagine what they are like during the Carnival! You see some bacchanals, as well as brutal carnage.

I joined an exclusive club. I thought that to be rich, it was enough to live as a rich person. I tried to get into the milieu where you can meet the beautiful people that matter, make useful friends for my purposes, so that I could return to France rich, ruthless and powerful. I had made up my mind that I had to make some easy money. To live in a big way, you need to have spades of money, no regard for anybody and rip off the neighbours. It became an obsession.

I waited for the right moment, without haste. I had time to burn. I had to sniff around to find out how to invest money, how to increase my capital. The money I had was safely parked in the Bahamas, because in Brazil there was no economic stability. One day you were rich, another day you were poor.

I presented myself as a builder with property in France and I stayed in five star hotels. I changed them often because I was afraid of being recognized by someone on vacation. Also for safety reasons I gave everyone a false name. I met the real wealthy people, but what a life they lead! Armoured cars with bullet-proof glass. Bodyguards. The children are escorted to school. The servants go to the grocery store or order by phone. Where they live looks like a fortress—electronic security systems everywhere. They are afraid of kidnapping by the organized gangs. But what kind of life is this? They live in a gilded cage.

Every now and then I met some compatriot. But I was alert; I avoided being photographed. Often you cannot classify them—how they live, what they do. During the Carnival I struck up a friendship with a group of French youths with ponytails. They enjoyed throwing their money away, with the air of those who have too much, of the arrogant conquerors that move the world at will. We went from place to place. There are also clubs that organize parties twenty days before the Carnival. I've seen so many of these places! Women in miniskirts dancing on a small platform and black men all around them groping under their skirts. Hands from all sides, on their ass, on their tits, in their pussy. They drink, get all excited by the music and then go wild.

I remember an elegant club. At the exit there was a bunch of blacks. About 4AM people began to emerge. A woman came out and some men took her around the side of the club and fucked her among the trees. But it wasn't a tragedy because the woman was already out of her head—they had all been drinking. They go out to dance, then during the evening, after drinking, they become loose. Some women don't have the strength to say no, or perhaps they are excited.

My friends also took part but I remained on the sidelines. I did not want to join in. I did not give a damn. But it did me good to see that brothel, and the anarchic chaos. Strangely, it relaxed me.

In Brazil people don't understand moderation. Everything has a strong, violent impact. It's like a glass of whiskey in the morning on an empty stomach. Who knows why, but Brazilians seem to want to live up to their reputation of losing all control, all restraint, all inhibitions. I always sensed beneath something that coincided with my own state of mind—a sort of general despair.

A cliché defines Brazilians as frivolous people, all samba, sex and football. In Brazil you get a sense of the fleeting quality of life. Their exaggerated joy, the wish to live life to excess is a reaction to the precarious nature of life that Brazilians inherited from the time of slavery. In Europe we have more certainties—or false certainties: family, career, social image, duty. They have drugs; the rest doesn't matter. They drug themselves with football, with samba, with sex.

I too took every opportunity to get drunk, to avoid thinking. I let myself become involved and I followed my friends on their nightly raids. But there was nothing I could do—even in the midst of an orgy, I thought of her, my wife. Often I dreamed about her. And in my sleep nothing had changed. We talked about banal things in the kitchen or living room; my son's homework or his marks at school. Everything happened in a normal routine way, as it did before, to the point that I felt a terrible sense of emptiness when I woke in the morning and she was not there.

My friends spoke only of millions of dollars. But it was difficult to distinguish the truth from bragging. If there was a deal to be done, even not a very clean one, I wouldn't restrain myself, as I was convinced that honesty guarantees only a modest life. In the front of my mind, I had a successful and arrogant model—that bastard who took my wife to bed.

I was introduced to a certain Mr. Tony, a Frenchman who made his fortune in Brazil. Here there are many who have made a fortune, like the Venetian family Guerra who control the biggest trucking business in Brazil. Tony was between a gorilla of a bodyguard and a mind-blowing blonde. Both of us were from Provence. We empathized with each other and he gave me his business card. He lived in São Paolo. During the Carnival one of their acquaintances was murdered. They didn't talk particularly about it and I refrained from asking. I realized that in Brazil crime was easier and often went unpunished. Especially during the Carnival, they kill one another to settle accounts. They wait for the right moment, all masked in the confusion.

Carnival is a holiday all day and night long and it goes on for five days. You put on some shorts, a few feathers on your head, a shirt and away you go! I remember that I called my mother-in-law and began to insult that bitch of a daughter. I had been drinking. My mother-in-law reacted: "You are a coward! It's very easy to escape." She screamed that my wife had to talk to me. I gave her a raspberry and hung up. I had arrived at a different view of life, and did not to give a damn about the universe. I was no longer myself. I was there, hypnotized, watching the samba schools go by, a parade lasting for hours and hours. You see some beautiful chicks! All half-naked. The best are the mulattos, with the very long legs and high butts. Then the Queen of Carnival is elected. For three years they have elected the same one. I have the pictures. Her husband is German. She is completely naked, only painted blue, yellow and green, like the Brazilian flag.

The Brazilian women are full of *carinho*. Carinho is a much used word here. It's a sweet way of doing things. However, I could not settle down with any woman. It was always my wife that I wanted terribly, although I was always hoping to wake up one morning not wanting her any more. Yet there was one that almost made me lose my head.

Near the center of the city there was a beautiful restaurant with an orchestra. One night I went there, I sat, I ordered. A little further on, there was a Brazilian family and among them a very attractive woman. I fixed my eyes on her, and she reciprocated. Since there was only one old man and the rest women, I gave her a sign to invite her to dance. We went onto the dance floor. You know how that is? As you touch her, you know right away if she responds. She responded very strongly. She was in Rio on vacation with her family and her husband had remained in Sao Paulo. She was jogging every morning on the Avenida Atlantica and about noon she would come to see me. I lived right on the bay, in front of Sugar Loaf Mountain. I would put on a little music—Chico Buarque, Gaetano Veloso, Roberto Carlos. She went right into orbit when she heard Roberto Carlos, the best known singer in Brazil. He was often on tour in France. He sang: "I just fell in love with my friend's wife...". We did a nice jog in bed and then she went back to her hotel. I thought it would end there, but when she left, I missed her. We got on well together, we talked well. She was a worldly-wise and intelligent chick. She did not want to leave her address, but I was able to figure out the general area where she worked and the places she frequented. Then I said to myself, "Yes, I will try; I am going to look for her. While there I'm also going to look up Tony, the rich guy from Provence with the bodyguard."

So in a jiffy I took the plane—São Paolo is close enough to Rio. Every half hour there is a plane, like the buses. When the plane began to fly over São Paolo, it was dark and I could see a lot of lights. I thought it was the suburbs but instead, the lights never ended. Over twenty million people!

I realized I was doing something foolish. It was like trying to find a needle in a haystack. São Paolo is the opposite of Rio. As you arrive, you feel you've immediately plunged back into a productive and dynamic world. People in suits. All work, offices and industry. I went to the places where I thought I could find her with no luck. Then I began to lose hope. Only running around, crisscrossing the city is crazy. The traffic and pollution are dreadful. At a traffic light you can be stuck for two hours. Sometimes the taxi driver will refuse to take you to some part of the city. "Por l'amor de deos!" he might say.

Tony had a private plane. Every time we went out, I was afraid. Maybe they would think I was a relative and they would kidnap me.

He mixed some Provençal words in with his Brazilian. He had a modest appearance but he didn't need to raise his voice; everything else spoke for him: the CCTV cameras in the house that made you feel uncomfortable, the private plane, the bodyguards, big cars in the garage... seven or eight, just for fun.

He often invited me to his ranch; we would go hunting crocodiles. A river crossed his ranch. He didn't even know how much land he had. Such a rich guy should stay in Europe, where you're not surrounded by hungry people! Yet he was generous. He was a friend of Ayrton Senna, the race-driver and spoke of him with great admiration. Senna now has a monument in Sao Paulo—a sculpture of him driving a car—Brazilians were proud when he won. You don't know how many charities he has supported! The biggest orphanage in São Paolo bears his name. When they had the funeral, it was as if a pope had died.

In Brazil it is not easy to distinguish the underworld from an honest person. Corruption has so penetrated the social fabric that, at times, even an honest person needs the help of the underworld. Tony was a friend of the police chief of Sao Paulo and also of a guy arrested for international trafficking of cocaine, who controlled more than fifty massage establishments.

I tried to make him understand that I was a reliable person, able to commit anything for friends.

He once took me to a nice massage center. There were many very pretty girls. After an hour or two of massage, I gave the girl some extra money. Can you imagine her saying no? She pulled down her panties, and produced creams and condoms. Everything was perfect. You're in a quiet area—if you want to participate, that's fine; otherwise she does everything. I could really relax. The massage was real, but you could not resist the extras. You paid when you went out but you gave the other money to her when you were inside. Around the Italian consulate there was a string of massage saloons.

Every now and then I went back to Republic Square because Maddalene, the lady I met in Rio, worked around there. I walked around for hours and then I consoled myself with the "massage clinic". Not far from the massage houses there was the Japanese area. There are even more massage houses there, only you pay triple. The girls are Japanese, born in Brazil; they call them the Nissei. Tony went there often and felt at home in the area. He joked with the girls; you may as well have been in Japan—everything is Japanese: The roads, the streetlights, the buildings... some houses are even in the shape of a pagoda. They come out in kimonos with wooden sandals when they have their parties. Often I bought things there, like rice noodles. Very good! The Japanese have their own ranches and fresh food comes in every morning.

Tony found me a job in a massage parlour. It was a two-storey house, hidden by a hedge of creepers. It had a "blind" gate, so you could not see the inside. I never understood what kind of ties Tony had with that center. Rich clients were coming and we had to ensure their privacy. There was a lot of coke in circulation. I was responsible for managing the center; I slept upstairs.

One day a masseuse threatened to report to my bosses my too personal way of managing the center. I had sent another masseuse to a customer to deliver cocaine that I had bought on my own. She did not stop threatening so I gave her a slap. As she continued to stand up to me, I knocked her to the ground and pinned her with one arm behind her back. She started to squirm and scream. I beat her up, then dragged her into the closet of my flat and locked her inside. Half an hour later I went and sat in silence in front of her. She was crying. I took the disinfectant and dressed her wounds. Then I began to fondle her; we made love gently. I had her tamed. She was reserved, a rather sad woman, in her thirties; her name was Sonia. She began to talk, to confide in me and could not stop. She too was in São Paolo in search of someone. For months she had had no news of her 14 year old brother. She thought he had finished up on the street, in the hands of a criminal gang.

She came from the Northeast, the desert region, the poorest part of Brazil, on the coast in the state of Sergipe. Her family there was made up of grandmother, mother and children.

The typical Brazilian man, when he realizes that he cannot support his wife and children, melts away. The women remain with their children and they have plenty of them. They are as tough as men. And the children grow up on the streets. There are so many situations like that; their education is only enough to make them semi-literate. The children leave after they grow up—what the fuck are they going to do? There is nothing to do.

The masseuse's brother had come to São Paolo and had vanished. Imagine one of these kids arriving in São Paolo with no profession. At home he was a fisherman, or maybe a goatherd. Both in Rio and in Sao Paulo I have seen gangs of seven or eight boys all about eleven or twelve years old. They call them *menignos de rua*—street children. There is even a special police team set up to control then.

They are policemen wearing hoodies, in São Paolo I saw them. They know where to find the boys in the night. They can kill them on the spot. In the morning there is a van that takes them to an institution; they harvest the organs and the rest is thrown away.

It's likely that her brother met that sort of end. Others are controlled by organized criminals, who send them to the front lines. They are drugged and armed, and they can kill you in an instant. And they are just little boys!

One night going home I heard some screams. They had attacked a gentleman and tried to rip off his watch. It was like when ants attack a cockroach. I couldn't see anything with all those kids around him. They cleaned that man out and left him, half bloodied. They attack you like a pack of wolves.

I liked Sonia. Another time I could have fallen in love with her. But I reasoned coldly, in fact, I liked to feel like a bastard. When I wanted to make love, I didn't allow any refusal. I closed the door and slammed her on the bed, skipped the preamble. I treated her like a whore, precisely for that superb look she displayed. She was a proud woman and reminded me of my wife. Maybe that's the reason why I treated her the way I did. I was excited that she feared me, but I was wrong to go too far. The more I liked her, the more I humiliated her, but at the appropriate time, I also used sweetness. I deceived her. I let her believe that, thanks to my friends, I was the only one who could find her brother or at least to find out what had happened. But when I spoke to Tony about it, he dismissed me with a joke: "Who cares what happens to a menigno de rua?"

Meanwhile I was making a lot of money and my day of vengeance was approaching. I had my feet back on the ground... I had to find someone who would dispatch my enemy to his Creator. I would return to France to set it up and then I would go back to Brazil before the murder so that I had a safe alibi. Then, through my good contacts here, I would rebuild my identity as a successful man, send a lot of money to support my son and humiliate my wife. I felt that, with the money, I could have her again, when and how I wanted. But in that event I would do so just to humiliate and destroy her.

One day I was approached by two policemen, who discovered well sealed packages of cocaine in my bag. I don't know who had tucked them in my bag. I was about to return to France and instead I ended up in jail, where I was sodomized.

Released from prison, I went to a clinic because I was freaked out. I don't know how many kilos I lost. I also had paid a penalty for passing as a Brazilian, by giving a false name to avoid being deported to France. I wanted to see Sonia but I didn't call her; I was too afraid of falling into some trap. I avoided even calling Tony to ask why he did not come and visit me during my detention and I had no idea if he was still on my side. I took refuge with a French friend I had met in São Paulo, who had moved to Olinda, near Recife, in the Northeast. There I recovered, with difficulty. I thought back over my life and everything that had happened to me. It was as if it had happened to another person, as if it had nothing to do with the normal and simple life that I had once led with my wife and my son.

I was demoralized, dejected. Once I called my mother-in-law's house and my wife answered. I got a lump in my throat, I could not speak and hung up. I had wanted to say simply: "Hello, I'm coming home!" I began to think that I had been a coward to flee. The day that I had left, she sought my eyes. Perhaps she had expected a backlash, the violent reaction of a tough man, willing to do anything to win her back. But I had not wanted to do that. Within me, at that time, there was only hatred and a desire to erase her from my life.

My friend had a girlfriend at that time. She was thirty and he was already retired—who knows if he is still alive! There are many retirees in these fishing villages, living with a younger partner who also acts as nurse for them. Olinda is a paradise; the name means 'How wonderful'! At that time, the Indians living there stayed in huts; they were probably quite comfortable. Olinda has coral reefs. The water is very calm; it's quite a liveable place. Portuguese colonial style, full of churches.

It is no accident that I met the woman who steered me into a new life in the Amazon, in Manhaus, where I moved to in order to spend some quiet time far away from everything. In Rio, you feel that everything is ephemeral and all human relationships are transient. Everything burns quickly, even in one night, as if there isn't a tomorrow. In Manhaus, when they see that you're a foreigner, the girls would strike up a chat with you, not for prostitution but because they hope that you will take them away. They feel separated from the rest of the world. Manhaus is like an island in the middle of a seemingly endless forest; it is isolated because it's within the Amazon area. Aircraft or the river are the only means of transportation. The mestizos, the Indios, live there. They don't have many contacts with the outside world and just remain there by the river—the Amazon River, Rio Amazonas, the Father of Rivers. It's like a sea. In some places you cannot see the other side. She, Katia, has blue eyes; her grandfather was Dutch. He arrived, like many other Europeans, at the time when rubber was a path to a fortune, when Manhaus was the only place in the world where rubber trees were growing. The Siringhero were the ones who knew how to extract this substance from the rubber trees. They built fine buildings in that period. There is a beautiful theater there, where even Caruso sang. Then an Englishman took the rubber tree seeds to Malaya, where the trees grew well and thus began the ruin of Manhaus.

I started to make plans with Katia. She wanted to open a restaurant in a tourist area of Brazil. I was aware of the danger of being detected by any French customers, but I enjoyed planning the restaurant with her, dedicating myself to harmless, family pleasures. We went shopping together, we spent the morning searching for ingredients to cook a dish. I rediscovered the pleasure of sharing something with a woman.

We moved around often as we had to choose the place where to open the restaurant. We always took the plane because railroads in Brazil are very few. A simple life, without great ambitions or desires to arrive who knows where. It was not difficult to make her happy because she didn't have any big demands. I was managing to leave the past behind me and I no longer thought about returning to France. I had given my address to my mother-in-law, so that my son could come to see me. It was a postal address near the airport. Meanwhile, my mother-in-law insisted that my wife wanted to talk to me at all costs but I regularly blew her off.

We were in Porto Alegre, where Katia's married brother lives, when I realized that she was expecting a child. I had a new life in front of me and a child was near to being born; my enthusiasm for life was returning. In those years we lived well in Porto Alegre, there was no crime. Now Porto Alegre is like Rio. There are favelas but there they are called *malocas*.

We went to the Guaia Rio, a huge, freshwater lagoon 100 km by 70 km, that's also called the Inland Sea. Porto Allegre reminds me a little of life in France; even the climate is similar to some French winters. People are more solid; Europeans think about tomorrow.

In the evening we went to dance those traditional frontier dances—the milonga, the tango, the waltz... The milonga is beautiful to see; it's a typical dance of the southern gauchos. A friend of mine has a lot of trophies in her house. She participated in a folk group with those colourful clothes, full of flowers, even on her head. The pictures are beautiful, from a time before she started drinking.

I have even gone out as a herdsmen with the so-called gauchos. They have a lot of sheep; the merinos: big sheep with large ears. I stayed with them and slept outdoors. I went riding, sitting on a leather saddle, wearing spurs, gun and belt, out on the pampas. A sea of grass and wild meadows. At that time the car driven by the poor and the Negroes was the Beetle. I bought one because I liked it. But I was mixing with well-off people and they said to me, "What are you doing? Are you crazy? The Beetle is the Negro's car." That was the best that the Negro could buy. The gauchos are racist and just tolerate the black man, but it is nothing like South Africa.

I made a lot of new friends. There was a European community with a lot of French people. It's a mixture of races, Germans, Poles, Italians and people from Provence and Burgundy who still speak their local dialects. You can even find aspects of a country that no longer exists back home. A group from Mestre University came to hear the Venetian dialect, as it used to be spoken, because here the dialect hasn't changed in a hundred years.

We opened a restaurant in Porto Alegre. Then there was an unforeseen turn of events and now I am no longer there. My son sent me a telegram to the mailbox in which he informed me of the time and date of his arrival. I went to the airport, eager to embrace him, trying to imagine what he looked like. But instead I found myself in front of my wife. I could barely breathe; the words were choking in my throat. She was no longer the same person! A simple woman; humble, anonymous—far from the memory of the girl I kept in my imagination, who had been seductive, provocative, disruptive in her sensuality. We sat in a bar. I did not know what to say, what to do; so much time had passed. I almost could not believe that for her I had raised hell. I couldn't feel any emotion, only a slight tremor in my hands and legs. I feared that all of those memories, my torments and suffering of the past might resurface. She did everything to retrieve the intimacy of that earlier time. She said that she had spent whole days at her mother's house, next to the phone, waiting for my call. Now that woman was in front of me and too many things separated us. I had another house, another family. Yet while she was talking, I realized that, in all that time, I had been unable to forget her. I still had a strong desire for her. I thought that I loved her despite everything that she had done to me. I was scared and felt trapped. Now I would never escape from her, even if I flew into space. I didn't reveal to her that I had another woman and child.

The next day we were on the plane headed to Rio. Being far away from France, in the crazy atmosphere of Rio, we felt like two kids, who had just met for the first time. We went on the cable car to the Sugar Loaf. I took her to the exclusive places of Rio, to the most outrageous clubs. We danced, laughed until three in the morning, talking, drinking, joking. We even forgot everything that had happened in the past. We were completely out of this world, just like the first day when I met her at the party of a mutual friend and we chatted all evening long in a park.

I felt a strange sensation. I was with her, I enjoyed every moment and I wanted to prolong those moments as something isolated from the rest of the world, but at the same time, inside me I felt that it was the right moment to say good-bye to each other once and for all.

I restrained myself because I saw her unguarded and confident that she had won me back. It would have been too easy to destroy her. She was so happy that I thought I had been wrong to escape and to leave her. It seemed that she had suffered and missed me very much.

One evening we went to the restaurant Antiquarius of Rio. I intentionally chose a dream location. Leaving her just at the climax of our rediscovered love, I could keep pleasant memories in my mind. Sooner or later, living together, we would have watched our relationship fading again, as before, and I would have reproached her for our past. In some paradoxical way it seemed to me that I wanted to save our fine last days spent together in Rio.

I told her I would leave her, while she was savouring the chocolate mousse, when I saw her eyes full of happiness, when she was completely sure of keeping me in her grasp. I confessed that I had loved her too much and for too much love I had become a fool, a criminal and a fugitive. Then I revealed I had another woman and another son. She burst out crying; she begged my forgiveness. She said I did not deserve what she had done to me but she had paid enough. She repeated: "What do we care about the past?" In the evening, in that restaurant, she stammered; she could not articulate the words. She swallowed a handful of tranquilizers and the race to the hospital began. I spent the night in the hospital holding her hand. I stayed a few more days with her. It was hard to leave her because that strong attraction was still there. I was very sweet to her but inside I was resolute. I told her it would be foolish to commit suicide. That would be very selfish for our child. The last day I left her on the road in the rain and she stood still without shelter while

I walked away. To the last she tried to move me to pity her, to make me change my mind. I left without looking back and I have not seen her again. There was another family waiting for me now.

I know that now she lives with a man much older than her, who took in my son to work in his company. My son will come to meet me this year. We will spend the 2004 New Year together.

In all these years, Brazil has changed. You see skyscrapers in Copacabana, 300 square foot apartments with 60 square feet just for the servants, and you say, "Who are those people, living on the twelfth floor of those palaces on Avenida Atlantica? If I am afraid to walk around with $100 in my pocket, how do they survive?"

I love this country as I love Jorge Amado. I have a lot of books by Jorge Amado in Portuguese. His soul was black because he was together with the people of the port. Brazil has given me the desire to enjoy life just as it is—so absurd, so crazy, so cynical, so cruel and yet so beautiful!

A Psychological Perspective

Michel has fled from a no-win situation. The fraud and the stolen money are just an opportunity, not his goal or purpose. He is torn between his enduring love for his wife and his difficulty to forgive her, particularly after having been humiliated in front of his rival.

But can we describe him as a man unable to forgive? In fact, forgiveness is an emotion—no-one can decide rationally to forgive, just as no-one can decide rationally to love or to hate. If he had succumbed to his still-strong attraction to her and had just forgiven her with words, but not in his heart, then most likely the problem would have flared up again, when their relationship suffered further tension or decline in future. Under such circumstances, the risk would have been the slow, merciless annihilation of their love. Hence the sudden, instinctive solution that he took instead—to break off and end their relationship at its most beautiful moment.

When you are romantically involved, you are more contradicted, more passionate and more vulnerable. In the present case, the love between Michel and his wife is as great as the pain they have inflicted on each other.

4

From Italy to Cambodia
Screwed by The System

A man from Rome:

I lived alone in a 200 square meter penthouse on a side street off the Via Cassia in Rome. My house was always filled with friends, nice people, beautiful women and even an occasional showbiz personality. My world consisted of parties, a mobile phone, trendy bars, restaurants and hours of work spent with architects, engineers and investment bankers. I also had a love affair with a rather famous television actress, at that time early in her career.

What was about to happen was unimaginable to me, like an axe cutting down the life I had built with one clean stroke. When catastrophe strikes, you realize for the first time how much your world, those places, those walls, that circle of friends, those faces you see every day, even the more insignificant objects in your house, are a real part of you. In this terrible bout of misfortune I even lost my mother and a love affair was suddenly ended. Needless to say, I found myself surrounded by emptiness and solitude, dumped from a comfortable, brilliant life, into an existence filled with deprivation. And this happened under the indifferent eyes of institutions you depended on and people you counted as friends, because, in the end, no one is really interested in your personal drama.

There is nothing that can more readily drive a man to insanity then taking away the familiar ground from under his feet and tossing him into an alien reality which ignores his very existence. I cannot imagine how I didn't go mad—or maybe I really have gone mad! Either way I was knocking at the door.

I owned a construction company and I purchased two buildings from a business that had been inherited from its founder. The buildings were to be renovated and I staked my entire liquidity on the project, including all the funds I had in a bank in Luxembourg. The company that sold me the buildings failed in the following few months and the court seized the buildings which I had legally purchased. In addition I had to fork out additional money because I was in default of the contracts that I had signed with sub-contractors and their employees for the restructuring.

Italy is the only country in Europe and perhaps the world where, after purchasing a property and your vendor failing within two years after your purchase, your property can simply be confiscated without any compensation. I lost a cool seven million euros on the purchase of the buildings and was left without money to pay my taxes. And since my company was now in bankruptcy, the bank wouldn't loan me anything more. In other words, I was robbed of the buildings I had legally purchased and at the same time I became a tax dodger.

The money lost was mostly my own. A modest family fortune from my grandfather, who had emigrated to South America, had provided the foundation capital for my construction firm. Back in Italy he and my father had opened a hardware store that I had grown into a retail building materials business. After buying the adjacent land to expand the business, I left university to devote myself full time to this venture that was beginning to do really well.

I responded to this misfortune with all the anger and despair I could muster. I appealed to the highest authorities, but it was all to no avail! The law proved to be a mockery; its sentence condemned the healthy business that I had built with my own sacrifice! Now I had come into disfavour, was lost, even stripped of my very identity. I had considered myself to be a clever man, self assured, thoroughly vetted, even envied. In my own small way I had been a successful person. Wherever I went, I had enjoyed attention and respect. Now I was a failure, a mediocrity, just one of the many, anonymous and without worth.

Within my circle of contacts I sensed a subtle change towards me—a disconnect around me, a feeling of aloofness, and an air of mock participation. Some of my real friends did their best to comfort me but I could read in their faces that they didn't know what to say or how to act. They struggled to find the right words. I knew I needed to respond but it was difficult for me to know how. I tried to find direction in the high-school memory of the metaphor of Lucretius, who impassively observed a shipwreck taking place on the sea in front of him. But nothing could erase from my mind the reality of my economic collapse and the end of everything that had become part of me.

Since the amount of tax owed to the state was extensive and above the threshold that would mandate a jail sentence if not settled, I decided to gather what little was owed me and disappear. I could not afford to lose the crumbs of what had once been a small fortune. I had other matters pending besides the taxes and my company. Even if I didn't end up in jail, I risked losing even my other personal properties. The liquidation of my other possessions had not yet been frozen, because the tax department had not instituted their controls. The judicial process would, however, run its slow and inexorable course. I still had more or less four hundred thousand euros of value in personal assets. If I had lost those as well I might as well have dug my own grave.

And what could I do about the process of defending myself? How could I pay the lawyers? I might have been acquitted of the criminal charges, but I could not avoid the cost of the process, the fines, many surrounding issues, the disqualifications and I'm sure a good deal of other things unforeseen. I needed to say goodbye to my apartments. I could have turned them over to relatives, but then I would have committed the crime of misappropriation of funds, for not having paid fines to the state first.

As it turned out, I did manage to sell my studios and I funnelled the money into my Luxembourg bank account through a trust company. They then had the money sent abroad. Thus I managed to transfer my personal capital out of Italy, to prevent it from being gobbled up by the voracious tax authority. And I am now a felon on the run.

I had to find a place where I could live comfortably with my now meagre means and start a new life. That is easy to say, but harder to do. I had chosen Cambodia by chance while watching TV. They spoke of a terrorist who had taken refuge in Cambodia for several years. Since my offense, by comparison, was relatively minor, I thought that it would be a good place for me to go as well. Because part of the nightmare had been the evaporation of most of my monetary assets, Cambodia seemed better suited than the poor countries of Latin America where life is much more expensive.

The idea of starting a new life outside of Italy terrified me. It took a titanic effort to make such a decision. But what else could I do? Could I start to look for work at forty-four? Maybe a kind friend would hire me at his office for a 1000 euros a month, of which half would go to payroll deductions. Think of how much fun that would be! I might have to leave my attic hovel because the rent would be too much. I couldn't even afford comfortable shoes. In Cambodia, however, beach sandals would suffice.

And how exactly do you prepare, if you're leaving, likely never to return? So I sold everything, including my valuable paintings and antiques. It was like dismembering myself into a thousand pieces! I had immersed myself lovingly into every detail of my house. And yet before my journey could begin, I had to get rid of many things to which I was fondly attached. Everybody raved against it—after all my house was a reflection of me. It represented my alter-ego; I had spent more than one year furnishing and decorating it. Whenever there was a modification, a new idea applied, a minor change at perhaps the suggestion of an architect friend, or of an interior designer, it was attended to with utmost care.

I remember, the first day in April 2004 after having just landed at Phnom Penh airport, that my first impulse was to return immediately to Italy. It was sticky and suffocating hot! There I was, on a dusty road, gawking at the buses which were spewing people and billowing smoke. Many were hanging outside the bus because it was too full. I was overcome with nausea.

It was probably at just that moment and for the first time I realized that my life had really changed. I could feel the change on my face, my skin, in my eyes, my throat, and my stomach. Before, the change was known merely through sheets of stamped papers or numbers on bank statements. Now it had become soberingly real.

Through the Lonely Planet guidebook I found the address of a budget guesthouse with air conditioning. It was an empty room, with two wooden cases over which were two mattresses with no sheets. When I moved the bed I saw a used condom, which served as a lesson to me to avoid cheap places. You might risk finding roaches and such walking on your neck. Fortunately, there were also some colonial style luxury hotels built by the French, such as the Raffles Hotel, Le Royal, or the Sunway where I ended up.

I was careful not to waste my money. Now I was beginning to fear ending up on the streets. This was quite normal after what had happened to me, so I allowed myself some distractions, but no luxuries.

When I looked out of the window of the guest house, I felt that I had landed on another planet. There was incredible animation on the street, a continuous coming and going. Since the streets aren't very wide, a person in one house can look straight across the street into another's front room. There are not even curtains like a tent flap, so there isn't a concept or practice of privacy as in our countries. One can see in the neighbouring apartment who sleeps on the floor or who does the cooking, who eats when or who washes and irons the clothes. Everyday life inside the houses is lived out as if on a stage for anyone to see. If someone outside looks in at us, we immediately lower the curtains. Here, however, they do not care.

Despite this mixture of people, scooters, stray dogs, barefoot children and street vendors' stalls, it struck me that the people here were well versed in civility, behaving politely and bowing with folded hands out of respect for one another. On the common balcony of the guest house, a Cambodian girl sat down next to me and asked me if I had enough money to get her something to eat. She appeared so poor and acted so humbly that I couldn't say no. We both ate noodle soup from a pushcart peddler and it cost a dollar. Between gestures and a little of her rough English, I could sort of understand her. Her name was Pen and she had two brothers and two sisters. She sold eggs in the market and her mother had been murdered by the Khmer Rouge. I was amazed to realize that the important day of her life had been the one on which she had sold some mangos she had collected in a village, and bought her first eggs. Thus began her livelihood.

At the beginning of my sojourn I rarely went out from the guest house. Intimidated by what was outside I was reluctant to venture out. I would read or watch movies all day. The same scenes continually haunted my thoughts; while wearing a tracksuit, scenes of my past paraded in front of my eyes from morning to night. Scenes like the bank director making me sit in his office, or my being elected organizer of the tennis tournament imprisoned my mind.

Pen, my new-found friend, did not understand what I was going through. She could not; she watched me as mute as a beast. She did not understand why I suffered but she understood that I was in great pain. Sometimes I would wake up at night and find her lying on the floor at my feet because she was not used to sleeping in a bed. She made every effort to cheer me up. This was disconcerting at best. Any little thing was enough to make her laugh like a child, who laughs at any absurdity!

When we visited the market, foods were often completely covered with flies and some desserts even had flies under the plastic wrap! I would feel disgusted by what I would see but she just joked about it. I saw big rats still alive or partially so, hung by their legs on little sticks. It reminded me of African films where they carried prisoners with their hands and feet bound to a pole. The rats were gasping but there were those who bought them. Since other uses didn't come to mind, they surely must have purchased them for food. Maybe they were not sewer mice, but they weren't squirrels either. This was confirmation of what I had read, that Cambodians ate anything that moved, from grasshoppers to mice—apart from human beings of course.

I rented a scooter. Pen was driving, while I visited Buddhist monasteries, the Silver Pagoda, the Royal Palace and many buildings built by the French. I observed life along the Mekong—the fishermen, the souvenir sellers and the girls at sunset dressed in rags, but with wicker hats full of flowers or fruits on their heads. The hats they wore were a French classic worn by grandmothers of the early twentieth century that you can see in old photographs—here they are still in fashion after fifty years.

But besides the touristy, picture postcard scenes, I also saw people in a state of abandonment and poverty; a misery alive and chaotic! One senses the feeling of a world in evolution, trying to change but stuck between good and evil. I even tried to devote myself to the nightlife, built exclusively by foreigners. There were a few bars, some shabby nightclubs, restaurants of various nationalities, minimarkets with some international products and the casino. They were like islands of refuges within the city. But you are reminded continually of discomfort, difficulties and the lack of regular services and the truth of this was always driven home by the vignettes of misery and misfortune one could see everywhere.

I was deeply affected by a former school in Phnom Penh that had been used as a prison—the 'horror museum' as it was called, because it had been the torture and killing ground for thousands under the Pol Pot regime. They have basically left everything as it was. It is not a museum of glass showcases, but simply the place where the victims had been bound and tortured, left as it was. There are chains, blood-covered floors, photos of the condemned taken before, during and after torture, beds without mattresses and the irons that were heated to brand the prisoners.

Even though I loved to eat at Italian restaurants, for breakfast I frequented a bakery run by an old retired French colonel, named Gerard. He happily churned out croissants with almonds and granulated sugar while on his face, sketched like a map, one could read the vicissitudes of an intense life. He was the first person to introduce me to real Cambodian life. He instructed me on how to move and behave and in which places to hang out. Unfortunately he has recently passed away, and it was a loss to me.

"You see, Cambodia has a thousand resources," Gerard would say, "and theoretically could have an enviable food sufficiency. Cambodia has enormous lowlands with very few inhabitants and from an agricultural point of view it is ideal. It has a land area slightly greater than Bangladesh, but with only 12 million inhabitants, just a tenth of the Bangladesh population. It has an enormous tourism potential, with many islands and pristine beaches. Traveling on the Mekong one can visit Laos, China and Thailand by boat. In theory, anything you plant in Cambodia will flourish. Start any kind of establishment and it will thrive. Since there is so little production here most products come from Thailand or China, even including the soft drinks! But unfortunately there is also no reliable government structure either. The judicial and police systems are untrustworthy. One is often exposed to illegitimate rackets where you either pay up or end up pushing up daisies.

If there were reliable laws, law enforcers and security, Cambodia would flourish like a desert spring. A Thai company once bought sea-front property in Sihanoukville, with the plan of constructing some hotels. Suddenly the government proclaimed that the land belonged to the state and the Thai company was dispossessed of their legally purchased property."

But I thought, "Maybe I could be a pioneer, one of the first to invest here with very little money and if the situation changed, I would strike it rich."

Gerard's answer struck me like a boulder; "What you have now is the best. There is nothing more here for you. The truth is that you're not really in Cambodia. You heart is still in Italy. Your world is there. Your life is there. Your yardstick of comparison comes from there and is the best. You don't see the reality around you. You don't have eyes for this country. Cambodians don't exist for you. It's all only local fauna. You are too refined to lower yourself to the level of these beggars. You don't care a lick about this country.

You need to delude yourself that you're still rich or to tell yourself how powerful you are."

Pen became loquacious, speaking often of her economic difficulties and trying through pity to scrounge some money. But she seemed to be light years away from my reality. She lived from day to day, without any apparent interests, ambition or cultural curiosity. She stoically took life as it came.

Despite her constant attention to me, she seemed to me a stranger, more like a nurse or a house servant. She also neglected some small body details that generally women see as important. It's not that she wasn't clean but she neglected things like shaving her armpits. Eventually I found an excuse to leave her. Yet soon after, perhaps because of boredom, fatigue or total paranoia, I began to look for her.

I located her father's hut. The sewers close to his hut formed rivulets that overflowed from various places under the foundation. The raised floor was made from rickety boards and reeked with the smell of sewage, while bugs emerged from one crack and re-entered another. The father was about 70 years old—a formal type and badly off. He was skinny and at most one meter sixty tall, and he had few teeth left in his mouth, but he smiled a lot. We sat cross-legged on the floor, where he told me that Pen was not there, but that I could take another of his daughters. He extracted a photo from a box showing Pen with her younger sister, in traditional costumes of thin plant leaves and sequins; they were miming a folk dance with the movements of their hands. They displayed a candid air—two solemn and proper little girls who studied at a school of classical dance.

While he was looking in the box for other pictures of the sisters to show me, I noticed a photo of a soldier in uniform. Sensing my curiosity, he told me that it was a photo of himself. He had been a soldier of the Khmer Rouge, a Communist political organization that ruled Cambodia between 1975 and 1979. He then showed me the photos of his wife and his brother-in-law. Through gestures and a few words of English I understood that they were murdered by the Khmer Rouge on the very floor where we sat. He had been considered a traitor for having hidden his brother-in-law, who was an active anti-communist, in his house. He managed to escape because he was not at home the day when his wife and her brother were killed.

He showed me the photos of his classmates and his teacher, who was also murdered by the Khmer Rouge. He said that when he was a soldier of the Khmer Rouge he never looked in the face of his victims; he did not want to meet someone he might know. The political arm of the Khmer Rouge was responsible for the Cambodian genocide that resulted in the deaths of 2.5 million people through starvation, forced labour and executions. It was a real massacre of Cambodians, by Cambodians! Both friends and relatives were often on opposite sides; sometimes one had to kill a friend in order not to be killed oneself. The Khmer Rouge forced the entire population of the city into the countryside to work on common farms. They abolished hospitals, schools, banks, the use of money, and 'bourgeois' careers such as teachers, doctors, lawyers, etc.

I understood through the gestures of the father that Pen had some handicap or illness, perhaps in her back. I recalled that I had once found her trembling with her eyes damp with tears. She had run away to avoid being seen by me. A strange expression was used by her father to convince me that it was better to give up Pen, especially now that she was at her grandmother's house in Siem Reap. At the same time he insistently bombarded me with photos of the little sister. I politely declined the offer and was about to leave when he asked me for some money to buy cigarettes. I bought him enough cigarettes to enjoy for a week and he thanked me without end.

The meeting with Pen's father had disturbed me. His persistence at wanting to give me his little daughter seemed like an attempt to distract me from looking for Pen and the mention of her alleged illness raised some feelings of suspicion in me. I decided on the spot to go to Siem Reap, to look for her and to be with her—after all I had nothing better to do. And she had been the only person who had managed to make me smile; in return I had given her a fistful of dollars, her marching orders and relegated her to the task of nursing her grandmother.

I traveled via the Tonle Sap River, which flows both north and south and eventually into the great Tonle Sap Lake. Moving by river in Cambodia is a standard way of traveling. Often we had to get out and push the boat, with feet planted in the mud, because there was little water. Then where the river was high, the boat began to move very quickly. We encountered a constant wind of fifty kilometers an hour and had to crouch down one behind the other for relief. More than once the boat quit in the middle of the river until a punt arrived and funnelled gas to us. Cans dripped streams of gasoline while the operator was smoking away! When there was no wind, we breathed gasoline fumes. And during the last half hour a storm broke—a nice shower driven by fifty km an hour winds! They covered the boat with a tarp, but things didn't change much. Then, after the river episode, we traveled about ten miles by truck. It felt like you were dancing all the time because the ground was full of potholes and broken curbs. It was truly only a cattle truck in which all the occupants were standing.

All that nightmarish travel was for Pen, who in Italy would have been no more than a cleaning lady. Siem Reap, the small village where I arrived the first time, had two traffic lights that signalled the seconds to the next colour change. When they were installed, the news was reported in all the Cambodian newspapers. In the evening, one walked the main street, which was the public walkway. Suddenly there was a power outage and since there was no moon or starlight we were enveloped in total darkness. Within minutes, the little shops on the street were animated with candles.

Most of the restaurants are simply outdoor kitchens, with lots of pots. By lifting a lid you can see what's for dinner inside the pot. The candles did help to see into the pot but inevitably a few drops of wax landed in the food. Groups of three or four people would suddenly appear out of the darkness right next to you. It was spooky! Sometimes girls appeared in brightly coloured silk pyjamas, because Cambodians often go out in their pyjamas in the evening. I walked on in the dark and heard strange noises. After about an hour the lights came on again. Those strange noises turned out to be bicycles with their riders going around in their pyjamas in the dark.

During the day girls normally walk barefoot but with the usual flower adorned hat. I stopped to chat with a girl in pyjamas about Pen while her friends approached, but no one had ever heard of a girl by that name. Then after I moved on, one of them accompanied by a boy came up to me on a motor scooter. The boy said that he knew Pen and volunteered to accompany me to her for three dollars. I immediately jumped on the motorbike without further discussing the price, which was rather daring. We left Siem Reap behind, between potholes and puddles. Trash fires illuminated huts of tin plate and cardboard, surrounded by pieces of wreckage, uprooted sofas and numerous car seats. The bike was traveling farther and farther, until I began to suspect that I had fallen into some kind of nasty trap.

Finally he stopped in front of a gate and we entered a small door. There were many girls in pyjamas and one of them was rubbing her eyes. It was clear she had been awakened. She was at most fifteen. They made me sit in a room that was less than two meters wide. There was a single bed and while passing my hand over a sheet, I felt something like sand. On the wall over the bed were some nails with wet towels hanging on them so you had to be careful not to impale your head on the nails. On a shelf opposite the bed there was a fan, a light bulb and a plastic bottle cut in half, full of condoms. Magazine pictures were stuck haphazardly around the walls.

I waited almost half an hour, all the while putting up with the moans coming from the next room. I imagined one of the occupants to be sexually gifted. Then a girl with a towel wrapped around her head and slippers on entered the room. She said her name was Pen but was not the Pen I was looking for. Before leaving the brothel I peeked in the next room where I could still hear the gifted one. It was really a pigsty full of pigs!

I resolved to just forget Pen, especially since it was proving so difficult to find her! I stopped back in Siem Reap because, just two kilometers from this insignificant village, was the UNESCO-protected site of Angkor Wat containing the ruins of one of the most famous temples in Asia.

I needed to lose myself in something timeless. Angkor communicates a sense of the supernatural which dwarfs your life, helping you to look beyond your seemingly insignificant journey. It makes you realize that something here was truly remarkable even a thousand years ago. Buddhists from all over Asia have gone on pilgrimages over the years so that many stories are carved in bas-relief representations on the walls as well as in the hearts of the many visitors. The Wat is a series of temples spread over a vast area of forest and the forest itself is eating away the site. Trees grow right through the stones and their roots cause the blocks of stone to shift all over the temple. The roots can move anything—when a tree grows, it breaks the cement like broken ice while making lumps in the walkways. These trees are devouring the temples, just like in the Lara Croft movie. The whole place has the feel of an Indiana Jones scene, where one is lost in the forest with a little monkey jumping around in front of you. One is almost afraid to touch a stone lest everything around it comes crashing down.

Angkor Wat now has the new airport at Siem Reap to serve it and tourist traffic has grown, prompting the opening of many new shops, hotels and restaurants; people of many nations stop for a day or two. There is a cosmopolitan air about the place now.

When I returned to Siem Reap to take a plane back to Phnom Penh, I met one of the girls that I had seen the first evening I arrived there. She told me that she had done some snooping around and had located Mui, Pen's sister and her family. She said she would be glad to accompany me to her house for two dollars. I followed her, quite sceptically, through a swamp full of bushes, brambles and thorns. The family lived in a small wooden construction raised off the ground. It was a single room divided by rags hung from a wire and there were mats on the floor where Mui, her two sons and husband slept. They told me that Pen was in a small village a short distance away, which did not even have a name because it was only a hamlet with a few huts. From things spoken and descriptions offered, I realized that we were finally speaking of the Pen I was looking for. I expected to encounter somewhat emotionless people but instead I received a festive, vivacious and warm welcome.

The Cambodians are a tough people because while you know what they have suffered they do not burden you with it. They have endured years and years of misery and bloodshed, so how they can exhibit displays of joy and happiness remains a mystery. Their kindness is genuine and not yet polluted by tourist cynicism, as in neighbouring Thailand. This was despite the fact that during the Khmer Rouge regime, two of the total seven million Cambodians had been ruthlessly murdered. In the West we continually speak of the plight of the Jews, but it seems that few in the world take notice of these lost two million Cambodians.

Their culture had been all but destroyed when Pol Pot wiped out the intellectual promise of a whole generation, so the country lacks national cohesion. They are a people at the mercy of those who arrive and know how to speak; they seem easily manipulated. The country lacks a strong identity like Thailand, Vietnam or China. There is a king but he is without power or direction and does not really count in the daily lives of the people. There is a democracy but the real power lies at the mercy of those most cunning and rich.

With some general directions from the sister, I found Pen tending to her sick grandmother at a place about 15 km from Siem Reap. There I found the grandmother, a dog and Pen, who was coughing all the time, in a hut raised from the ground on piles, with a crooked floor, an old wardrobe and blinking lights around an image of a Buddha. The latrine was outside and consisted of four walls with tin roof with a place to squat in the center. My immediate thought was to go buy a sharp razor and slit my wrists. I was psychologically torn up, but having found a bit of family warmth I decided to stay a few days.

I ended up staying almost six months.

Pen looked after me like a mother. She comforted me with her naïve joy, generated by the smallest of things. She had a special antenna that alerted her to when I wanted to be alone. Some nights when I rambled on or was delirious, I took some Rohypnol that you can buy here as readily as noodles and without prescription. She spent her nights watching over both me and her grandma, often rubbing me down with a wet cloth. I could not get used to their food and spent more than one night inhabiting the outhouse. I nursed thoughts of dying. Once I put my hands in their open air water tank and they reprimanded me because it was the source of their drinking water. I occasionally went to Seam Reap to stock up on bottled water.

A neighbour who had an old, battered, windowless Mercedes became my chauffeur. There was no city-generated electricity and only a few individual generators but the starlight was sufficient for walking. Having lived in a city, I had never noticed that the stars give out so much light.

The family was used to throwing everything on the floor; however they do wash clothes three times a day. Pen washed a shirt for me after having worn it only once. But they let cobwebs form all over the house and give little notice to a cockroach slipping under a mat. You have to adapt yourself and not try to change them. They often eat their little bag of fried beetles or larvae like they were potato chips.

It's important not to get bitten by mosquitoes here as you risk malaria. The standard protections are mosquito nets on the bed, the wearing of long pants, using shirts with long sleeves and applying lots of insect repellent!

A obvious question arises at this point. How can one reject the Western lifestyle? How can you voluntarily ban yourself from city life with its cinemas, restaurants and shops? Living here like this has been a challenge to me and I tell myself repeatedly that if I keep my head about me I will emerge stronger. The whole day you have in front of you four rundown huts, a mangy dog that strolls around in circles, two grubby children playing and an old man sleeping on a mat.

What strikes me, however, is the advanced civility and lack of vulgarity of these modest people. We in the West expect slum people to be rude and profane—they, on the contrary, are very decent. The collars of their shirts may be torn but they are rarely dirty.

I had never been in the midst of rice fields! There were also little rivers; I went fishing. I discovered that even some fish sleep. In a sense I lost myself in the act of fishing.

I once saw a duck in the mouth of a dog. I saved her and grew attached to her. One day Pen made me find other ducks. She said, "You have to clip their wings, otherwise they would escape." But that was not necessary; they always returned because I treated them so well.

More than once I tried to mention to Pen the illness that her father had mentioned to me. She always dismissed the matter with a laugh, pretending that I had completely misunderstood what he said. Instead she made efforts to convince me that she was as healthy as a horse. For the most part her behaviour seemed normal. She did all that she could to comfort me and her grandmother. It almost seemed that her purpose for living was to take care of others and not herself.

I honestly felt that I wouldn't be able to survive in this environment without music and films on CDs and in English of course. So I took a trip to Siem Reap and bought a whole suitcase full of entertainment media. Sometimes I watched as many as three or four films a day. In the evening the whole village gathered to watch the movies that I had purchased. The generator was noisy so I watched the movies with headphones. Some movies I watched more than once. I now know many lines from *Back to the Future* from memory. I am fascinated by the third film in the series where Michael J. Fox, the star of the movie, finds himself back in a previous time more than one hundred years in the past. He didn't even have a fridge!

On only one occasion was the tranquility of the village upset. A father had refused to give consent to his son to marry a girl. He wanted the son to become a Buddhist monk, which for a Cambodian family is a cause for great pride. His son, torn between love for his girl and respect for his father, decided to get drunk on rice wine in one of those shacks that they call a karaoke. Then he paraded in front of his father completely drunk and burned his moped. The newspaper gave prominence to this news, especially because respect for elders has great value in the community. The boy ended up marrying the girl anyway.

It became an event in the village when I went to Siem Reap and bought Pen a flowered dress, rubber boots and a nightgown. She liked to be watched but considered me strange when I made her wear and model sexy underwear. She wore panties with puppets on them. One night to make me happy she put on the Tom Jones CD, *What's New Pussycat?*, one of those songs that defined my days in Rome, and she attempted to add to my delight by doing a striptease to the song. She did her very best but she was quite inadequate, pathetic and even clumsy. For Cambodians sex is a natural thing and they don't understand our making it complicated and depraved. Who knows what I would have done to relive one of those escapades in the attic on Via Cassia, surrounded by exquisite objects, antique furniture, silk sheets, and my last partner?

The intrigue of our relationship was founded in mutual understanding, heightened by hints, allusions and both physical and mental provocations. Pen doesn't know the seductiveness of a neckline, of a skin-tight skirt, or of stiletto heels while, for me, the ability to dress up and put on dazzling make-up is part of the feminine mystique of seduction.

At a restaurant in Siem Reap, Pen spent a quarter of an hour trying to read and understand the menu. She then ordered a copious number of dishes and as she did not eat everything, she packed the leftovers to go. This was carted home and distributed to her family members and some of her neighbours. Strangely, I appreciated that over-abundance of food, because maybe in a special way I identified with Pen but I also enjoyed the pleasure of seeing her satisfied. But maybe there was another deeper reason. Having reached rock bottom in my life, I now appreciated things that once I took for granted.

By now she considered me her man. But I knew that one day I would have to leave her. Our relationship lacked the entente made of affinity, interests and common experiences. She was attentive but I sensed in her a lack of passion, a trait which perhaps does not even exist here, but is a necessary complicity between lovers. But how I could tell that to her? Her new-found world would certainly collapse. I had become the livelihood for her father, brothers, sister and grandmother. Even without asking me for anything, I could feel their need wrapped around my neck like a hangman's noose. Yet I regretted the thought of leaving her, because I would feel alone again. Relationships here are based more on roles than on connections. A Westerner accustomed to sharing problems with his partner, or willing to cooperate on domestic jobs is interpreted here as weak, because he is surrendering part of his power to his woman. The Cambodian girls are simple. When they eat, they sit on the floor with their feet on one side and not in the lotus position as men do, because it is assumed that when something is needed they will be the ones to get up and get it or do it. Some girls have men who beat them. One woman went to the village chief to protest such a beating and he simply replied, "It's your husband. So what do you want me to do about it?"

When I heard that another Italian had come to live in a nearby village, I jumped on the bike and ran to look for him. The direct road was seven kilometers but had not yet been cleared of landmines, and in order to avoid them I cycled about ten extra kilometers under the hot sun. A man who was working in the fields asked me for a ride and I subsequently took him to his home, a kilometer away, sitting on the crossbar. He lived in a shack behind a couple of trees. The inside of his abode consisted of nothing more than a mat, two pots and a charcoal stove. He was not a bum but rather like many other Cambodians who lived the same way.

Further down the road I encountered a woman emerging from a rice-field, carrying on her shoulder a boy who had lost a leg. Throughout Cambodia there are nearly two million unexploded landmines still buried in the ground and too often someone loses a limb on that account. Needless to say you get used to seeing amputees in many places and yet that particular scene remains engraved on my mind, perhaps because of the desolation of the place.

According to the directions I had, I recognized the Italian's house, which was built partly of brick masonry and was surrounded by a large yard, where a battered pickup truck was parked. Scattered around here and there was a tricycle, a couple of mangy teddy bears and a number of issues of the Italian magazine, *Gente*. The latter were piled on a washing machine which had a clever but obviously homemade external pipe connection. Then I saw him, standing out in the sun, inserting a broomstick in a bush. My first thought was, "What is an Italian wearing a cowboy hat and a Barilla shirt doing in a place like this? Why wasn't he in Phnom Penh, where there is at least a modicum of life?" Then it struck me that I was here too.

I leaned over and yelled: "Hello, can I bother you a minute? Are you Italian?" He looked at me with a hard expression. "Yes, why?" he replied. I told him that I was Italian too and lived just a few kilometers down the road. He looked me up and down, not overly convinced and eventually invited me to come into his home. "Are you that one with the sexy lingerie?" he asked. I didn't understand, but then he added, "The voices here run like the wind. It may look like a deserted place but there are people where you don't expect anyone to be." My mania for sexy lingerie had gone around the rice fields, but it had not aroused animosity, only curiosity! There is no morbidity for sexual things here in Cambodia.

My countryman showed me in and merely one glance around was enough to prove the resident of this abode was an Italian. The place was the only one with shutters, a coffeepot and a mound of Lavazza sachets. In addition he was a member of the financial police!

To describe his place as desolate would have been an understatement. George's home was well situated in a slightly raised area, sheltered by trees, which overlooked rice fields and scattered hovels. There were no further questions to ask each other. The only one question was, "What were we doing in this ass-end of the world?" I immediately blurted out my entire history. I felt instinctively or naively that I could trust him, even if he was an off-duty cop!

He offered me some homemade popcorn. Every so often, like an apparition, someone timid but curious would poke their head into the room. George seemed to be surrounded by a tribe of Cambodians. One by one he introduced me to them all. There was his wife of about forty, some young children, the brothers of his wife, the mother-in-law, the wives of the brothers and their respective children, some neighbours and a few dogs and chickens. There was even an adopted child. He related to me that once, at a gas station, a man on a motorbike in line in front of George, after having filled his tank full of gas realized that he didn't have enough money. He asked George to loan him the money to pay the gas station attendant and told him that he would leave his son as collateral. He did not come back for the boy and George, without blinking, kept the child who is now part of his whole clan. The child's father probably imagined that since George was a rich foreigner he could offer the child a better and more prosperous life. George pointed him out to me playing in a corner with the other children. He seemed perfectly at ease, cheerful and without a problem in the world. He was growing up, together with the others and like the others. I had the feeling that many problems that we encounter in our country are not even considered problems here—for example the different treatment that the parents can accord to an illegitimate son. In Cambodia there are thousands of cases of abandoned children. Sometime when a family is not able to support them, they merely abandon them, hoping that someone with more substance will take care of them.

We had started to relate to each other our mutual misadventures when the village chief arrived—a typical Cambodian like so many! He dressed in sandals, trousers at least one size too large, and an undershirt torn at the back. He arrived on a dilapidated moped with a broken headlight. He bowed with folded hands and then took his gun and put it in George's hands as a sign of trust and respect. According to George he was a half-hearted lush and so every time that he came, George offered him a beer. To repay the kindness, the chief had come to propose that George act as judge in disputes between Cambodians.

The village chief here is normally the mayor, the police chief and the judge. When two people have a disagreement, they go to him and he decides who is right. There aren't any lawyers, official documents or processes that will last a lifetime. But George declined the offer, preferring not to make any enemies in the village.

George was my opposite physically. Being originally from Mestre he was stocky, muscular and dark-skinned and limped a little as a result of an accident on a motorbike. In contrast I'm tall, thin and have pale skin. It seemed that Italy did not concern him anymore, having put his native land completely out of mind. How could he be so comfortable with the Cambodian environment? So integrated? I found in him an attitude which repulsed me, yet at the same time fascinated me. He had to be a very simple-minded person to be so at ease among culturally backward people. Certainly, in Italy we would never have become friends. Here the fact that one is a fellow-countryman is usually sufficient reason to become friends. Yet many of his ways of doing things charmed me. He had some words for each Cambodian—he joked with them, he harangued them, he exhorted them, he reprimanded them. I almost envied him.

He was the type who told you things when he decided to and not when you asked him. He soon began to talk freely about himself, almost non-stop, as if I were there to record his memoirs. He related stories from when he was ten years old. He remembered a girl named Elisa and how they had sent kisses to each other out through a window because she could not come out. Then he continued by telling the story of a schoolmate of his that he eventually married. Once married they bought a detached house with two floors which he registered in his new wife's name. They had two children together. Later he had an affair with a much younger girl whom he married in a quickie ceremony in Las Vegas. He returned to Italy with her and had another child with her. For years he was the head of these two families simultaneously. He had always managed to make everyone feel good, although at times he made some mistakes like buying a shampoo for one house and bringing it to the other. He reasoned that he was a generous person—with his feelings, his body and his wallet. He preferred that his women were in need of nothing and he loved especially to see them happy. He liked large families and with every woman he intended to build something special.

After he retired in Italy, he was arrested for bigamy. For years he had lived in two families, each unknown to the other. According to him he was a model father, but now he had been discovered and denounced.

He let me know that that was not his only debacle. He also told me that he not only had that house but had created yet another. He maintained an apartment in Phnom Penh where he kept another, younger Cambodian wife who was also pregnant. Who knows what convoluted mental mechanism convinced him to take on the burden of two families, each with their own multitude of problems. Was it a delusion of grandeur? Did it arise out of a need to make family life exciting? Was he enamoured with the myth of the patriarch, the head of the tribe?

The house in Phnom Penh, which I did subsequently see after we got to know one another better, was the sort of place that resembled a status symbol of a poor Cambodian who had achieved a significant standard of living. It revealed its owner as a town person who was almost educated. "Here in Cambodia I don't carry guilty feelings or a fear of being discovered," George told me. "It is sufficient to ensure that my family has the essentials, a bit of economic tranquility and after that they overlook so many things. I do my best to give everyone what he needs. Sometimes in the middle of the night I wake up wondering how much longer I can still manage this lifestyle. You are almost sixty years old now, George!"

There is an area in the northeast, near Vietnam, where there are lakes full of fresh water, with frolicking dolphins. I went there with Pen, George and Soi, his Phnom Penh wife. Soi's purpose to go there was to scatter the ashes of her dad in the river. I followed George passively, because I needed to understand his acceptance, and his way, of living a Cambodian lifestyle.

We carried Soi's father's coffin to a temple for cremation. We traveled by bamboo train, which is a simple trolley with a bamboo base, without sides or railing, acting almost like a raft on wheels and track. A Cambodian commanded the first 'coach' with a powered cultivator motor, connected to the carriage. It was almost like putting a fan on a boat to propel it. While we were travelling along, another train approached from the opposite direction with a bigger load and more wagons. So since there was only one track, we had to unload the corpse, dismantle the train and stack the pieces along the edge of the rail. After letting the other 'convoy' pass, the funeral train was reassembled! Corruption raised its head when two policemen had to be bribed to allow our illegal train to pass. When foreigners are involved, the police always seize the opportunity to make a little extra money.

Most real locomotives and wagons were destroyed by the Khmer Rouge in their attempt to return Cambodia to the Stone Age. The jungle has covered most of the tracks. The locals have resurrected this train route, built by the French in 1930 and have dug up the lines from the jungle.

Pen, George, his wife, his family, their relatives and friends and I ate dinner together. It almost seemed that the fact of the father's death had been forgotten. But in reality a funeral, for the Cambodians, does not exclude manifestations of life and becomes an opportunity to share in the unity of life and family through simple events such as sharing a meal. They use any occasion to practice poise, unity and group cohesion that promotes a sense of oneness. George tried to explain the principle by giving the following example: In Cambodia if there are ten people, another one is easily absorbed in the midst of so many. Where one eats, ten can eat. They readily divide the food for ten to feed a hundred.

By contrast, in Italy, we are die-hard individualists and resist attempts to share. Yet when a father dies, filthy greed appears among the heirs. As soon as there is a meatball to be divided, the heirs start acting like a pack of hungry dogs. They hardly give the deceased a proper time of mourning.

Here all are brothers and try to help each other. If you make one enemy, you make all of them enemies. If you favour one, you favour everybody. The Cambodian woman never separates herself from her family. As you become decrepit they are all willing to do right for you. They all assist with washing you, without any regret for your old age or any disgust at your wrinkles. Respect for life shines through clearly. There aren't the media influences that cause you to see an old man as hideous, or to worship only the young and smooth.

After a few days Pen suffered a respiratory crisis. I called a doctor who gave her anti-inflammatory drugs and administered oxygen. She has a lung infection, possibly from being exposed to 'Agent Orange', a chemical weapon used by the Americans in Vietnam and widely used in Cambodia as well. Medical sources give little hope of recovery but the disease can be controlled with medication, unless there is a sudden acute crisis.

I took her to a specialist in Phnom Penh where we bought drugs coming out of Thailand. Now her condition is under control, though lately her respiratory crises have increased. The doctor did not give her more than a year to live. I began to understand why she had hidden her illness from me, because in Cambodia no one would take a sick woman as a wife.

One of the unbelievable paradoxes in this country is that despite overwhelming evidence of humanity, there are also episodes of incomprehensible cynicism. This truth was exemplified by a neighbour's situation—they had a daughter who was three years old and who had stopped eating. Her skin had wrinkled pitiably and she had become nothing more than a skeleton. She looked like a little monster, so that George and I cruelly used to call her E.T. The mother, who had been deserted by her husband and left with three children, abandoned the child alone in a corner of the house to die slowly. It was unbelievable that a parent could do such a thing, but since she could not maintain all the children, she calculated that she had to sacrifice one.

In Europe a parent is scandalized if the school finds an infestation of head lice. Here people don't even take notice unless someone is dying—and maybe not even then. If we go to war in Iraq and somebody dies there, there is an uproar. Public opinion is mobilized; the Pope sends messages from his balcony and people with placards run screaming through the streets.

George and I offered to bring the baby to Phnom Penh and to pay the hospital costs. In cases of serious medical need, it is better to resolve them in Phnom Penh where there are effective, though expensive, medical centers and you can find appropriate care. In the rest of the nation it is better not to get hurt as there is a chronic shortage of physicians in Cambodia, most having been killed by Pol Pot because they were educated people. You can buy any medicine here without a doctor's prescription but sometimes the box may have the usual colours and markings, and can contain only well packaged sugar.

The next morning George and I went to take the baby but the mother was not there. The baby looked cadaverous with her eyes closed. It seemed she was destined to expire at any moment so we had to leave as soon as possible. She had maybe only a matter of hours to live.

The journey of about eight hours became twenty, because the bus never follows a planned route. Arrival times are always uncertain. With the bus bouncing around on the road, the red earth arose in clouds of dust, came through open windows and stained everything. This red grit gets into your teeth, your eyes, your ears—and this is when it's not raining; otherwise you're covered with mud. If the bus breaks down, you risk stopping in the middle of nothingness and nowhere. If you're lucky, as happened to us, you stay overnight in a nearby village.

After dark there is absolutely no intercity travel. One never knows what strange things can happen to you. In Cambodia, one dares to travel only on certain routes. If one travels by taxi or motorbike he never leaves the road even for a quick relief stop. I learned through experience not to put too much trust in information about the security of a given place or the usability of a certain road. The Cambodians don't have a realistic view of the danger of travel.

I found myself riding a motorcycle on a road recommended to me by a Cambodian friend and I almost broke my neck! I also risked spending a night in the terrifying company of wild animals. But for Cambodians a night outdoors can be quite a normal thing. If you stop to eat somewhere, make sure that the restaurant help opens a bottle of water in front of you and only brush your teeth with bottled water. Observe that meat and fish have not been spoiled and eat as much as possible in well frequented places. Don't touch any strange items on the roadside; there are landmines and unexploded artillery everywhere. Beware also of snakes, including the deadly Hanuman, which are easily camouflaged because of their green color.

In Phnom Penh, after a few days of intravenous drip and a few hundred dollars of assorted treatments, the baby survived and thrived. She now lives with me and Pen. She is a beautiful little girl, lively and smiling. The mother is happy too because we have taken a load off her mind. The girl's upbringing doesn't cost me too much because she grows up among the other kids. With so many others around there is no need of a babysitter or of kindergarten. This was one potentially devastating story with a happy ending.

Now George and I are like brothers. Even though I moved with Pen to Sihanoukville, he often comes to see me with one of his wives, and I know that I can count on him anytime. For the very few residents and tourists who can afford it, Sihanoukville is becoming the vacation place *par excellence* of Cambodia. It is developing day by day. One of the few good two-lane asphalted roads in the country connects Phnom Penh to Sihanoukville. Don't imagine that it is the promenade of Rimini, for at night the streets are almost deserted except for some central places. There is some music on the beach, two nightclubs in the red-light area, a Mercedes or two of dubious origin cruising around and a 24-hour casino. Normally there is nothing around here but desert and degradation. But when there are festivities, Sihanoukville comes alive.

Here I've opened a simple dining place with four tables attached to a four bedroom guesthouse. I had been an entrepreneur before and I wanted to be one here now. What I earn allows me to survive here, consuming only a small part of my capital.

The sea in this area is clean and clear and so transparent that you can easily see a wheel, a bottle, a shoe or other objects underwater. This place makes a positive impression on you—stretching out before you is a beautiful white beach with clean water, despite a little underwater trash. It's not polluted, without flecks of sea foam or sewage that pours out into the sea. It's full of innocence and ignorant of what might be.

Obviously I have different problems now than from those I had in Italy. There are few real roads, little drinking water and electricity that is intermittent at best. It is better to have a generator, but where can you buy one? You may buy it overseas but then how do you get it to where you are? And be sure and get two of them in case one breaks down, because it is unlikely to get fixed. Foreign money here is worth a lot, so obtaining certain things is not so difficult.

Just for fun, I started making some handmade ice cream. I didn't know where else to get a good lemon sorbet, which goes so well with grilled fish. I started with recipes found on the internet. At first the results were quite disgusting, only fit to be thrown away. I had to do the discarding secretly since it's not good practice to throw food away publicly. Now the ice cream is delicious and there are girls who come by to buy it, for resale on the beach. They keep the ice cream in plastic boxes inside other boxes of polystyrene. I have now built an ice-cream making machine by modifying an old freezer.

Eventually every real entrepreneur wants to work. Give him some tools and he has a good time. But if you muzzle, cheat or discourage him, he won't work anymore. Here there are valid, objective difficulties. For example if I have to climb a tree and there are no footholds I simply find some wood and form a makeshift ladder.

By contrast in Italy I suffered from bureaucratic difficulties that could not be solved with talented thinking but only with contracts and lawyers. I was a businessman and not a lawyer, but I found myself struggling to find legal solutions to many situations. I often had to delegate problems relating to my work (which in itself was a problem of construction and renovation) to other professionals because I had no time to worry about shuffling paperwork. Then there were other annoyances. They considered me a sort of Uncle Scrooge and every occasion was an opportunity to tap me for money. One time a fire broke out in the meadow behind my business and when the firemen arrived, they asked me for money to extinguish the fire.

One evening by chance I found a letter in a drawer, written by Pen with my name on it. Though it was written in barely decipherable English, she said that she had loved me and thanked me for everything I had done for her and for her family. In it she also expressed the desire that I would marry her little sister. I asked her to explain but she dodged any real answers, implying that it was only a joke. Only after I become angry, did she admit that she had no intention of leaving me. She had written the letter because she thought she was going to die and that I was supposed to find the letter after her death. Then she confided with emotional sarcasm that she was sorry that she was unable to give me what an Italian woman could. I did not know what to say. We remained for a long time in a silent embrace.

I am delighted when I find someone who speaks Italian here. We talk a lot. Characteristic of life in Cambodia are long, almost interminable, conversations between fellow countrymen. Being far removed from their country, the chatter becomes like a ritual of sorts. And, of course, Italian is the language of argument. A friend of mine, Mario from Naples and who travels the world, summed up my life and consoled me by telling me, "You are richer than Berlusconi and you don't know it. It is a real privilege staying on this beach and talking with everyone who passes by. The best thing in life is to live without too much fuss. Berlusconi cannot say that he has the pleasure of lounging under the sun or lying in front of the sea. He may have some votes, the Congress, bodyguards, bouncers and villas. Many famous artists I have known are unhappy—almost all of them are drug addicts! Lucio Battisti was always camouflaging his life. He could not even go out of his house to buy cigarettes, and then they shot him in his house anyway. Here they bring you fruit, adjust your deckchair, arrange your towel and move your umbrella when the sun moves. Does Berlusconi live like this?"

By now I can finally manage the Cambodian language. It has a different alphabet from ours but it is not so hard because it is not a tonal language. There are no words that change their meaning with changing intonations. I have now lived in Cambodia for two years. Even cable TV has arrived and now I can watch an Italian station, changing the inside of my house into a little piece of Italy. They discuss the poor men of Africa, the lack of human rights in China, the death penalty in America, even the rights of dogs, but they rarely talk about Italian injustice. How many people in Italy have waited for over twelve years for judgments in civil suits?

I could go back to Italy now because my accountant has arranged a tax amnesty, but my buildings are lost and it would not be the same as before. The strange thing is that I miss some places more than the people; for example the center of Rome or the street where my house was and the cafe on the corner where I used to sit and eat my breakfast. Wherever you go in Italy, you're surrounded by beautiful works of art but if you live there, you rarely notice them. Not often do you linger in a square or on a street or at a monument. Everybody is caught up with many other distractions. But you only understand that when you're far away.

After what happened to me, I tried to deny the country that nurtured my downfall. But here, much more so than in Italy, I realize that to be Italian is very different from being Chinese. Yet I can say now that I feel integrated into this country, and no longer feel like an outsider. Cambodia has changed me. The continuous sight of poverty and misfortune but also the serenity of the Cambodians has given me a new view of existence, both fatalistic and at the same time peaceful.

I recently returned to Italy with Pen because I had to satisfy two desires. First I wanted to go back to Italy just as a tourist and secondly I wanted to give Pen a wonderful and final dream-like present. I showed her the Colosseum in Rome, the Arena in Verona, San Marco Square in Venice—and she begged to have her photo taken in front of the automatic car washing machine in Mestre!

A Psychological Perspective

This is a situation which occurs frequently, in which one goes to live in a poor country to feel rich. The main motivation in this story was not to escape from a bad financial situation, but instead from a country that reminded him of his loss of social standing.

He chooses a new country where he can remain in a relatively privileged position. But why seek a state of degradation in a village where the conditions are so poor? Emerging from the bottom, even going to eat in a modest restaurant, can be appealing.

The continual sight of misery and misfortune—and also the fundamental serenity of the Cambodians—have introduced him to a more fatalistic and peaceful vision of life.

5

From Romania to America
I met a man with a secret

A country girl from Romania:

Hi!! My name is Alexandra.
One day I met a strange guy who was sleeping in a pickup truck. He was from Colorado and was traveling around Europe. By his neglected way of dressing, his long hair, and being tall and thin, he looked Romanian. There was a strange, almost sinister aura about him, although he actually turned out to be a kind person. I liked listening to his stories about America.
He eventually came with me to Transylvania to visit Dracula's castle. I think he thought I was one of the many young girls who go to the cities of Constance or Neptune on the Black Sea in the summer, in search of foreigners with loads of money. He was surprised when I didn't yield to his advances. I don't know if I was more attracted to him for his personality or because he came from America. He told me that his work in America was as a coach driver and that he had won a healthy sum of money in a lottery. With that he had decided to travel in Europe for a year.
My American friend Robert had a hat like Humphrey Bogart, wore sunglasses even at night and turned the collar of his shirt up. He reasoned that he suffered from a lack of melanin and did not want expose his skin to the sun. In addition he ate carrots all the time, like a rabbit. He filled his refrigerator with Coca Cola, tea, coffee and had many colourful watches. He gave me four different watches, so I even gave one to my neighbour. He supplied me with cheese for a month too.
I'm from the Transylvanian countryside, where most people make a living by what comes from the earth. Even during the communist regime, although there wasn't much money, there was always food. Our neighbour milked his cows and gave us milk and we in turn gave him rabbits. We also had some chickens and exchanged these for wood from someone who lived near the forest.

With Robert I tasted the rich side of Romania. He took me to some luxurious restaurants and tossed around money like waste paper. He didn't have a wallet but rather just put his hands into his pocket and pulled out handfuls of money. He was generous but also pretty much full of himself. I think that he loved showing off his new-found wealth. In Romania you couldn't just eat anything you wanted, anytime you wanted it. Rather, four cucumbers and two eggs might be a typical meal for someone who was not a farmer.

Then the revolution came and Robert disappeared.

One day at the station in Brasciov, I suddenly saw him in front of me, saying hello. I hardly recognized him. I could not believe it; his face was unrecognizable. His nose was different, more subtle. His whole face was changed. I thought immediately, "Robert, what have you done?" He told me that, in America, it's not unusual to change one's features, or get a facelift.

Travelling around Transylvania, we always acted dramatically. One time we stopped in front of a farm and Robert raised the hood of the truck, pretending to work on the engine. Then I approached the farmer and secretly whispered in his ear that the foreigner would pay in dollars and that he would like to eat. Owning a chicken coop, the man killed some chickens and prepared a feast for us. The two of us ate like royalty for five dollars.

Once, Robert took me to the mouth of the Danube just to catch sturgeons. He knew Romania better than me. While he was fishing, a gentleman approached him and they had a quiet conversation between themselves. That meeting seemed to both excite and relax him at the same time.

Traveling around, we arrived in the town of Aiud. Robert saw a castle with a church on the grounds—it was right out of the 1500's! All the towers were crenelated and there was also a stable. Amazed at the place, he confided in me that he wanted to speak with the mayor and intended to offer $600 per month to rent the castle, where he would establish himself. His goal was to open an art school, with paintings and frescoes everywhere! He would tidy up the battlements, refresh the stable and restore everything. So he persuaded me to organize a dinner for the mayor. The mayor's response to Robert's dream was to say, "by all means,"—as long as he hired people to work and maintain the property. Robert told me, "I will become a Lord in Aiud and you will be my chatelaine." My father was not so optimistic, telling me that all men were pigs just out to get the girls and that this man was no different. Robert hired six labourers at $50 per month each, while he, himself did the work of architect and designer. I was his secretary.

Then he did something strange. He built within the castle a secret passage that connected to the forest. At my own suggestion he hid the entrance to the passage in the fireplace in the hallway. It had a mantel two meters high! One could enter the secret passage even when a fire was burning. He convincingly adopted the lifestyle of the middle ages. He organized dinners with waiters in uniform, plenty of food, friends, and beautiful women. Local farmers came to visit him, bringing eggs, chickens and cheese. He earned the respect of all in the area by distributing a few dollars every now and then to the poor people. He reconstructed his bedroom with a majestic canopy bed and created a royal ambience inside the castle.

Sometimes he sat in a rocking chair and looked with self-satisfaction at his furniture, the chandeliers, the paintings, carpets and the general decor. He rarely left the castle. There were those who also brought him women—he wanted to be with me but to take other girls to bed as well. He said that he behaved in this way because I hadn't yielded to his advances but I just couldn't, because he seemed so strange and unstable. In spite of my clear-cut refusal, he was insistent. In the end I left him to his delusions of grandeur!

I went to Bucharest to attend the university there, even though he pleaded with me to stay. He enticed me with all sorts of material gifts, but I was determined to go away from him and to get on with life on my own.

In Bucharest I lived in a block of big apartment buildings constructed during the dictatorship. The main door didn't lock and as a result it slammed against its hinges constantly, and the iron lift creaked annoyingly. It was better to walk up anyway because if the electricity failed—which it did regularly—you would get stuck in the lift and be forgotten forever. Each floor had long corridors like a prison, without illumination, with iron doors, each one different from the others. I lived in an apartment of 20 square meters. The entire city itself was like a building site, and when it was windy, clouds of sand arose and came swirling into my room.

After the fall of the communist dictator Ceausescu, Bucharest had begun to develop. There were new opportunities for work; malls were built; shops were opening around the clock. There were also cars of all kinds on the streets and these became symbols of a new economic revival. There was no longer just the old Russian Dacia cars on the street. Romania was living in a euphoria of change and renewal. Later it would be discovered that it was not all a bed of roses; freedom and rampant consumerism also has a downside. For example, there was an increase in crime. The government would no longer provide everything as before, when all medicine and education were free of charge, and there was no unemployment.

As a memorial of the dictatorship, a wonderful palace was left to the people—a towering luxury block, colossal in size, with large rooms and marble staircases. It had been Ceausescu's home! Today it is the seat of the Parliament and also a great tourist attraction. Ceausescu had allocated 25% of the state budget to build what everyone had dubbed 'the monster'. Consisting of a maze of twelve floors with about 5000 rooms, it has gilded ceilings, crystal chandeliers, marble everywhere, and was built all the while the people were exhorted to 'diet'! But even after all the heartache caused during its construction, it turned out to be well worth the bother. The building is the second largest in the world after the Pentagon and has a reception hall as large as an airfield. Apparently, there are still three storeys in the basement that the government hasn't yet told anyone about.

Romania was emerging from significant poverty and near starvation. I remember, before the fall of Ceausescu, sitting outdoors on a terrace drinking only water or something with a vague taste of orange juice. There were no Coca Colas or tea or even lighting in the streets. We were allowed the use of only one household light bulb. For entertainment there was only one television channel, which played just a few hours each day, often showing Russian songs and dances; at school we studied the Russian language.

It was during this time that I met Daniel, a wealthy divorced Romanian. He was in the used car trade. Although he was full of himself, he knew how to handle me. My feelings about Daniel are at best mixed. He often decided on what I should do and was terribly jealous. As such, he did not want me to travel around alone. We broke up and patched up many times. I left him regularly, but then he would phone me or send me flowers and would wait for me downstairs at my condo with his excitment visible through his trousers, and we would be together again.

In the meantime I graduated with a Masters in economics and became an employee in an insurance company, with a good position. My company also gave me a car, a mouse-grey Citroen, and I began to enjoy the pleasure of being an independent woman. Although going around alone was always a risk for a woman, a car fills you with a sense of freedom. I liked discovering many new places, stopping where I wanted and traveling in the car with my CDs playing. In the evening one was careful never to drive on the right. Everyone drove in the middle of the roadway, because on the right there might be potholes, or chasms or even men with carts without lights.

With Daniel I visited various tourist areas such as Brasciov, Constance and Neptune on the Black Sea and we traveled in the mountains. When I was a child I had gone with my parents to Neptune, where many restaurants didn't even have a menu. Now in Brasciov, which rises to over 2000 meters, I took my first ski lessons. There are numerous ski lifts, hotels and lodges; some people have a second home there. Romania no longer leaves an impression of being an underdeveloped country. However, when I drove my car from Bucharest to Constanta it was like crossing a wasteland. The contrast was stark. Settlements of high rise buildings made during the regime and other sad places dotted the landscape, such as a mega-refinery surrounded by the bleak dwellings of those who worked there. There was no real life there; nothing but sleep and work. They call them the amorphous cities.

I took the only Romanian highway toward Constanta. It was only 30 km long and then it ends and turns into a normal road, full of holes, made for horse carts that are even now still used. These sometimes transport whole gypsy families. You cross a series of villages in the countryside that, seen from afar, appear idyllic, but viewed closely are only few poor huts. Women still draw water from the wells and carry baskets on their heads. At the same time you can also see numerous parabolic antennas, signs of a modernization that's advancing there.

I returned once to Aiud because Robert had a high fever. He was lying feverish on his bed; I cared for him for two days. I couldn't say no to his insistent calls. I felt that I represented a stabilizing figure in his life. He told me that, even from a distance, he felt close to me. He lamented that he would do anything for me and even arrange for me to immigrate to America through his connections, if I wished. He spoke to me so much about America; it was as if a fit of homesickness had overtaken him. Since I liked his amusing way of describing his country, I could have listened to him for hours.

He said that in America new ideas were encouraged. Every city has a City Hall. One can go there and tell them, "I want to open a highway that goes from here to there," and they will say, "Okay, here's the license". He said also that in America the visual, aesthetic effect is the most important consideration. Everything is for show. Even corpses are beautified. They colour their cheeks, comb their hair, trim their nails and dress them in their finest.

My feelings for Robert had always been contradictory. On the one hand I felt something inside me prompting me to walk away; on the other hand, he amused me. America, for me, at that time, was still a dream, so I went the way it led. Something was holding me back from trying to get to know him more deeply. I came to understand that there was more to his story than I knew.

I remember one day going to take the bus to Bucharest when I heard a drum and I saw two men in armour. One of them had a loudspeaker and was shouting that Robert wanted me to marry him. By now I had no doubts that Robert was completely raving mad.

For many girls in Romania, the first goal of self-fulfillment is a sentimental one. They grow up with the idea of finding a guy with a lot of money who will take care of them. I did not fit that image of a Romanian girl, and did so even less after Ceausescu. I didn't subscribe to the mob mentality that says that a woman must always be under a powerful man and that she always had to follow the money. Daniel was one of them, but despite this, I felt a strong attraction for him.

One day Robert called to tell me that there was the possibility of obtaining a visa for me to the United States. I realized that this time he was talking seriously. I felt excited—America seemed within reach! What perplexed me was Robert's enthusiasm in giving me the news. What kind of interest could he have in sending me to America? But because I was excited I did not pay much attention. I thought that probably he was trying to get me away from Daniel. Normally there is a long wait to obtain a visa and Daniel was furious. He tried in every way to dissuade me but I was resolute. Although I loved him, I knew there was no future for us. He was too different from me and thought like an old man. I was fascinated by the American dream: the possibility of a career, of owning a house with a garden and having and using a pile of credit cards. All those are distant dreams in the heart of a girl from a small country.

Soon the visa arrived. It still surprised me although I had waited for it anxiously. Before departure I found that I was somewhat nervous. It was becoming clear to me how much I was attached to my country and to the people I loved. Daniel wanted to accompany me to the airport but the parting was painful. On the plane I shed some tears. I sensed that I was somehow sacrificing a person that I cared for. The confidence that I had flaunted before leaving was flagging dramatically.

Fortunately upon arriving, I received a warm welcome from a landlady known and sent by Robert. She lived in Boulder, Colorado about thirty miles from Denver, the state capital. I didn't suffer the initial discomfort of loneliness that usually accompanies one's arrival in a new and strange place, because my phone was ringing all the time. Robert kept me glued to the device even during my initial drive around the city.

Boulder is a model, quiet town, of about 150,000 inhabitants. It is in the Midwest and reveals another face of America. It has an aura of wealth and ease. There is a bike path, which is actually an excellent road, right in the heart of the city. It's wide, full of bicycles, pedestrians, people skating and policemen in shorts and maybe even an angler. You may see two or three men playing jazz on the grass or people having picnics. In the gardens there are barbeques. You may spot a fifty year old woman passing by on skates in a bikini, with a propeller spinning on the cap on her head. It's just how Americans are; a little eccentric and often dressed in gaudy colours and strange costumes.

Many people move here from New York because they have had enough of the big city. They want to go to a place where there are gardens and lots of flowers, where nobody spoils anything and everything is undisturbed. This is the countryside. You almost get the impression of being in a little village because you see small houses everywhere. Of course we are in America—malls are everywhere, foods of all kinds are available and vitamins and dietary supplements are in abundance. It seems that all Americans take dietary food supplements like water.

Once, along a bike path in the woods, visible from the city, I saw a sign that said, "If you see a mountain lion, don't run away because he could eat you. Better to throw some rocks at him and then warn the wild animal protection hotline." By phone, Robert explained to me that pumas kill about four people per year. These are mostly runners who go jogging at dawn using earphones and listening to music. If there is a hungry puma, he may catch and eat you, even if you are not easy to digest. The story is told that if a mountain lion eats a human being, the cat must then be taken to a hospital where they will give him indigestion tablets. Nobody wants to eliminate the pumas because they are part of nature and are a protected species, but the Rocky Mountains cannot be fenced—they traverse the whole country! I always carry some stones in my pocket...

There is a reported case of a girl captured by a puma, scratched in the face, and then taken by the neck into its den to be eaten later. While the puma went out hunting again, she managed to escape. Since then she has shown a great respect for wild animals yet still doesn't fear them.

There are additional warnings not to be bitten by spiders. It may happen by putting your hand into a shirt hung unused perhaps for a few days. Be sure to shake the shirt first or the shoe or whatever piece of clothing where a spider might have nested while the item was unused. The spider does not care about attacking you, but if he builds his web in your shoe and you then put your foot inside, he will bite you. Most signs or books say that there is little reason to panic if you go to hospital within a half an hour. Otherwise you could lose the use of your limb. Wow—that's what it says!

I also started jogging along Boulder Creek, a river flowing down from the mountains. It is full of people running! The Americans here seem very health-conscious, obsessed with jogging. One day while I was sitting on a bench a lady arrived, jogging with her dog. The dog, panting deeply with his tongue hanging out, stopped and stood beside me to rest, while his owner continued to run in place. Yet despite this fetish for running, many will still die of a heart attack.

While I was taking a walk one day, Robert asked me to visit a friend of his who lived not far from where I was. I took a little-used path and when I came upon a house, I glimpsed a muscular young fellow who was playing ball with a child in the garden. I called out and the man approached the gate. I told him that I was a friend of Robert's and his face lit up. I gave him the mobile and he looked quite happy to speak with Robert. While walking in the garden, he spoke for a long time with Robert, and I waited on a bench. I was quite surprised that after talking with Robert that he did not invite me into his house. He just thanked me with a smile and returned the cell phone.

Robert told me that I could travel around the city carefree, because there wasn't much crime in Boulder. Yet, on the first pages of a local newspaper, there was a story of the theft of an old lady's television, even describing the TV model. The article ended with this announcement: "If you find it in any market, please call the police toll-free number!" Then, at the bottom of the page, cases of murder were listed. These are often committed as a result of banal quarrels or out of jealousy! Shootings seem to take place as if it were the Wild West. Behind the houses here there are the alleys, which are the narrow streets where they put the dustbins. Many senseless killings take place in such alleys, when two cars confront each other and cannot pass. The car owners get out and start telling each other to move, which ends up in a yelling match and ultimately in gunfire. Often the story is a brief article in the local papers, because if you don't want to be shot you could have just backed up! Unlike California, many men here travel around armed. At a supermarket if a person bumps into you, he immediately says, "sorry, sorry". There is a lot of cordiality displayed because people are afraid of getting shot.

My first job, which was suggested by Robert, was in a ghost town resort. He explained to me that nearby were abandoned mines surrounded by ghost towns which had become attractions. One of these places had been resurrected into a casino. Another, designed for tourists, presented reproductions of the life of the Old West, with lots of shootings, bank robberies, chases and recoveries of loot, and visitors could even participate. I worked as a Can-Can dancer in a fake brothel. There was also a real saloon there where customers were served canned beans. Another man played someone who was escaping on horseback with the proceeds of a bank robbery in his hand and a brothel girl holding on behind.

As part of another tourist attraction out of Durango, in southern Colorado (which is at the end of the 'one million dollar highway'), I rode on an old steam engine train and pretended to be assaulted on the train, which had been stopped by trunks on the tracks. All of this was staged! Even some tourists were 'abducted'. Tourists knew exactly what to expect, as there was even a kidnapping schedule. I also experienced the thrill of the pioneers who were attacked by Indians while in a caravan in the middle of the prairie. The wagons were placed in a circle to defend themselves from the Indians' attack. Being part of the Indian band costs more but was great fun. This entire trip lasted three or four days and all the while the customers lived like pioneers.

Later I enrolled in a marketing course at the famous University of Boulder. Occasionally while I attended there I visited Denver. Commuter buses connect the two cities on a regular schedule. In Denver there is a well known mint where coins are stamped. There are always great queues outside ready to take the tour and see how the money is made.

Robert and I conversed by phone about all the places I had visited and the things I did and saw. I used him as a mobile guide, with the phone stuck to my ear. I passed nearby his hotel-management school where he had got a degree and saw the stadium where he played basketball with his university team. I saw the church where he was an altar boy and his old cinema, now just about to be demolished. They were building a shopping mall.

It felt as if Robert was really with me because they were very long phone calls. Then, after he hung up, not a half an hour would pass and he would call me again wanting to know what I had done. I often asked him why he was spending so much money on the phone. He merely replied that he liked to and money was certainly not a problem! Once he said that the voice of our inner selves expresses more than the body can. It speaks directly from our heart and can communicate over distant oceans or continents.

Robert gave me the address of his brother and asked me to visit him; he told me that the brother could help me in case any problem arose. His brother Peter was in a wheelchair, but despite this seeming handicap, he was cheerful and optimistic. Elly, his wife, was a witty, intelligent woman. Though she had some white hair, she had a young and firm body. She played piano by ear. Together they radiated a positive atmosphere. I considered myself fortunate to have met them but glad not to be in a wheelchair.

I celebrated my birthday at their house and received a surprise present from Robert—it was a lovely necklace of red pearls. I imagine that Peter bought it and Robert simply reimbursed him. I began to appreciate Robert's unusual and unpredictable behaviour. But, at the same time, he was present and physically absent, like a ghost. I started to wish that I could be close to him in the flesh.

Peter and Elly gave me advice about Boulder since they had lived there a long time. I even became fond of the place where they lived. It was almost a part of the surrounding woods! Their place was so fairy tale-like that it seemed to come right out of a storybook for children. Once, strolling down their street, I saw a small line of cars waiting, as a deer was in the road calmly eating leaves from the hedge of a garden. The cars simply turned around while the deer continued to eat the hedge uninterrupted. Whenever I went to visit them, I felt Robert's presence more clearly because of the many photos of him around the house.

I began to feel myself part of a family consisting of Robert's brother, sister-in-law and nephews. Yet in their house there was the continuous shouting of kids, toys thrown everywhere, crayons and paints scattered about and blankets and pillows strewn on the floor. Outside, in the garden, they had a huge caravan made of steel, where the parents slept in turns to avoid hearing the children cry at night. Their room in the house was used only for piling up dirty laundry which was then washed on Wednesdays.

But inside I consoled and restrained myself, with the thought of being an independent woman without family responsibility. I loved my orderly house and the fact that life in Boulder was serene, without stress. In the evening I was free to enjoy a brisk walk. While I lived in Bucharest, I would never go out alone at night. In Romania there is much more discrimination between men and women, even if that thinking is rapidly changing.

Peter and Elly appeared to be less than forthcoming when speaking of Robert. I attributed this to their own obvious reserve and discretion. For example they never did ask me too many personal questions. Only once did Peter let slip a revelation about Robert, saying that he was a person who asked too much from life.

Peter had a penetrating way of looking at people which sometimes embarrassed me. It was the look of a man who had many things to say but kept them to himself. Despite this I was at my ease in their house because I knew that Robert had lived there and the children sometimes mentioned his name. And then my telephone rang so often! Robert tried to keep in touch by phone even when I was in the bathroom or shower. I liked his folly, his questioning about all the details of my day, his willingness to spend so much money on me. Who else would have done it even with money to burn? Then when I entered the bedroom he would tell me to imagine that his hand was caressing me. We made love many times by phone.

Occasionally when Robert called me, I would pass the phone to his brother who would wander out of earshot and speak with Robert for a long time.

One day Elly fainted. Yet Peter was composed in his reaction, almost as if he were accustomed to this behaviour. I later learned that she suffered from epilepsy and I felt a bit responsible. Maybe they needed my help. So I found myself staying overnight more often. One morning I heard a noise outside the door which was a bear rolling an overturned garbage can! In the winter bears often came down from their mountain homes when their food supply was limited due to heavy snowfalls. Elly called the wildlife patrol and two women in uniform would come and drug him.

Bears are dangerous. Bear cubs come down into neighbourhoods because they are inexperienced hunters. Sometimes food is dropped in the mountains for them by helicopter. In Romania we eat bears and there are restaurants specializing in bear meat, especially in the mountains.

One day I was stopped by two undercover FBI agents. They took me into their office and I was interrogated for a long time. A few days before this Robert had escaped arrest by Interpol, in Aiud in Romania. Apparently he was wanted for several murders that occurred during bank and post office robberies in Tennessee and Alabama. These robberies yielded a lot of money! The FBI was trying to reconstruct his movements and wanted to know what my role might be. Why had I come to America? Why had I picked his city of origin? Since I was a long time friend, did I know where the loot was hidden? Did I know his accomplices? They had found his refuge in the castle at Aiud. The local police surrounded the castle but Robert managed to escape.

I remembered the secret passage. I thought I was playing with an eccentric, but was instead helping a dangerous murderer to build an escape route.

I also learned that Robert had changed his name. His real name was Denis Collerman. After the robbery, Denis had fled to Ohio, to a remote place in the countryside near Findlay, 2000 kilometers north of the location of his last robbery. He met a little known person named Robert Gundeborg and cloned all his data, from his identity card to his social security number. Gundeborg was a farmer who would never travel outside of his own country. Denis, alias Robert, filed for a passport, having affixed his own photo in it, and fled to Europe. The Interpol information spoke about a meeting on the shores of the Black Sea, between him and an accomplice who gave him part of the loot. They had thought it was in the form of gold. I remembered the fishing trip to the mouth of the Danube! I decided to tell everything to the police, including information about the secret passage, and my spontaneity finally convinced them that I was not involved in the matter.

I have since learned the truth about Robert's brother Peter and his wife, who turned out to be the accomplices. Peter was in a wheelchair because he had been wounded in a gunfight with police and was under house arrest. The Police have exonerated me from any blame. Robert had used me to contact those people, who probably did not have free access to a phone. After I moved from Aiud to Bucharest, he had persistently suggested to me that I should go to America, and particularly to Boulder. I was beginning to understand that I had not come here of my own free will, but rather as a result of his clever persuasion and manipulation. Was I used just to put a phone into the hands of his accomplices, who couldn't trust the use of their own? Did he ever really want me to see Boulder, the place of his childhood, and stay in touch with me? I thought that Robert really loved me, but now I longed to speak to him again, to find out about his real feelings for me. It's been a long time since he's called me. Most likely he is afraid that the police could trace his whereabouts through my phone.

It seems too silent in my home, without Robert's calls. While in Romania, there was always someone knocking at my door. It might be the tenant upstairs who came to ask for a cigarette or the lady next door who came to retrieve her cat which had wandered onto my balcony. It might be the owner, who sometimes brought me some furniture when he didn't know where else to put it.

Here, however, the relationships are different. It's merely "good morning" and "good evening"! The neighbours at most watch your house when you're not there and report strangers to the police. This is called the 'neighbourhood watch'. There are signs to alert thieves that neighbours look after each other's homes.

Since my arrival in the States some years have passed and recently an idea occurred to me. I would like to write a small book for dog owners. A page for the master, with tips for the care of the dog and another page for the dog that, after a little rubbing, would emit a smell, reassuring or exciting to the dog and making him bark. This could be a book that the owner would read sitting in a chair with his dog in his arms; a book for dogs and people!

A vet once showed me some substances that are used to ward off dogs, so that they won't pee in certain places of the house. He also told me of other smells that would simulate positive dog responses. After searching animal and veterinary association sites on the internet, I prepared a feasibility study, including my ideas on how to advertise and market the book. I found a publishing company in Denver that also produced games. They proposed that if I provided them with a mock-up of my book, they would fund its publication and advertising, subject to some testing. The whole process worked out. The book was sold mainly at Christmas as a gift item and I earned enough money so that now I'm sniffing around to invent something else, perhaps a book on Transylvanian bats.

At the moment I'm sitting at my computer, a cat on my knees, while a light rain taps softly on the window. Every evening I surf the internet. It is so nice to dream about new places and travels, to be tucked away in a corner of the world, with intimate access to someone who lives far away. One day I may go to see George or maybe he'll come to visit me. It's been more than one year since we started our nightly chats. We have many interests in common, traveling above all! I like his sense of humour, his cheerfulness and his ability to communicate to me his enthusiasm for everything. He is a pharmacist, living with his mother and his younger sister in a secluded lane, in the suburbs of Launceston, in Tasmania, an island in south Australia. He is too far—to get to him one must cross Mexico, the Pacific Ocean, many Polynesian islands and all of Australia from north to south. I'm in love with a ghost but does this mean that my love is less real?

A Psychological Perspective

America, in this case, represents Alexandra's desire for female emancipation. She fears male power and the loss of independence. Robert, like many criminals, is prone to megalomania and mythomania. The castle, the medieval public manifestations, the impressive festivals, the secret passage with which he ridicules Interpol, represent a need for omnipotence. No wonder one day he reappears in a different way and in an unpredictable situation.

6

From America to Japan
The geisho

A man from New York, age 43:

After the last war, if German or Italian citizens were travelling to Japan, they didn't need a visa. Still today, the Japanese have fixed in their minds the famous "Ro-Ber-To" alliance—Rome, Berlin, Tokyo—the alliance among Italy, Germany and Japan, during the Second World War. Imagine what kind of loyalty they have! In America a guy working for you is a mercenary. If someone offers him 100 dollars more, he goes to them. Here, no way! In extreme cases a worker may come to you, saying, "Forgive me, boss... I've received a better offer. May I ask you for permission to go and work there?" If the boss says no, even refusing him a penny of increase, he won't go.

Absolute faithfulness!

Once a hotel receptionist gave me the key for a room that had not been cleaned and prepared. I went back down to reception to complain. He kept stammering, "don't worry, sir," while offering a stream of apologies.

They have a hallucinatory sense of duty.

In Japan there is a deep sense of fidelity between friends. If you start a relationship with a person, man or woman, your acquaintance will be forever.

In our country, on the contrary, it's 'out of sight, out of mind'.

For instance I have been in touch with a wealthy lady, named Mikui, for the past seven years: she lives in a villa in Shinyuko with two Porsches in the garage. Shinyuko is the equivalent of Fifth Avenue in New York.

In the past I was her escort. Now we seldom see each other—maybe even six months might pass without meeting one another. But we retain our friendship. When we go out to a restaurant, she always takes me to the most expensive one and when I invite her, we normally go to cheap ones. Once she took me to a typical top level Japanese restaurant. Try to imagine: a woman dressed in traditional kimono who opens the door, kneels on the ground and takes off my shoes. Of course, my friend takes her shoes off by herself because a geisha doesn't kneel for a woman. We entered a Zen courtyard—a courtyard of combed gravel in the form of waves, with a log of dry wood in the center.

I offer an aside here: Zen is the culture of nothingness; the objective is to clear the mind of bullshit. So this rich woman had a Zen room, where you entered and there was nothing except a niche with a vase of flowers and that arrangement represented the expression of absolute beauty. Hey, don't ask me! Every two or three days she paid an artist to refresh the floral display inside of this completely empty room. This is Zen!

It's the same sort of thing at the restaurant. In this Zen courtyard, where one follows a wooden path to avoid disturbing the gravel with your feet, there were doors of rice paper and every door led into a private room where we could sit down and eat. The geisha opens the door. I see the low table and I'm dismayed when I realize I will have to eat on the floor with crossed legs. But they know that not all foreigners have this ability, so my geisha moves the small table, removes a cap from a square hole on the floor and I put my legs inside the hole. After seating, they move the table close to me. Mikui kneels to my left side! This very rich woman kneeling to my side! They served us a dinner of about twenty courses. The largest morsel of food was the size of a walnut. All courses were beautifully presented. Every different shaped dish was accompanied by sake, from a blown glass pitcher with crushed ice inside. And this woman waited on me for every course! When she finally paid, I peeked: 100,000 yen, about $950.

I got a real shock. But she was already prepared. With confidence she pulled out her credit card and settled the bill. Just think: a very rich woman, accustomed to giving orders, who has meetings with ministers and ambassadors, paying to serve me on her knees. I calculated the money she was carrying on her: ten thousand dollars, including clothing and jewelry.

She once took the Shinkansen (literally the 'flash train')—the Tokyo-Osaka train which costs more than an airplane flight—to come and see me, and then, in the same evening, returned on the train to Osaka.

Japanese women have a tremendous respect for their men. But then, perhaps she has other flaws. She is absolutely free and sometimes she doesn't relate in a total way to the man by her side. If you've been fucking her for the past ten years, it's likely that another man has been fucking her for the past fifteen.

Another defect is her way of being so precise that it clips your wings. But then she conforms to your wishes. For instance, I am a motorcycle buff and she will ride for hours seated curved behind me. I like boating, and she says 'yes'! Because you like it, she likes it too.

Of course, as a Westerner, you think she is crazy about you. On the contrary she can be a perfect geisha at the right time, then after she is an independent woman. Betrayal is not as bad a thing among them as it is for us. Japanese men often have two or three lovers and even with each of them he appears loyal!

They have a great love for foreign things but also harbour an inferiority complex. I remember one of my first Japanese ladies who was often complaining about her "flat face." In fact if you see their profile it is flat, without a protruding nose. They always strive for the European ideal.

They have copied virtually everything and have tried to absorb the very best. They've sent people around the world to study lutherie, to develop the art of making guitars like Ibanez. Or they've gone to the great Italian or French kitchens, to work as chefs. Nikon sent its employees to work at Leica. Everything that was possible to copy in Europe, was copied, improved upon and put onto the market. The moment they decide to do something, they aim for the best.

If someone says he knows a wine, he knows it seriously. He requests, for example, a 1997 Barolo because he knows that it was an excellent year.

When I arrived in Japan the first time in 1999, I went to live on the outskirts of Tokyo in a typically Japanese district, in a Japanese house, in a room with a tatami, that straw mat for a floor. And I slept on a futon; that's a mattress that lies right on the mat. In this expensive house, the bathroom was a hole in the floor, a squat toilet. Today they use technology also in the home, but at one time they only exported it. Now they have reached a good standard of living. But compare it with a country like Thailand—they have twice the population of the Thais—one hundred and twenty million. And there are many remote and inaccessible areas, such as volcanoes and mountains. So you can imagine how densely populated a Japanese city can be.

Consider then that in Japan construction of buildings must be of a standard that is earthquake proof. Yet they tie their valuable ornaments with wire to avoid them falling down as a result of the continuous tremors.

Some things you might take for granted cannot be in Japan. For example, you can see electrical outlets for 110 volts, in a country where the national standard is 220. When you leave a tip for a waiter, he runs after you, to return your money, because here people do not tip. There aren't street names and house numbers. Residential areas are divided into districts and sub-districts, like the Russian *matryoshka* dolls. You turn into an alley, stop by a tavern for a drink and find people listening to classical music, all absorbed in religious silence. Or you wander down an alley with paper lanterns and incense, where company employees in uniform and tie stand in a long and disciplined line to munch something from a street vendor, perhaps *tonkatsu*, consisting of pork chops or breaded chicken with rice.

When you enter the subway during rush hour, there are attendants with white gloves, pushing you into the cars, because passenger are too polite to push in. So they're just pushed in, one against another. Then as soon as the train leaves the city, people thin out and you can see them falling asleep. They spend up to three hours in the train to commute to and from work. They take advantage of this spare time to sleep. They live in the suburbs of the city because houses are cheaper there. They look like a horde of worker ants but that's a mistaken impression. A friend of mine told me, "You are individualists. We are one people." If they work in a company, every few hours they all do five minutes of exercise together, or they go down to the yard before the lunch break.

Everybody has a uniform. The bank staff wear bank uniforms. The building site has its own uniform and the building site the other side of the street has another uniform. So it is for every kind of shop, any workplace! Even the baker and his assistant! They are very proud to wear that uniform, to belong to that group, to that company.

The first times I visited Roppongi, a neighbourhood in Tokyo full of bars, restaurants, discos, casinos, I went into the Hard Rock Cafe, full of strangers. You could feel as though you were in London or New York. You arrive by violet subway line, or the blue one. There are a dozen lines, all of different colors. You can imagine Tokyo as a city described by science fiction writers, where everything works like a Swiss watch; everyone precise, perfect and all equal. The trains and other public transport are punctual and drivers wear white gloves! An almost surreal city, where everybody vanishes into the mass, each equal to the next one!

At first, to save money, I slept in a capsule hotel. The rooms are practically niches, one stacked on the other, each space one meter high by one meter sixty wide. As comfortable as a coffin! You open the door of your niche that looks like a mortuary refrigerator. Besides the bed there is TV, a little light for reading and one alarm clock. You have to leave your stuff in another room where there are combination lockers. They are like hives used by people who have missed their train or something like that. So no baggage! In the collective bathrooms you find everything; disposable razor, soap, toothbrush, shaving foam dispensers. There is also a very expensive version, where you are immersed in a mixture of salt water at body temperature. And they say that one hour of sleep in these corresponds to four hours of normal sleep. I don't have these problems. I like to get up at ten o'clock and have breakfast quietly. I practice the habit of idleness, of "the siesta", of having long chats. I think the ultimate goal of existence is to sit in a bar watching the world go by. How on earth did I, arriving here by chance as a tourist, then decide to stay? How did it happened that someone like me, who shuns stability and bonds, has chosen Japan, where people have a strong sense of duty?

Anyhow, Japan is not a goal or an end point for me. And there's nothing like Japan to make you feel unstable. Here you'll never fit in a hundred percent; you will never be Japanese. You're an alien—and I like to feel like an alien. You are less responsible. And they make you feel stranger still by the way they look at you and talk to you. The Japanese accept you as different and they want you to be different. They accept as well a certain degree of extravagance in you. Your diversity, as long as doesn't annoy, is justified by the fact that you are a foreigner. Basically you are allowed to be and to do what is not allowed for them. For instance, I am easily noticed; let's say, they run, I walk. But I do not stir up trouble or discomfort. Once, among friends in a restaurant, I started singing. It's one of my habits. Since I have a great baritone voice, I like to show it off whenever I can. The Japanese at first watched me open-mouthed, and then began to be amused, so much so that they even asked me to sing another song I knew.

In my family I was the black sheep—impatient with rules, duties, considered odd and in need of re-education—and I did try to change. I have always been carrying around an inferiority complex; a feeling that I was unlike others. So, paradoxically, I have done everything to try to be like others. I married. I went into banking. But I was just a distorted image of my father. He was a judge and I wanted to follow his example: have a family with strong principles, marry a typical wife from my own background. Without thinking, I was living contrary to my nature and I was torturing myself. For years I tried to make everyone believe that I was what I wasn't. I was doing things that I had no interest in. It even bothered me to come home to a dinner prepared by my wife, as this forced me to return home always at the same time.

Then my father passed away and I sold off all the property I inherited—exactly as he had feared when he was alive. In fact, he never wanted to register even a closet in my name. Then my marriage broke down and ended in divorce. The end of my marriage unlocked the latent wish that I had kept inside me for such a long time—to follow my free nature, to live a life of no commitment, no obligations. If, until that moment I had tried to be like others and believed my inner feelings to be wrong, for the first time I started to accept within me that sort of personality that I always tried to suppress. The pretext, or rather the straw that broke the camel's back, was a court judgment demanding that I support my wife for life. Every month she would have sucked away a third of my salary: a life sentence for the mistake I made.

So I gave up my job in the bank, joined the ranks of the unemployed and demanded financial support from her. She came to me on all fours, all conciliatory. How can divorce in America mean that you are obliged by law to support a person who has become a stranger, for a lifetime? She wasn't my wife any longer. She was a young lady with arms, legs and a brain—quite fit to work. The Catholic Church never accepted divorce. Still they try to pound into you that marriage and family are sacred and inseparable. However, priests are the first ones to avoid marriage! A priest friend of mine and I were sleeping with a mother and daughter—he took the mother and I the daughter. Here in Japan, however, all are agnostics and don't give a damn.

The first thing I appreciated in this country is the lack of intrusiveness. Some customs may seem a little ceremonious and even contrived and ridiculous. Then you realize there is a real sense of harmony and respect for others. They bow to you, they smile. We Westerners do not understand. To understand it, you have to live here.

In our culture we notice the one who raises his voice, the person who stretches his feet out on the table, sinks into a sofa, makes noise at inappropriate hours, sprays graffiti on the wall, the street peddler who, if you're with a woman, sticks flowers under your nose and will not go away until you give him money. America is the land of the pain in the ass. There is a real license, even if undeclared, for people to get on your nerves. But here, everyone tries not to be intrusive, noisy, not to harass or embarrass others. I've never liked conventions but here I've learned to appreciate them, even though it took me a little while to understand when to apologize when I was acting inappropriately. You have to find common ground on which to communicate, even in diversity, without invading others' space and without offending. After several months I felt a desire to fit into this world of friendly extraterrestrials: of course on my own terms. Meanwhile, as far as work is concerned, you are treated like a gentleman. They have great respect for professionalism—if you do something well, you are overpaid. A friend of mine who runs a French restaurant has become a celebrity. In France, he ran a cheap tavern. Here he has been a resounding success. He is sought after, interviewed. Having learned to speak a little Japanese, I invented a job that was made for me: a guide—but of a special sort. I ran an announcement in the foreign language newspapers: "American with car offers his services as a companion and personal guide, sharing his insights into Japanese life." I accompany clients around town showing them the hidden Tokyo—the city from a resident's point of view. That is, I show them my Japan, the one I've discovered while living here.

Instead of joining a group and being taken around by guides who show you the usual tourist places, I tailor my tours to a customer's specific needs. Lately one has asked me to take him to visit a *kimbaku* studio, (this translates into 'the art of bondage' and is a unique sort of Japanese striptease). Sometimes a businessman asks to be taken to a special little place or places connected with his job, for instance, to an office for a couple of days, or I assist him in a search for a company or some specific material. A personal guide in Tokyo, especially for the first few visits, is indispensable if you can afford it, because it's hard to get around alone. For example, you go to eat and they hardly speak a word of English. You point to a dish, saying "I don't want rice with this," and they are all in a panic because they don't know how much discount they have to give, without rice.

Once I brought a Dutch woman to a restaurant frequented only by Japanese people, where the writer Yukio Mishima used to eat, and she went into raptures. She wanted to know where Mishima sat and what time he had dinner. She liked to have a guide just for her, to feel as though she was one of the local people. We were going to a restaurant where there were no tourists, where they knew me and greeted me and she was happy to feel a little special, in a family environment. I show my clients not only Japan, but also the Japanese people. I'll take you to my Japanese home, I'll introduce you to my Japanese next-door neighbour, my Japanese cat and I'll make Japanese tea for you.

She was an architect. She started to give me tips on how to decorate my home. She had some crazy ideas but they were fun. On the wall of my bedroom she designed little birds with a background of the blue sky to match little blue little flowers painted on the dresser.

And then she decided, by herself, to paint the walls of my home. We went to buy paints and brushes and she painted the living room in a pale salmon color. While walking in Tokyo, I always held her hand. Her name was Jan. She had to return to Holland to have chemotherapy for her cancer.

In fourteen days I took her everywhere: classic restaurants where there is a theatrical ceremony to prepare and cut the fish before you eat, as well as those traditional little restaurants, less frequented by tourists, where they try to revive the old Japan.

When the time of the samurai ended, and they discovered that they were unable to do a damn thing apart from being warriors, many of these samurai recycled themselves as innkeepers. If you go to one of those run-of-the-mill restaurants where they cook in the traditional way, cheap and simple, with no special flavours, what are you eating—something you could get at a canteen? But in a restaurant managed by a samurai, dressed in samurai regalia, you feel as though you are reliving the time of the samurai. You slide open the rice paper door... there is a curtain. You find yourself in a stark, black, smoky, environment—it reminds you of some old kitchen blackened by soot. Then when you leave, reeking and cleaned out of a lot of money, you have experienced real tradition.

I took Jan to attend a sumo wrestling match. Each fight lasts thirty seconds. I noted that Jan was happy because, every moment, I was explaining what was going on. Japanese sumo wrestlers never engage in vulgarity or violence. Sumo is a struggle between two fatties in underwear—the winner is the one who throws the other fighter out of the ring. Under those lard-balls there is a bodybuilder's physique. Otherwise how could they lift another wrestler who may weight up to 500 kg?

Jan was fat too. She was 1.75 meters tall and weighed 120 kg. Imagine seeing her in the ring, fighting with another fat woman like herself? But here wrestling matches are forbidden to women. Lately there has been a TV debate on the possibility of letting women fight and it became almost a national scandal, because, for many Japanese, it would have shamed the entire country.

A Japanese man has a very strong sense of femininity and virility. To understand sumo, a sport four centuries old, you need to have a Japanese mind. Just think that to maintain a heavy physique, the wrestlers have to constantly overeat and this leads to certain death before they turn fifty. And despite this, there are Japanese people wanting to become sumo wrestlers!

I even took Jan to some infamous places, such as Sanya or Ikebukuro, where you can actually find a few bums: an anomaly in a country like Japan. A Japanese guide would never take you to such a place. Then I took Jan to classic places, such as the Sensoji Buddhist temple, the Tsukiji Fish Market, Tokyo Disneyland, and then to a place where she had fun to die for: the Ski Dome, an artificial ski slope, where even in summer it's minus 4 degrees. Jan told me that in Holland they don't have mountains but they dream about them so much that, in "Mini-Holland", a park with miniature replicas of their most important monuments, they also added lovely mountains, complete with cable cars. To me, who learned to ski in Nevada, the Ski Dome looks like an exercise yard in a some sort of prison for Eskimos.

Then we visited the love hotels. They're everywhere, but apart from the presence of condom vending machines, they aren't squalid places like our motels. These hotels are visited by all sorts of people, even married couples looking for a diversion from everyday life. Every hotel has theme rooms. For example, one room would be decked out like a sheriff's office with Old West furnishings. Another one might have a bathtub that was a huge clear glass globe, like a goblet of champagne. Japanese people like to play. And these rooms are a triumph of fantasy. They associate sex with childhood, with a carefree world, with no rules: quite the opposite of adult life, full of duties and formalities.

One room was a real jail cell with bars and handcuffs available, and Jan liked to spend the night there. Sometimes she had a mania for gruesome things: probably a result of her past life in Holland and her illness. That night she needed to be cuddled. She, just like the Japanese, associated sex with childhood.

I don't want to be confused with a gigolo. I have set as my objective the well-being of my customers and, when sex occurs, I do my best to satisfy them. Japan taught me the pleasure of serving others and putting people at ease, of creating around them an atmosphere of harmony and serenity.

I was inspired by the Japanese *geisha*, who would attend a school where she studied for years to master the arts of ceremony and entertainment, the art of flower arrangement, such as *ikebana* or the art of *origami*, transforming slips of paper into dolls, animals, etc. In Japan these are considered noble arts and strict disciplines, for which rules apply and training is essential. For us it may seem ridiculous that a *geisha* entertains her guests making paper dolls. But again, it demonstrates that, for Japanese people, childhood is the realm of happiness.

I started giving Jan some lessons in etiquette. I made her repeat the gestures, to observe how the Japanese grasp an object with harmony, as if their hands were performing a take-off and landing. She asked me, "What should I do?" all the time. But eventually she was doing things her way. Once, in the lobby of a hotel, we heard a Leonard Cohen song playing in the background. She literally dragged me across the floor and forced me to dance in front of the strangers in the lobby, who had a great laugh over it.

Then she took me to a shop to buy a Damascus knife. And only after she had done this, she explained to me that she wanted to commit suicide. Who knows why she wanted to do it with a Damascus knife? Maybe it gave the act a romantic aura. The seller did not want to sell us the Damascus knife. We had to prove him that we were able to sharpen the blade; otherwise, in his opinion, we could not appreciate the knife in the right way. Then, in the street, she told me she wanted to go to the hotel to commit suicide. Luckily we ran into a long parade of children in kimonos for the festival of Shichi-go-san: all walking in line for hours, only to have their kimonos blessed by the priest. So I had plenty of time to change her mind. I said, "Let's go to the park to rest a little—you commit suicide after dinner." In the park we got to singing *O sole mio*. I taught her the words and then we sang it together. Meanwhile a group of Japanese had gathered around us and were roaring with laughter. For them, any unusual behaviour, actions beyond the ordinary, provided great entertainment.

When we headed home, Jan was very quiet. I knew that such an unpredictable and sensitive woman could be capable of anything.

Of course, an incurable disease and the prospect of an ordeal of suffering can justify suicide, but I wasn't ready to face such a situation. We entered my home and, without exchanging a single word, we plopped down in the armchair in front of the TV. There was a documentary on the behaviour of parrots. I changed the channel. The Japanese news was describing, in detail, the slowly changing shades of color in the leaves and flowers with the arrival of spring. I explained her that they have an obsession with small changes in nature and they have many words to describe them. Even the rain has different names, depending on the sound. I made her repeat the different words for the rain, hoping that I could distract her from committing a reckless act.

Instead, she fell asleep on the couch, snoring, with the cat in her arms. The day she left, I expected more of her usual eccentric behaviour; however, she remained composed, dignified, contained in her silence. Just a few tears. She left me a lot of money, much more than what she owed to me and she kept only some small change for the taxi in Amsterdam.

In my opinion, these days in Japan, there is a need for a figure similar to the *geisha*, that of the 'geisho,' a man who dedicates his attentions to women. Men are so devoted to their work that they sometimes neglect their women. And for women, this is very emotionally disturbing, because sex is communication. There is even a voluntary sexual organization for women here, which is called the Sex Volunteer Corp. It offers free sex to women who cannot find a man. As for me, I do what I can, thanks to Viagra.

Japanese men frequent brothels, but it's not a degrading thing. For example, under the office of a company nearby, there is a prostitution service for employees, paid for by the company. So at lunchtime, after a steam dumpling and a quickie, they return to the office to be productive. In Western countries they make you run like a donkey being led by a carrot on a stick; for example, those sexy ladies that you can sniff in magazine ads. Here they give you a tiny piece of carrot every day.

They also visit prostitutes in groups. A company recently paid for its employees to go on a holiday in China. They organized an orgy in a five-star Chinese hotel. There were one hundred and fifty Japanese and one hundred and sixty prostitutes. The Chinese got pissed off, because that day was the anniversary of the occupation of China by Japan.

There are also shops selling girls' used panties and Japanese men put their noses inside, to sniff the pussy. This lingerie is sold complete with warranty and photos of the former owner. And sometimes the girls in karaoke clubs offer customers a well packaged pubic hair as a souvenir. A hostess, a friend of mine, had a house with a garden in Narita. She hangs clothes to dry in her garden and occasionally panties disappear. The only thing that disappeared were the panties—in this case, they belonged to a European woman! I even remember reading an ad by a coprophage who guaranteed his sincerity and ensured that he would clean up after!

For the past two months I've had a new client who had responded to my usual advertisement. I am her personal driver and companion. She has two children; a boy of eleven and a girl of seventeen, who both strike you as educated and refined. In the West you can often hear young men using foul language. Here there aren't any vulgar words. Schools are very strict. The boy is a fan of video games and so here he is in his element, as Japan is the home of video games. The daughter wants to stand out and be trendy, like other girls. She dresses, like many young people her age, in an unconventional way and follows all of the latest local fashions.

When we are out too late, Soko sometimes sleeps over at my house. Let me tell you about the first time she stayed over. At two in the morning I heard her calling me.

"What's happening?" I said.
"I want to go to the bus."
"At this hour? There isn't any bus. Wait until tomorrow morning."
At four o'clock she called out to me again.
"I want the bus."
I reply, "But there isn't the bus at this time."
In the morning, when I woke up, she was on about this damned bus.
I said, "Wait. I'll make you breakfast."
Then in the kitchen I noticed that her legs were trembling. So finally I understood—it was 'the bath' that she was asking for, not 'the bus'! The bathroom! But she accepted my refusals because she did not want to risk disturbing me.

Another time we slept at a friend's house. The bed wasn't very big, and I'm not a small man. When I woke up, I found her sleeping on the floor. She felt like she was taking too much of my space and so she gave way. A Western woman would have kicked you out of bed.

One of Soko's favourite things, common to many Japanese, is her garden. She even has a website dedicated to it. She knows all about particular forms of rocks or dwarf trees, *bonsai* trees, and that they symbolize this or that. As the seasons change, I help her to move the position of the rocks in a 'sea' of gravel without water. Then she spends her evenings combing the gravel with a rake. She even involved me in stealing fresh moss from the park, for which she was caught and fined.

She likes to admire a certain little plant. After observing it for five minutes, she will move it just a few inches. "It's better that way," she says. What the hell is the point of moving four green leaves! She also organizes evening gatherings at home with landscape architects. Their culture is made up of small things, and tends to change with the seasons. I also take care of her house. I put things in order, following an aesthetic concept of harmony and spiritual vision. Sometimes we lose ourselves studying the angle of a particular vessel, the arrangement of the dishes at the table. Everything must be perfect, and express outer and inner harmony. Of course, in all the things Soko does, I am always by her side. She is an intelligent woman who has not yet overcome the loss of her husband, after a car accident in which she also lost an arm.

In Shinjuku, near the railway, there was a lane that has now been demolished. There was a very small bar, run by two Russian women selling vodka. There were six chairs and perhaps two or three customers. I often went there and sang Italian songs like *Torna a Sorrento* with great passion and the few dozing costumers immediately revived and went into raptures, in this infamous place with half a dozen chairs.

A Psychological Perspective

The Japanese are so different in their way of being, of living, of thinking, but they avoid judgment and accept the geisho, with his eccentricity and his diversity as a foreigner. The feeling of being a foreigner—an outsider—becomes for him an advantage, a way to find freedom in a country governed by strict rules.

The protagonist, having suffered as he grew up under the strong will of his father, lacks a sense of duty and has a pathological aversion to any form of bonding or commitment. He even creates a bespoke service—personalized guidance tailored to the needs of a single individual. This, too, is the result of an unconscious attempt to rebel against any sort of imposed rule or model of life.

7

From Italy to India
A life, a hundred lives

Piero, from Rome:

I began my career as an outsider while babysitting. I had a friend who was working as a nightclub hostess. She went to work and I stayed home with her one and a half year old son. I changed his diapers, prepared the baby food and sang a lullaby.

We lived in Rome, in Trastevere, at Vicolo del Cinque. Everybody looked at me when I went out with the baby. A man pushing a child in a pram was pitied at that time, especially if he had long hair like me! Today no one would pay attention. But times were different. At night-time, the mother went to the nightclub. I still remember the name of that club—the Pipistrello. It was somewhere near Via Veneto. Her name was Susan and her son, Nico.

I took the baby and went to someone's house. I put him to sleep somewhere and we smoked marijuana until dawn, listening to Pink Floyd, the Beatles, the Rolling Stones, Bob Dylan, Led Zeppelin, the Iron Butterfly. At that time it was fashionable to talk about politics. There was the myth of freedom, to do what the fuck you wanted. We had just come out of an authoritarian age.

I attended the secondary school at Orazio Flacco in Montesacro. I remember the classroom being dead silent—even if you laughed a little bit, the teacher threw you out of the class. Then, by 1968, every rule seemed to be overturned. The teachers did not count for anything. Students put their own marks on their work. They had all become revolutionaries and were wearing green parkas. They used the same language, the same expressions, so you could no longer distinguish a dickhead from somebody smart. Every now and then someone said that it was necessary to revolt, to blow up the system, to throw bombs. And you never knew which side he was on; if he was a madman, a terrorist, a fascist or an undercover policeman. At that time everything was possible.

At my house, in Trastevere, sometimes people turned up and I couldn't even remember where I had met them. You saw one putting on music and starting to dance alone or a couple who, without asking me, went into another room to fuck. Sometimes a friend came with his woman just to fuck. Half of Rome have fucked on the bed where I slept with Susan. Occasionally Susan's husband, Nico's father happened to come by—he was a photographer. He played a bit with his son, then he gave him back to us. Somebody still remembers Nico in Trastevere. We have all brought him up.

I slept under bridges and in the villas of the rich. I have come to know beggars and billionaires, the homeless and showbiz people. I tried all kinds of drugs without becoming addicted. I am able to live six days without eating. I arrived in San Diego, California with two hundred thousand liras in my pocket and stayed there two years.

Whenever I felt threatened and it looked like I might come to a bad end, there was always a woman to rescue me. I have also been kept by a fagot. He was an undeclared fag; he liked to act as my mommy. He brought me breakfast in bed every morning. He chased me away because he found out that, when he was out, I let a woman come into his home. Before leaving, I beat him. I was violent; I don't know why.

Once, as a kid, I let a rock roll down a slope, on the head of a big boy while he was leaning down to pick up pebbles, which he fired at me with his slingshot. The mother took her son to my house with blood still trickling from his head, and my father nearly killed me. He could not stop beating me!

Many aspects of my life have gone wrong, starting with my family. I have never belonged to anything or anyone. I don't know fidelity—I have always betrayed everything. I had a rage which I didn't understand. I ran away from everything. I always had this urge to throw everything away and start again somewhere else, as if I wanted to live a hundred lives. That's my karma.

For some years I managed a club in Los Angeles. Then I sold everything and traveled all over Latin America. I used to sell cars imported from Europe. I also lost my roots. Sometimes I can get lost in Rome but in Los Angeles, never.

I had three children with three different women. The last child is here in India and is two years old.

India was the destination of my first trip. I was a hippy, one of the flower children. That was the real India! I remember the first day I arrived in Bombay. In the morning we went along a road next to a canal from the airport to the hotel. There was a long line of men and women with their asses in the air, as they had no inside toilets. Every morning they leaned over and crapped in the canal. For them it was normal. Now the situation has changed a little.

Indira Gandhi did not solve the problem of poverty but has distributed it in the middle of the country. Just outside of the city center, you see slum after slum with open sewers. The slums in Italy have a semblance of home. Here you see huge bundles with a nylon cloth on the roof. Clay makes up the floor and there are rivulets of sewage, while they cook over a fire with faggots. You can still see all of this if you go to the outskirts of Bombay or Old Delhi. Bombay center, however, has been cleaned up now. You find luxurious shops and you wonder how these people can afford the expensive goods—brand names costing twice as much as in Italy. There are luxurious show windows and unique shops that have nothing to envy those of Paris or New York.

I have been in India three times. Now I live in Goa. Lately I have been back to Italy and found a world completely different from what I had left. I had trouble figuring out where I was, among Moroccans, Tunisians, Algerians, Albanians and I don't know what other races. I didn't seem to be in Italy. I have also been branded as a racist because I didn't want them to wash the windscreen of my hire car. Racist! To me, who's been roaming around the world for thirty years!

Now, in Italy, they talk only about money. They work their asses off to buy cars from one hundred thousand euros up. Money is God! But nobody talks about it. Politicians make humanitarian speeches, the Pope goes around preaching against hunger but there is little room for humanity, for friendship. An honest person, in Italy, has a hard time. Today, at school, if you have a father in jail it's almost a virtue.

The foreigners in Italy do what they want. Maradona drove his car without a license. Cicciolina, the porn star, was unknown in her native Hungary, but in Italy they elected her Member of Parliament.

I am still an anarchist but I no longer wear my hair long, also because now I have only a little remaining. Moreover, long hair has lost the significance it once had. I was one of the first to wear long hair. At that time, letting it grow was like a declaration of war; you aroused insults, mocking comments. For me it was a way to attract attention. I was a narcissist. I felt almost pretty, with this long hair over my shoulders.

The first hippies created a terrible scandal. You were considered a reprobate, one who does not wash, even effeminate. When a long-haired boy appeared in a family, it was a tragedy, a misfortune for the family. I was the only one of my brothers to send money home, to attempt a reconciliation with my parents. They thought that I peddled drugs. Now, behind the counters of banks, you find clerks with an earring and long hair. Everything is fashionable now. I rebelled when there was no rebellion or protest. I remember fierce quarrels which came to blows.

I was a character. I always had a lot of people around me.

Today, anyone who lives outside of society, if he has no money, is just a beggar. Imagine now a penniless hippie on the Spanish Steps. He is a failure, an outcast. From this you can understand how much society has changed.

We had the fascination of outsiders, because we lived outside the system. I was starving, I drove an old clunker, I dressed in rags, I went around with a stubble and long hair, but I had success with women. I learned a lot just meeting people of all types, including writers and famous persons. At that time there were no barriers. The student, the drug dealer, the worker, the actor, the common people, the lawyer were integrated, were in contact with each other. Walking in Trastevere, I stopped to talk with high society types and pimps. I was friends with everyone and I managed to stay clean.

I worked for six months at the Treasury. When I fired myself, my father cried. He wanted to commit me to a mental hospital. He had managed to get me into the Treasury by pulling strings, of which he felt proud. He reproached me like a broken record. "For you I kissed the ass of that politician!" But there was a force stronger than me. I felt like an alien in that place; I went around the office in a trance. I couldn't even get the most basic work done. Once the boss gave me some cards to give to a guy who I had never seen. Then he became angry and told me, "You still don't know your colleagues, after four months here?" Another time the department head told me, "We've decided to give you some important and challenging work." I replied, "No, no, give me a rubber stamp. I prefer stamping papers while listening to music on my headphones. I can stamp anything you want."

I couldn't care less about what happened in that office. I still remember the face that the department head had made. Then I signed my resignation. When I left the Treasury, I also left home. I couldn't bear to listen to my father saying, every day, "You're a parasite, an exploiter, a failure." When I sat at the table, I felt like I was stealing the meal. As I left the house, he was still shouting from the door. And I never went back.

At first I suffered a little. My father had the classic mentality of the bureaucrat. When he came home from the office, he did some extra work. But he never got rich. I could see he was not happy, but even he didn't know why. Maybe he would have liked to travel the world, but he didn't have the time to think about it.

At that time dialogue among members of the family was not easy. If you said something unconventional they took you for a madman. Once he discovered in my room a scientific book on sexuality and he asked me, "You need these things?".

Once, in the Grand Central Station that was my house in Trastevere, the mother of one of the fellows who had been hanging out with us came by. She wanted to get to know us. She was about 45—her name was Maria Pia. Under the guise of being a democratic and open-minded person she wanted to see what her son, Alvise, was up to—and of course to check on him. Her son was always stoned on grass, coke and anything else that he could get his hands on.

You could see that Maria Pia was from the 'upper crust'—those people with true money, one of the types who don't mix with the masses and feel superior. And just following her son, she ended up in the middle of this gang of kids—hippies, druggies, perverts, people on the left, political provocateurs.

Her turning up in our midst was like the icing on a cake. My companions put her on trial. For them, owning a house, servants, a yacht, designer clothes, was a serious affront to the working class. At the time some really idiotic ideas circulated, so that some of the rich were ashamed of their wealth. She tried to apologize; "I can do without worldliness," she said, "and I don't even go crazy for furs and jewels."

It was difficult to understand why her son agreed to see his mother in that environment. There must have been some underlying, sadistic game. It amazed me that she never lost her air of snobbish superiority. It really stuck to her. Hers was a true public drama—she had found a syringe needle on the carpet in Alvise's room. Alvise! He who was educated in the best schools, enjoyed exclusive trips, had access to golf courses, had ended up in the middle of some nasty drug addicts. She didn't say it outright, but she thought it. She then tried to gain her son's trust, treating him more like a friend and an accomplice than as a son. But to stay among us, she had to divest herself of her bourgeois shell, sympathize a little with all of us and pretend to be more open than she really was.

She smoked grass with us. She danced, sang, played with us. At one point a couple began to make out heavily; at that time kissing in public shocked the conformists. And Maria Pia was a classic conservative thinker.

Sometimes we took the piss out of her; she pretended not to understand. She tried to laugh, even to adapt herself to our taste in clothes. She almost managed to look like one of us. Often she wore jeans. Her son continued to smoke grass and listen to music somewhere but he did not understand a fucking thing. All this was against his father's will, who wanted to put him into a clinic. But Alvise was not a beast to be tamed.

One fine day Maria Pia made me a tempting proposal—to go to India with her and Alvise, all at her expense, but to commit to control her child and report everything back to her. With this offer, her mask fell away. She had come to us with the sole purpose of taking her child out of an environment she considered to be depraved. I was just the right pawn. She knew that Alvise was very attracted by India and that he also felt close to me. As a friend, I had to stick to Alvise like a shadow and prevent him from getting into trouble.

Besides, she was ashamed of her son. He wore long hair over his shoulders and a strange, big hat. He was dressed in a very extravagant way, with bright colours. Wherever they went, everybody stared at him. In India they would have paid less attention.

I told her it was a full time job and that's why I deserved a salary. She agreed. She had no choice and no financial problems. India was also the perfect opportunity for me to free myself from the motley crowd around me. I had been playing my part—I'd been involved in some minor drug deals and there was a risk of me being drawn into more serious trafficking. In Trastevere, both police and revolutionaries were hanging around. I didn't feel like a revolutionary, nor a police informer. I didn't give a damn about anything; I was a blockhead, but I felt I had to put something different inside my head. I didn't understand who the fuck I was or what I really wanted.

It was 1972 when we arrived in Bombay. Coloured stripes were hanging outside the windows of the houses. They contained prayers that were carried away by the wind. We went to live in a nice hotel, opposite the Gate of India, just nearby the port. The Gate of India is an arch, like l'Arc de Triomphe in Paris, or l'Arco di Constantino in Rome. It's the gateway to India.

Waiters brought us baskets of fruit and greeted us with "Namaste," which means, "I salute the divinity within you".

Opposite the gate there was a beautiful lawn. In the night-time this meadow was full of a thousand colours because people were sleeping there. They were covered with cloths that expanded to blanket the entire lawn. These people ate and defecated on the sidewalk where they lived. There was widespread poverty. Families were living on the sidewalk; the sidewalk was a latrine—there were no sewers. When there were monsoons, the rainy season, everything came up. The streets were flooded with up to half a meter of water.

We rented a big, old, colonial car with a driver. We drove at walking pace. In the middle of the streets there were carts, flocks of sheep, rickshaws, elephants, cows, pigs eating from the garbage, pedestrians, bicycles, very slow trucks, paper trash flying in the wind. India has not changed much. Now plastic bags are also flying around and the streets are filled with more traffic than before. So you have to maintain a defensive driving style, especially in the dark at night, as you jostle between cyclists, pedestrians and animals. You have to constantly dodge them like in a videogame. Furthermore there are no rules defining right of way. The cars arrive tooting and trying to gain position, slipping between other vehicles. The one who resists and does not give way, wins. Every now and then they slam into one another. They scream, they fight, but no one asks the other to pay for the damage. In India you have to fight for everything, because the state isn't present, least of all to maintain public order.

Outside the hotel where we were staying, little kids were strolling about and we gave them nicknames. There was Gambadilegno who had a wooden leg, and occasionally we bought some food for him. We did not give him money because we knew that would not go to him. There were people who bought kids like in the market. Once Maria Pia said, "Let's take one of them off the street," and the choice fell on a girl five years of age. We handed her over to an institution run by nuns and we paid the fees. We have involved some of the regulars in the hotel. I took on the task of collecting the money and went around asking, "What do you give for Ghira?" And another was charged with bringing the money to the nuns. There was a register where everything was written down. Ghira stayed with the nuns from the age of five up to eighteen. Even when we lost touch, I know that Maria Pia has always sent money. Then Ghira decided it was best to go and become a whore to the Arabs. It's the latest news that I have—probably the Arabs bought her from the nuns. Anything is possible. It's also possible that the nuns gave her to someone else to look after. Even the nuns give the kids away and then they don't care how they end up.

Both in Mumbai and Delhi there was the 'court of miracles'; that is, the beggar factory. When a poor family had too many children, they sell one to some shady individual, who then almost always maims him. Of course a cripple arouses pity and is guaranteed to collect some charity money.

This world of the wretched can be seen at the intersections of the more crowded roads. They were there then and there are still many. Starting with the leper, who does not need additional intervention, then the cripple, whose lips had been cut, with teeth exposed and drool dripping from his mouth—a disgusting and pitiful vision, pushing passers-by to leave some alms. Of course the more money you gave the more they produced cripples. Some unfortunate ones had their bones broken in such a way that they would heal at an angle. You could see kids walking like spiders. Even today in India they continue to create eunuchs, who are taught to dance and sing with the only purpose of begging. They are castrated with forceps, and many of them die. Obviously there aren't volunteers.

Maria Pia looked different in India—less uptight, more sporty. She also started to question herself. After twenty years of marriage, she needed the so-called 'period of reflection'.

She kept calling her husband. But as good intelligent bourgeois, they did not end their conversations with rude words and insults. It would have been stupid to look for faults and offenses. The truth is, feelings change, and life as well.

Sometimes I had lascivious thoughts about her. Something mysterious about her intrigued me. Maybe it was the age difference but perhaps also her delicate and aristocratic manners. At that time women had a greater aura of mystery; the sexes were more distant. Then in 1968 rebellious women arrived on the scene, and they were much closer to men in their behavior. Probably Maria Pia understood my embarrassed interest, but she was totally detached. She kept her distance and the age difference left me in some awe of her. Suddenly she, Alvise' mother, became my boss, but I was also still a part of that rabble of misfits from which she had pulled her son. She would never have had an affair with a street wretch, a half thug with no future, living hand to mouth.

I was a follower of the hippie philosophy, of life as a contemplation, to whom social climbing was anathema—perhaps also because I wasn't able to do anything, anyway. Then I became sick and tired of this philosophy and I became a businessman—but that's another story. I have been a hippy, an entrepreneur, an adventurer and a family man. I wanted to try everything. I would like to live another two hundred years. One lifetime is not enough to do everything, try everything. Old age scares me, especially for this reason. At a certain age you are obliged to hang up your gloves.

To Maria Pia I was indispensable. She knew that Alvise confided in me and that I could influence him better than she could. I fantasized about entering her room with some excuse and throwing her on the bed. More than anything else I wanted to remove her air of superiority, of belonging to a higher caste. If I didn't do this, I would feel a coward. I had somehow to prove to her that I didn't give a damn about her and her money. I had a crazy desire to treat her without respect.

But I was also getting used to living like a pasha, with waiters who filled my room with baskets of fruit and flowers, and served me breakfast in bed.

I began to think that her son could be a good means of blackmailing her. Alvise was more and more detached from the world. He seemed indifferent about whether his mother followed him or not. And he demonstrated more and more signs of strangeness. He spoke very little. Every now and then he disappeared and I had to go and find him. He was a maverick; he did not say, "Let's go," he said, "I go". His mother was anxious that he did not start to use stronger drugs and did not bungle things. Cannabis, inevitably, had been accepted by her.

We went by train to Varanasi. In India, you travel a lot in trains, which are cleaner than you might think. Even now, there are waiting rooms for women as well as women-only carriages. I saw Maria Pia in front of the ticket booth. She was scolding an Indian who had planted his hand on her butt. These are the things that a Western woman traveling alone in India must reckon with. Here they have the idea that foreign women are easy prey. I made a little joke about it; "All in all it should make you happy. It means that men like you." As usual I wasn't worthy of a glance from her. She had figured out by now that I would have gladly given her a special treat, but she showed no reaction. She had the ability to ignore you with elegance—typical of the rich snobs of every latitude.

This tickled me even more, so that in the train I stretched out my leg to play footsy with her. But she cooled me down; "Move your feet away, please. There is plenty of room."

Eventually I gave up; she was like a mummy. But vaguely I sensed her vulnerability. At 45 years of age, a woman still faced a difficult period of transition and was in need of re-assurance, especially during those times. "Too bad for you," I thought. "When you will have the chance for a nice young cock again?"

Maria Pia was a kind of puritan and Italy was still a puritanical country in the 1970s. Many girls were virgins when they married. There were no erotic films, pictures or books. Most women had no idea how a man looked naked before they married. It sounds strange now but it was like that then. And imagine what Maria Pia felt when she found out that, in India, there were special temples where they worshipped the phallus. There were giant statues of phalluses, in stone, metal, wood and so on. They were looked after by holy men; there were offerings of flowers and fruit around them. And there is milk and water flowing from some of them and collected in special bowls. Later the water and milk that went through these cocks are given to people as some kind of medicine—for women to get pregnant, for men not to have problems with sex. Then there were pictures from the Kama Sutra on the walls of temples and special holidays where they worship the phallus.

The contrast between the cleanliness of the temples and the filth of the street surprised me very much. The streets were awful, but when we went into some temple we were told to wear light coloured clothes—nothing dark. Maria Pia wore white socks; she took off her shoes before entering the temple and her white socks stayed white!

We arrived in Benares, the real name of which is Varanasi. A little to the north there is Sarnath, one of the five sacred places of the Buddha. Sarnath is part of Varanasi, which is considered to be a holy city. It rises on the left bank of the river where there are places of worship, the crematoria and various *ghats*, the slopes leading down to the river. It was the time of celebration of the full moon in November, when they turn on all the small lights. In the morning you get up before dawn because everyone wants to see the sunrise over the Ganges, which is an impressive spectacle. In November it was also chilly. There are so many things that confront you, that you can't sort them out in your mind—from the old man who says a prayer to thank the sun for rising, to women who tip the ashes of incense burned on altars into the Ganges. Necklaces of dried flowers are placed around the necks of divinities. Men brushing their teeth, with their pants made of cloth tucked under their butt, pulled up and then tied, like sumo wrestlers. Women washing themselves with their saris on. You see the tourist in ecstasy at the sight of people praying, the crematorium that never stops burning; corpses nonstop. I was astonished that in India relatives are present at a cremation and the burial fire is started by a child or some other relative.

Everything happens at dawn.

From the boat you can see the stairs leading down to the river. While the man rows, you see the crematorium where only adults burn, because the kids, wrapped in a rag and taken into the middle of the river, are sunk with a stone. Even people who have no money for a cremation are thrown into the river, so every now and then you see a body floating by, and carcasses of animals of various kinds. Sometimes you see the backs of animals emerge, perhaps dolphins swimming there. Within this river there is just about anything. All these images are crowding into your mind! But you don't understand—you can't understand why a man goes to Varanasi and waits to die, or why he goes there to be purified. The water is so dirty that if you drink it you'll die. Paradoxically, the same water of the Ganges is collected in pipes and after being filtered, they drink it.

One evening in the hotel, Maria Pia was euphoric, intoxicated by all the things she had seen. We were in the lobby of the hotel, with some other visitors. Alvise was absent as usual, listening to music. I whispered in Maria Pia's ear, "Come with me. I must show you something." She followed me, a bit puzzled, without asking questions. I remember that, just to give me courage, I had drank half a bottle of whisky. When we were in my room I told her to undress because I wanted to make love to her. This direct approach, almost brutal, was part of my way of doing things at that time. We avoided all forms of bourgeois language; courting was bourgeois. Any shit was bourgeois.

She gave me a sermon, in which she said she saw me as a child, maybe a bit crazy; that she was married and that her son was involved. I tried to convince her with good manners, "Sex is a beautiful thing. Why create all these feelings of guilt?" I gave her the stock phrases that were fashionable at the time. My goal was just to bang her, but I tried to disguise it with profound significance. I was as ignorant as a goat and continued piling on the clichés. She chatted freely and it took me a long while to figure out that she just expected me to jump on her. I remember that, as I took down her pants and then her panties, she kept saying, "No, please don't." It was normal. At that time many women, while you were banging them, cried, "No, please, no." You'd already put your tool into her and she'd continue to say: "No, please, no."

Maria Pia was a great fuck. She loved sex like crazy. When I think about her, my cock still gets hard. Now she must be over seventy. If I met her now I would likely get a real shock.

In my mind I see a lovely lady, still almost a girl. I have not seen her change because we lost contact after changing addresses. So my memory of her is just as she was a long time ago. I still have a picture of her, a snapshot, in front of the Taj Mahal in Agra, that famous monument to love. All three of us are there. She's wearing a sand-coloured sari. Alvise, a cowboy jacket and a hat with flowers, his eyes half-shut and his inscrutable smile. And me with my usual long hair and a bright shirt with an airplane type collar.

Maria Pia and I had nothing in common. India had the opposite effect on the two of us. She could not stand the filthy streets, excrement, nauseating odours, disfigured people and amputees following you like flies. She looked at all this misery with disgust and outrage.

To me, however, it pleased me to see that life didn't matter a fuck. I enjoyed seeing the destruction, the total decay of the human race. But it was not sadism; I did not enjoy the pain and suffering of the people. I enjoyed seeing life ridiculed, humiliated. We grew up with the myth of security, of welfare, prosperity, of a long life in the pink, attached to a beautiful house, to a car and a career. Here your life isn't worth a fig.

Once, while we were travelling in the car with a driver, we saw a man completely naked on the ground, covered in blood. Although the driver did not want to, we ordered him to stop the car and we went to see what had happened. The man complained and asked for help so we took him to the hospital. When he recovered we learned that he had been run over by a truck. While lying there fighting for his life he had been robbed—somebody had taken his shoes, another his pants and so on, until he was completely naked. The dead people that I saw on the street in India were almost all naked. It's not because they are inhuman but because for them life does not matter a damn. Life is a passage; it's a matter of religion. You're paying for your previous life. After death you will be reincarnated into a better life.

When they killed Indira Gandhi in 1984, I was in Bombay. The morning after the attack, I saw at least one hundred and fifty dead people on the road. The bombers, all Sikhs, were left to the dogs. In India, to see someone dying like a beast is the norm. You don't even stop. You see the naked reality—India tells you the truth. Every day reminds you of your own end. When you go into a cemetery and see an old man and you ask him, "What are you doing?", he'll reply, "I am waiting to die." You see the old men going to Varanasi to die. You see them praying with intense feeling. If you go to the Parsees' towers in Bombay, you can see the dead that are left there to be eaten by vultures. Or you see the crematoria with burning corpses and a big sign that advises that, for a cremation, you need two tons of firewood. More than that would be a useless ecological waste. In essence you are constantly reminded that life is a passage. When you see this, you feel infused by mysticism; you forget the trivialities of human life and, after all, you count for nothing in India. You are an animal to be milked.

The Indians are willing to do anything in exchange for money. So even here, if you have no money, you are worthless. But there is something that you cannot explain. Why is someone with two cars and a villa in Fregiene always pissed off and a starving man in India, rummaging in the rubbish, is peaceful? In the West, it is your fault if you are poor, while for an Indian it is right. They calmly accept having to pay for the sins of a previous life.

There are castes and there is no chance of jumping to a higher caste; there you are born and there you will die, so it's useless to get angry. In the West you are never satisfied with what you have. You wage an inner war every day against ghosts, parents, your colleagues, your boss, traffic, envious friends, continuously accumulating stress. Negative, uptight, competitive, aggressive people will give you negative influences. A simple smile, however, is a sign of confidence and encouragement. It is a message of non-belligerence. That's why you feel relaxed in India. I remember that my father never laughed. Next to him I was always uptight and I did not know why. Then when he was away, I felt my tension drain away.

In India I realized the importance of a person who smiles at you, of having a serene face next to you. You go out on the street and the doorman smiles to you, another says hello to you, the shopkeeper has a serene look. Whether you realise it or not, it affects your day. An angry, cold, detached person communicates to us the same feelings. Take this family that lives next door. They have a stand selling trinkets, incense, perfumes. They emanate serenity. They have a crippled son with no legs, with his feet attached to his knees. You see him barely walking and swaying. Yet he is undemanding.

With Maria Pia I lived a colonial life. We went to nice restaurants, frequented by wealthy Indians. She bought everything she wanted. I remember a merchant, a certain Mayawati, who often invited us to dinner. It was a clever way to ingratiate customers. He taught us how to eat without cutlery. In India you eat with your hands, even in wealthy families. Mayawati explained to us that the mother ate only from silver plates, because every time she ingested a little silver and this served to make her feel good. He showed us how to cook the various dishes of chicken masala, mutton and korma tandoori.

There is a difference between poor and rich cuisine. The cuisine of the poor is rubbish. The cuisine of the rich is very seasoned with ghee, a kind of butter. That's why the rich Indians are all fat—and that's also a status symbol.

There were no chairs in that house. There were mattresses on the floor where we sat cross-legged. Alvise smiled faintly and stood to one side. He was like a fish out of water. He just didn't seem cut out for this world. But in his way of talking he kept the delicacy, the composure, the manners that revealed his high-ranking origin. Mayawati's pride was to have a floor of Carrara marble in his home. It was surely a house that had cost millions, but the marble was chipped. The material was fine but they had no idea how to make it look well-finished. Some of the tiles were attached, some loose, some broken, despite being the home of a millionaire. The workmanship was inaccurate; I don't know why.

I feigned indifference toward that display of wealth and Maria Pia's sophisticated behaviour. It was part of my impudent, anarchist personality. We were prisoners of our own clichés; she, the upper-class women, a stuck-up snob, with her upturned nose. Me, the freak, not integrated, arrogant and nihilistic. In reality though, in India, her more hidden side came out. She seemed more youthful, less rigid. But I didn't care; I judged by categories. I saw only a chic and wealthy woman. And I thought of letting her live out a nice love story and fork over a boatload of money. What I did not understand about her, and I can understand now, was her desire to escape that formal context and high class to which she belonged. She suffered, after all, from feeling different, a marginalized woman of a certain age. Even when we were in Trastevere, she had tried to integrate, to be like us, to adopt our attitudes, our language, not just to be near her son, but also because of her need to feel like one of us. Although on the one hand she despised us, on the other hand she was fascinated by our challenge to the system and by our refusal to adapt, to conform to normal life. Beneath it all she envied us.

Once she told me, "India is like you—undisciplined, unreliable, violent and presumptuous." She had struck a bull's-eye. I was even presumptuous, like the Indians, who snubbed international aid after the last great flood. There was a kind of synergy between me and India.

By now Alvise hardly spoke a word. You could not have a conversation with him; if just a small thing bothered him, he walked away. He was very sensitive and vulnerable. But my presence did not bother him. Perhaps he felt a certain affinity with me, more than with his mother, who tormented him with questions and suffered because she could not communicate with him. In the end he rarely went out from his hotel room. We communicated with each other through long silences and the music we listened to together.

It occurred to me to record the sounds of India, the sounds of the street, rain, animals, drums, singing, chanting in the temples. The sound of the level crossing has a beat like a drum. The temple bells have a dull, muffled sound, as though heard from a distance when it snows. I had been right. This was the only thing in which I managed to involve him. We were there just to listen. We did not talk.

Alvise and Maria Pia returned to Italy. She wrote that Alvise had been admitted to a nursing home, diagnosed with schizophrenia. She had been forced to leave India suddenly because her son was now definitely out of touch with reality. In one of his moments of utter passivity, she had been able to take him on board the plane. I stayed, even though she asked me to leave with them. But our relationship was not only about her son. She promised that she would rent an apartment for me, where she would come to visit every so often.

Then, I don't know why, I felt a kind of annoyance towards every woman who clung to me. I assured her I'd be back soon to Italy. It seemed impossible that a woman like her, rich and intelligent, was in thrall to a dickhead like me.

She wrote that Alvise was now like a vegetable. He didn't communicate with anyone anymore. All day they filled him up with a deadly cocktail of drugs and left him alone in the garden, walking back and forth. He heard voices. He talked alone to himself and laughed alone. Reading the letter, I was reminded of when we were listening to music together. I am sure that, in those moments, he was fine. He was not alone. I had been better for him than those big doctors who were only able to dose him up with drugs.

India in the seventies was Gandhi's time, of nonviolence, and of flower children. Everyone was for non-violence, coming to India to smoke cannabis, which did not cost shit here. Without Alvise and Maria Pia, I continued wandering around India alone. Every now and then I joined up with some occasional traveling companion. When you travel alone you meet a sea of people. You easily become friends, then perhaps you never see them again. And you meet others. Everyone has his goals, his time, his 'trip', as it was called then. For a time I went around with a Belgian guy, one of those out and out hippies, always addicted to the core, and with a German girl, a lost freak, always with an inspired look, devoted to a holy man, a certain Rajneesh. When we were fucking she had visions. We both fucked her. There was no steady couple. Then, one day, she was lost. We didn't know what had happened to Karin—maybe she had met someone who had kidnapped her. We were convinced that something bad had happened to her because she had left her passport and her clothes in our room. The day before I had mistreated her because she was always glued to me. Sometimes I thought of giving up, but for sure she had come to a bad end. She was a completely helpless girl and a bit crazy. That's why I wanted to find her again. Everybody could do whatever he wanted with her. She was like a house with the door open. If she had found a master, she would let him treat her like a slave.

One month went by and no news of Karin.

Here, still today, for a few rupees they will provide you with hard drugs just so that they can take advantage of you. Someone told me about one of the more degraded places in Bombay where all the addicts hang out. The cages!

We went to look for Karin there. They were horrific places, with grates, behind which women were held captive, and offered for use as prostitutes. Each woman had a different price. A Tibetan, considered second-class, had a price. An Indian and a European had another price, so that way I knew if there was a European on offer. They took me to a girl in a straw bed, and I immediately recognized Karin, bloated with drugs. She was kept drugged with heroin, at the mercy of their desires and wishes.

I immediately said to myself, "I'll take her away. I won't leave them with the goose that lays golden eggs." It took a lot of money—luckily there was Maria Pia! I had a friend of mine call her, saying that I had had a serious accident and I was hospitalized. I continued this story for two months, getting her to send me money. So I had enough money also to help Karin. I received the correspondence as *poste restante* in a post office.

I returned to the place where the cages were located, determined to take Karin away. I was met by the pimp. "I'm here just to negotiate the purchase of a European girl." I said. He shot a frightful figure at me. "Two thousand," I replied "Not a dollar more," and I pulled out the wad of money. "But she can make even fifty dollars a day!" he protested. In the end he agreed to the money on the table. This happened in 1973 and I think that today nothing has changed. Like Karin, a lot of people have been lost in India, because they were made into slaves this way by unscrupulous, ruthless criminals.

Our friend went back to Belgium. When I took her with me, Karin was like a shadow. She had withdrawal symptoms; she had become like a three year old child. She was continually hugging me for hours, in silence. She also needed to have sex constantly. The psychiatrist explained to me that, in the absence of drugs, sex was a substitute for her.

We moved to Goa, to the myth of free love on the beach. We travelled around India for a year, and I lived a crazy life, with this wild girl who could make any kind of mess. Once, just as an example, I left her in a hospital run by nuns. She needed care, detoxification, and with me alone this was impossible. When I returned to my hotel, there she was standing in the lobby waiting for me. It was like a kind of hallucination—she had taken a taxi and had arrived before me. She couldn't stay away from me—I was the only person she could be with. Leaving her would have been like killing her. I was her bridge, keeping her in contact with the real world. Aside from me there was just the drugs. If I left, she would fall straight back into drug use, for sure. I wonder why drug addicts, weird or crazy people, always have had a certain attraction to me.

Karin and I also had our moments when we were happy. We could forget everything. We were in Goa and we went over the hills of Arpore, where there was a village of bungalows in the forest. Karin was very emotional. I liked the way she gave herself with total dedication, without reservation. Her body was full of sensuality.

We often watched cartoons on TV. I do not remember another woman with whom I could feel so distant from reality. We could laugh about nothing, even though we would later fall back into the usual paranoia. I remember those moments like an oasis in a desert.

We also amused ourselves watching those rambling, sentimental Indian love stories with magic and dance, those films that at other times would have bored me to tears. Everything made us laugh, especially when we were smoking marijuana. I almost managed to keep her from taking hard drugs, but she had continuous withdrawal symptoms. After several months I convinced her to return home to Germany, to be treated. Then I planned to join her. She also realized that she had made my life impossible, with her constant crises. And she needed a clinic to detox properly.

Getting her on the plane was an indescribable pain. I did not see her anymore, but we have always corresponded. Even from a distance she needed me. One day a photo arrived, with her holding a shrivelled brat. She wrote that it was her little girl, and she was glad that at last her life had some meaning. I thought about going to find her but then I found myself elsewhere.

I've lived in America for many years, again living like a hippy, drifting along. I went to rallies, concerts; I slept with a group in a

Westphalia, the famous Volkswagen van. Then I got bored of being a vagabond. I lived my little love story with the owner of a fast food restaurant in Los Angeles, and I married her. I have been a husband and a father—at least I have tried. The American dream hypnotized me for some years too. I hardly recognized myself—short hair and clean shaven every morning.

Los Angeles is the real America, and it soon swallows you into its system. In New York you can feel that you are in Europe. You see somebody going out for a stroll, or you spend evenings in the intellectual circle of the Village. In Los Angeles you go out to a specific place, or you go jogging. They are all fitness freaks, all perfect. There is no street life. The restaurant provided parking, even a post office has its own parking area, the bank has drive-in tellers, the supermarket has a car park. You go everywhere by car.

In New York there are popular, black neighbourhoods like Harlem. In Los Angeles popular means scum. You cannot ask for alms in Beverly Hills or Hollywood. In India you're a bum and that's that. There, besides being a bum, you're a disgusting, smelly piece of shit that society doesn't even want to see. America tends immediately to clean the streets, to take away the shit and corpses. Maybe a person could be robbed and murdered only because he stopped to change a tire on the highway.

In Los Angeles I also ran a bar, which attracted all-night wanderers because it closed at dawn. I always had to deal with arrogant assholes. There were a lot of gangs of kids who went to war with each other. They killed each other out of colossal stupidity. They exchanged heavy words, riots were a part of their lives. I have even been the object of some bombing attacks. They have also set fire to a part of my bar. This is characteristic of America. You are often a spectator to gratuitous violence: provocateurs, fights, gang wars. Then you would like to stab the man jumping the queue in the supermarket. I felt inside me a violence that I never felt in India. In that country they can steal your shoes, mutilate you and send you to beg, they can kidnap you, lock you in cages, but none of it's done in hatred. There is only self-interest, like a lion devouring a deer. There is no malice. It's just the way life is, in India.

You understand that violence is not inside the man. It is inside nature, in life itself. Nature is a slaughterhouse and you cannot help it. Existence itself is cruel. The Indian accepts violence as part of life.

In America someone attacks you in the subway, because you looked at him for more than six seconds. That's pure hatred, even pure idiocy. In the end you are convinced that violence is part of you. I even beat my wife, who then reported me. Our relationship ended many years ago; I don't know where my son is. Some years after the divorce, I came across my ex-wife in a parking lot in Los Angeles. We exchanged a smile. She looked gentle; a simple, plump lady.

I could not explain the cause of all that mess that had happened; the lawyers, the threats, knives, broken dishes—crazy things. We greeted each other like two people who have just met shortly before, without rancour or poison. Nothing at all. Then in the car park I found one tire of my car slashed. But perhaps it wasn't her.

My return to India was accidental. I accompanied a friend to Madras who had made up his mind to buy and organize a kidney transplant for his sick father. Madras is the biggest market for human organs. Even today, if you need a kidney or a lung, you go to Madras and buy the part you need with relatively little money. You give 5,000 euros to the one selling the organ, another 5,000 you will spend at the hospital for the doctor's work. One of those who had sold an organ was interviewed and asked, "But what can you do with 5,000 euros?"

This man, who was living in the middle of shit, replied that with 5,000 euros he could build a roof to sleep under, keep the TV and pay off his debts. With one kidney alone, a renal colic would be enough to kill him, but for him life is a passage. "Who cares if I die?" he says. A Christian, with eight tubes up his ass and two in his mouth, goes ahead anyway just to live another two months. But the Indian, with one kidney left, can get everything that he couldn't otherwise get in a lifetime of work.

The first day I arrived in Madras, I relived an episode that had happened to me in the past in India. I was getting a tonic massage. The little man started to touch my willy. I said: "What are you doing?"

"Do not worry Sir. I can do it for you."

He wanted to give me a blowjob for "the baksheesh", a tip. As single Indian males cannot fuck women, they sometimes arrange a homo session between themselves. They get blowjobs because women won't give you their pussy—starved as they are, they don't give it to you. Forget Indian pussy. Even today they arrange marriages where the woman has to be totally virgin. Even though the situation is changing a bit, living together without getting married is still a scandal, like it was with us in the 'fifties. To meet, couples have to hide or go to other cities to avoid being recognized.

I then started going out with a thirty year old Tibetan lady, of a lower caste. She was second class and remained second class. The Tibetans were always victims of persecution. They were routinely massacred in the past. In India they are second class citizens, like the Chinese.

We went to live in Goa. Then she died after giving birth. Now I live here in Goa with a little three year old baby. I play the role of father and mother, and now I really feel paternalistic. I change his diapers, prepare baby food and sing a lullaby. I started out babysitting many years ago and now I end up babysitting.

Last year a German girl came to Goa, to the residence where I live. I didn't understand why she looked at me so earnestly. I spoke to her; we became friends. Her name was Mila. A certain feeling developed. We went to the Doodhsagar Falls, south of Goa; we walked along the sea to the Chapora Fort. As she spoke more, I began to have doubts. There were special and strange coincidences. She too was from Frankfurt.

"But you're Karin's daughter?"

"Even your daughter," she replied.

Another person, perhaps, would have thrown his arms around her neck. However, I just wondered how I should behave in order not to disappoint her. I had no excuse; I was screwed. I told her that I was not her father before and I could not be now. To feel like you have a daughter, you must have seen her grow up, followed her every passage of life; otherwise she may as well be a stranger. But we could meet and get to know each other. I enjoyed talking with her; I found her beautiful and intelligent. Maybe a little cool, and reserved, one of those intellectual, serious and detached girls. She spoke about her mother, who had married, but remembered and always spoke about me.

Anyway, how could we forget the cages, all that mess trying to escape drug addiction and those moments lived outside of the real world—joints, alcohol, music, night bonfires, hippy parties. Mila wanted to see the places that her mother and I had frequented, like the lighthouse of Agada. We also went to the Shanta Durga temple. We returned late and slept in an Indian house along the road. The owners, in order to give us their bed, slept on the floor. Mila spent a few days with me and little Samir. When she went away I felt sorry, as if she had left something unfinished. I was beginning to get a feeling of... I don't know what.

I saw her again recently in Rome. She wanted me to be her guide. I tried to explain something about Rome but I knew very little about its history. I was more bewildered than her; me, born in Rome, reading the guidebook with her, just like a tourist! I felt a little uneasy by the side of this beautiful and sophisticated girl. I found it hard to consider her my daughter. Perhaps she felt my attitude was more gallant than paternal and she even seemed flattered. We spent some magic moments together. This, I thought, is the best Rome to live in; a city with something surreal. I said to myself, "How many inhabitants living in Rome really notice Rome, are aware of this city?" From the Colosseum, we walked under the Arch of Constantine, and we came to the Circus Maximus, where we stopped to look at the illuminated background of the Roman Forum. I told Mila, "I've never really seen this place, yet I've passed here who knows how many times?" Then we went up to Capitol Hill and we asked a Japanese tourist to take a photo of us in an embrace, under the statue of Marcus Aurelius on horseback.

We went on to Tiber Island and then we went down along the Tiber, where the Rome Summer Festival was in progress. And from there we went on to Trastevere, which is less of a popular neighbourhood for ordinary people than it once was. Now it's full of chic, refined cafes. All of Rome is different; it is more international and sophisticated but also full of poor people who I never used to pay attention to. We visited the Vatican, the Sistine Chapel, the Gianicolo, one of the seven hills of Rome, the Pantheon, Piazza di Spagna. Rome is the most beautiful city in the world and it was as though I was seeing it for the first time.

We sat at the bar Tre Scalini in Piazza Navona. Piazza Navona was once my playground but I couldn't find anybody I used to know there.

Mila wanted to confide in me, and tell me about her life, the things she'd done in all these years when I wasn't there, when I was wandering the world. She told me about University, her mother, her suitors, her programs, her ideas. She condensed her whole life into one week, almost to make up for lost time. After a few days, I had a deeper relationship with her than I had had with my other child in America, after years of cohabitation.

And then she was gone. Her life is in Germany where she is graduating in marketing.

I stayed another few days in Rome, walking alone aimlessly and I stumbled into a bar where I used to go when I worked at the Treasury. I went there every morning before going to the office and drank a cappuccino with the classic croissant. I found Ciro, the same barman of thirty years ago. He stared at me without recognizing me. He made the coffees, the cappuccinos and rinsed the glasses; the same gestures, the same movements, the same expression, just like thirty years ago. I watched him, almost in contemplation. He rinsed the cups with the same speed, the same face, a little more swollen with a few more wrinkles. Even the same sentences. "Hello, sir. Thank you. See you again, sir." And the same smile aimed at the customers in suits and ties who had come from their offices.

I've traveled around the world, turned the world upside down, changing places, jobs, situations, houses, countries, cities. Stories after stories, mess after mess. And he was always there. And after thirty years, I found myself in that bar, like before, as if nothing had happened, sitting and drinking the usual cappuccino and Ciro making coffees.

A Psychological Perspective

Piero had the choice available to his generation—to live as a hippie, to be free, to opt out of the system. For them, being "part of the system" was like a dirty word and any who were thus integrated, from the policemen to the clerk, were viewed as prisoners of society. Piero was a character of his times, a classic hippie, a dropout unwilling to commit to any traditional path.

He tries to do many things, but does not identify with anything. Every role, situation or job is just a game, one interchangeable with another. One life or one hundred lives are not enough. As in a game, he confronts the same bartender that he had known in his youth, in a sense his alter ego. Piero's is a case of escape from society and commitment, but he also feels the need to transcend life and to seek a deeper, more spiritual goal.

8

From Denmark to Thailand
I got a discount because she'd been in jail.

A man from Copenhagen, age 30:

As a child I remember having a big aquarium. I enjoyed watching the fish, especially their thin feces dangling down for five minutes before breaking away from their bodies. I loved the way all the fish glided in the water together almost as one body, as in a dance. But I was always fascinated when a little fish swam away from the group and faced the unknown by himself, exploring the bubbles of the oxygenator.

From an early age, like that fish, I never liked to follow the group, passively going along what others were doing. I always wanted to do my own thing, to swim against the current. But it took a long time for me to fully understand my true nature. Sometimes I felt I was living a life that was not mine and I couldn't even figure out what made me feel good and what made me feel bad. Each of us is exposed to a limited environment and perhaps we want something different but we don't know what it is. One grows up, goes to school, finds a girl and gets married, gets a job, buys a house and puts down a diamond-shaped tiled floor. That's the 'expected' script to follow!

The first time I arrived in Thailand with Amor, my Argentinean girlfriend, I saw Thailand through the eyes of a lover. Everything in Bangkok seemed to me almost beautiful despite it being a huge city with nightmarish traffic! Here, if you give a map of the city to a taxi driver, he looks at it like it is a map of Mars. Bangkok is nothing like a European city with beautiful squares, outdoor bars and evening strollers. In Bangkok you move around just to get from one place to another. You have to go to Lumpini Park for a stroll or to the malls—immense labyrinths of five or more air conditioned shopping floors. Places like Paragon, Central World or MBK become a common refuge from the humid, hot, sticky and polluted air of Bangkok, which is a year-round condition.

But if you travel on the Chao Praya river, you will see another world: the boats remind you a little of Venice. There is a special life on the river. You may see a man approaching by boat to sell fruit, or someone else washing clothes or even bathing in the river's dirty water. There are boats that have their own shops and boats that are restaurants and boats delivering food to those houses built on piles by the shore. The boat taxis embark and disembark so rapidly that Amor nearly fell into the river trying to get on. The boat handlers and veteran travelers get off while the boat is coming in and make a jump to get on when the boat moves away.

We also took a trip on a smaller boat that slipped into narrower channels and we had dinner on a steamboat. You may pass under various bridges and see all of Bangkok illuminated at night. In some places I have seen huge plants floating on the river like massive seaweed.

When we heard that there was a chance to go to Ayutthaya, the ancient capital, about 50 km from Bangkok, we seized the opportunity. Navigating by river to get there added spice to the journey. Having seen other tourists imprisoned by bus and umbrella-pointing tour guides, or using a rented motorbike, we freed ourselves to enjoy the city's sights at our own leisure and pace. We bought food with new and mysterious flavours, Amor using me as a guinea pig.

When we made it back to Bangkok we found that the banks were closed because it was the Queen's birthday. A true national holiday! I have never seen a people showing so much love for their monarchy. Throughout Thailand you will often see huge photos of the king, but also many in pocket-size. Everywhere you go, everywhere you turn, in any store, family dwelling, hotel, government house, lakeside hovels or means of transport, there is always a pictures of the King or Queen. In the cinema before the film begins, everybody stands up as the national anthem is played and photos of the King and His work in Thailand are projected on the screen.

Amor and I used to dress sloppily. We were like unkempt backpackers, clashing with the neatly-dressed Thais. Here you might expect to see people wearing wide, light pants or Bermuda shorts. Instead the girls go around with impeccable suits or skin tight jeans and well ironed blouses. They don't sweat!!

Amor and I had no schedule. Sometimes we went out in the middle of the night to eat a pizza, or we might stay in the hotel room all day making love and watching Thai television.

On the subject of TV, and in the case of accidents or murders, they let you see the dead bodies on the screen. They don't cover them with a sheet as in most countries. In some temples there are even photos of people killed in various accidents, showing scattered guts or people hanging with a rope around their necks. Once on television, a handcuffed killer was escorted by the police to the temple to make an offering for the deceased, and right under the eyes of camera and onlookers, the relatives of the victim kicked and slapped him. Then another time the newscasts talked about the state of health of an elephant, broadcasting live an operation on the elephant's foot. Since I was interested in watching it, Amor questioned me, saying, "I don't understand what you find so fascinating." But otherwise we were good together.

There are moments in life when you feel you don't need anything more—those absolutely self-sufficient moments. These aren't usually birthdays or a First Communion. Maybe you're washing your feet in a rundown boarding house and you sense for a moment that you are in paradise. In that moment you're totally away from the world and not thinking about the bucketful of manure that life is preparing for you. Maybe, out there, a distracted truck driver will run over you and your partner and you'll find yourself squashed like a bug, surrounded by police barriers, gawked at by tourists licking ice creams.

These moments, these holidays from reality, are beautiful because the moments are absolute. In your everyday life you are often anxious about what might await you. On vacation, however, you live everything to the full.

On vacation you can even think better of dogs. Dogs in Thailand walk around the streets freely just like people. In my country, however, we think that a dog is unhappy without its master. If you live here awhile, you realize that there is almost a co-existence with animals. You might meet an elephant on the street, pulled along by a kid. And Thais don't make a fuss if they have a house full of ants. Once I saw a flying cockroach in the hands of children (yes, here there are even flying cockroaches). I thought, "Now they will tear its wings off and then they will pierce it with some needle or something." Instead, after playing a little, they let it go.

Heading to Kanchanaburi, we encountered the bridge over the River Kuai, made famous by the film of that name. Now there is also a war cemetery there and a railway that runs through the countryside, up and down the hills, and ends by a magnificent waterfall. Nearby is Erawan National Park, a landscape of forests and waterfalls that seems to be something out of a movie.

On the bus ride there, the hostess gave us a snack with soy milk. That is just one of the touches that made the trip enjoyable. This culture of comfort, of care, of taking it easy, is created by many small things. For example, when you are in a barbershop someone may offer you a simple glass of water. When you buy a yogurt in a supermarket, they give you a spoon to eat it with. If you buy a fresh fish at the supermarket and you ask, they will often cook it for you and normally at no additional cost.

They pay particular attention to avoid causing discomfort to others. Even the last *coup d'état* in September 2006 created less inconvenience or disruption than a bus strike in Copenhagen.

We spent the last two weeks at the beach on Koh Samui (island) and in the lesser-known and lesser-developed Koh Pangan in southern Thailand. In Koh Pangan we rented a bungalow right on the beach and every morning, dreary eyed, we went tearing directly into the water. By the time we awoke fully, we were swimming in a warm and dreamy sea. We also rented a boat to go around to the nearby islands. Amor and I made it to an island inhabited only by monkeys. She did not want to disembark, because she was afraid of the monkeys. I almost dragged her. When we returned to the boat, the monkeys had stolen her glasses and she blamed me.

On the last day we took part in the famous full moon party, which is a monthly feast. They play music on the beach until early morning. The swaying palm trees, the ever-moving sea, the sparkling sun, the fish barbecued on the boat, the massage on the beach, the monkey stealing glasses are all things in our daily life there that gave me a sense of fullness. Everything matched perfectly. As I remember all this in my heart it becomes a reference point of contentment.

During the flight home, we spoke with a Danish girl sitting next to us. Her eyes were haunted by something crazy, almost magnetic. She talked about a spiritual retreat, the Varanasi, which she had done in a remote place in Thailand. For fifteen days she could not talk to anyone. She could only eat rice and some vegetables. There were a few lessons in Buddhist philosophy and meditation. No mobile phones or newspapers were allowed—if you slipped up on any of these rules, you were out. I was more than a little sceptical of these mystical sessions, but she seemed happy despite her schizophrenic look. So I asked her for the address of the meditation center.

Back in Denmark, Amor and I enjoyed a couple of happy years together before everything went to pieces. First, there was my dismissal from my job as a public relations officer for a company. Amor could spend an entire week with me, all the while remaining in a continual sulk. Sometimes one is in need of some time alone, but she wanted to do everything together, including shopping, shopping and more shopping. She criticized everything, even the cleaning of the mats in our car. She apparently liked unfortunate men who always needed her maternal protection, saving them from suicide. Eventually we separated. I returned to live with my mother and she with her grandfather from Argentina.

Then my mother became ill, which lasted for two years. I had to face this situation alone, as my sister was living in another city, and this added further hardship to my work problems. The last days before she died, my mother was rambling in a whisper. After a while she began to whisper poetry. We had spent the last few days trying to remember the verses of the poet Piet Hein. She would begin "Live while you've got life to live." I would respond with, "Love while you've got love to give." She died reciting poetry. She was in terrible pain, to the point that she hurled herself against the doctor who kept filling her with seemingly useless drugs. She raised her voice with maximum effort and said clearly: "Enough! I want to die."

The memory of my mother reciting these poems remains inside of me as a special message from her—one hard to explain. Her long illness and suffering shocked me so much that I promised myself not to die in a hospital bed trapped between doctors and treatments. I'd rather die quickly, like being blown up by an Islamic suicide bomber.

After the death of my mother, Amor called me every night, asking about my health. She often came to pick me up in her Fiat, which she had named Pablita, and would take me to a restaurant. I had awoken her maternal instincts once again. Soon we started going out again and immediately the strife began. When she went to visit her friends, she demanded that I go too. I went there to please her, but I hadn't the courage to tell her that I really didn't want to go. And she had this ongoing contrariness. She would ask, "What do you want for dinner?" I might reply, "Spaghetti" and so she made French fries without salt. I felt bad without her but even worse with her. So I decided to leave.

Everyone considered me irresponsible. We loved each other and could make, and be, a family, so why I was fleeing? But my crazy dream was to venture all over the world, to strengthen my mind and to tackle difficult and uncomfortable situations, to face the unknown, like the little fish I used to watch. I didn't know what I was doing with my life but I felt that I wanted to squeeze it dry. Maybe after a year I would come back. But I did not want to make a promise and thereby force her to wait for me. She didn't want me to leave. Then I told her, "I will marry you before leaving, so you can take Danish citizenship." I told her that just to make her happy, but instead she flew into a rage. She has an abnormal amount of pride. She desires others to need her but rejects the concept that she might be in need of others.

Well, I finally convinced her to get married but even then we quarrelled the day before the wedding. I did not give a damn about the marriage, but I would have been glad to see her happy. She had wanted everything to go well; the restaurant, gifts, photos, album, witnesses, and friends. After the wedding, I told her that I would be leaving soon, and she got angry, despite the fact that I had told her this before the ceremony. Somehow she thought I was joking. Since she insisted, we made another attempt to stay together, but we continued to have significant misunderstandings. I had thought of marrying her just to please her. However, according to her, I wanted to do it as an act of charity.

That night she hugged me. She did not want me to leave. But what was the point of staying? She was a whiner and with time would only become more so. And I too would become boring, argumentative and crabby, even more than I already was. Over time we had talked less and less. I told her that every plant withers but in our case the plant of our love would not wither. Our separations would make our relationship fresh each time I returned. I explained also that most marriages statistically end in divorce but our love was above everything and everyone and that any time she could turn to me for help.

Anger was her response; she verbally attacked me. She did not care that, statistically, married life was a disaster, or that living together could become a boring habit. She could not bear my theoretical discourses, since she only understood that she wanted to stay with me.

The tragedy was that I agonized over the idea of having to leave her but I still had this bug in me to be a solitary traveler. It was something stronger than me! As a child, my heroes were those who faced unknown worlds alone. I remember playing with toy soldiers. I would take one soldier and make him walk around the living room, under the bed, into the kitchen, in the bathtub, imagining that he had landed on another planet. I crawled on the floor with him in the unlikeliest places of the house. I even took him with me when I went outside and I imagined seeing with his eyes the courtyard of the house, the buses, the cars, the gigantic passers-by, the shops and the roads.

My sister and I had sold my mother's house and I took the half of money—about 111,000 euros. The day I left, Amor wanted to accompany me to the airport. I did not want her to, but she insisted and did so. We were both a bit sad and a little upset. But since I left, we phone each other about every four days.

Arriving in Thailand, I went to one of the lesser frequented islands, Koh Tao, in the south, where many divers go. It was a twelve-hour bus trip from Khaosan Road in Bangkok, and two additional hours by boat! The cost was a mere six euros. I had brought a guidebook for travelers who want to spend little money and also a book on meditation.

I studied and I practiced the meditation exercises from a bungalow on a cliff, with only candlelight. I did this all on just two euros a day. I spent the day watching the sea, trying to turn off my mind, to experience cosmic energy while taking deep breaths. Adding to the experience was a lady nearby who was continually smoking hashish.

Then I started to visit Thailand's less touristy, less popular, places. I saw scenes of backwardness, lives caught between tradition and ultra-modern life. I had a view of a country that, in only thirty years, had rushed from the hut to the skyscraper, from the jungle to the Mercedes.

There are highly organized localities for the tourists, but they do not really reflect the Thais' normal way of life. If you wander off the tourist circuit, you find squat toilets where you replace the toilet water with a saucepan, many annoying insects, strange noises everywhere, and signs in an alphabet all but incomprehensible.

But the one important thing that you will notice after arriving in Thailand is their special upbringing. For example, when a Thai passes in front of you, he will bow his head in order to not block your view. In a recent TV series, two Thai drug dealers, while exchanging goods and money, were continually bowing and thanking each other. Once I met a girl who, during sex, said, "More slowly, thank you; faster now, thank you... you are very kind."

I have met many Danish living in Thailand. They always hang around together every day like classmates. They often become a bit childish and sophomoric. This may occur because they are out of their normal, more formal surroundings. Many of them have built a little piece of Denmark there, with their coffee and croquette every day. But I started eating like a Thai. You may find tables and chairs everywhere because they almost always eat outside of the home—rarely do they cook.

I had never eaten anything so spicy. I went directly to the market and ate there. At the market you find everything. There are plenty of places where I eat for next to nothing, and where most of the foreigners do not venture. Many are afraid that it is not hygienic and in many cases they are right. But I knew that a stomach ache or two would improve my resistance. This possibility is also described in the book on meditation.

I went to several villages in the northeast, an area called Isan. It is a very poor and a much less touristy area. I immediately noticed the language barrier so I began studying Thai. They speak a little differently there, almost like in Laos. A word may have ten meanings, but verbs normally do not change as they do in English!

Once in a karaoke bar I met a girl named Nom, which means both breast and milk. She was a very pretty girl, well educated, refined, with proper manners. She had just been released from prison. Nom had had a little problem with some drugs. She went to make a new identity card and they arrested and held her for four months in prison. Now the prison she went to was not for dangerous people. There weren't any armed guards or security systems. To escape was easy. But if you did escape, then you earned time in the hard prison. She showed me a souvenir photo with her friends in prison. They were all smiling, wearing their yellow t-shirts.

We went to eat something which Nom claimed to be "Mai aloi", which means literally, "not tasty". She did not like it. Then we walked in front of a booth where she bought a bag of grasshoppers. They were on display behind a little plastic covering and perhaps they were precooked. The salesman dipped them in black frying oil, seasoned with some special flavour and then gave them to her in a bag. As she started munching on them, the claws came out of her mouth. A sachet of locusts, beetles, cockroaches, or larvae of worms costs more than a fried rice dish with chicken, but who knows why. It's probably because you can only buy them from stalls on the street and not in restaurants. I guess if it's possible and the world's population continues to grow, we all will end up eating cockroaches and grasshoppers. They are rich in protein and low in fat, *he he*! As I watched her, speechless, she felt compelled to share the meal with me. I said to myself that if she can survive then why can't I too, for after all I am not dependent on Danish food alone. When I slipped the first grasshopper into my mouth, I expected worse. It was almost appetizing; the flavor was a little like potato chips.

The next morning when I woke up with red blisters all over me, I looked like Edgar Allen Poe's *Masque of the Red Death*. It was an allergy attack, so I had to go to hospital. I spent a whole day there, and 60 euros as well. Nom came to visit me in the hospital and after took me to her home. She nursed me and kept close watch on my fever. There was an army of family members who occasionally stopped by to visit. I found myself so well looked after that I decided to stay on with full board, at a mere two hundred baht per day—equal to, at the time, about four dollars.

As her brother learned of the new entry into the family, he immediately quit his job as tire repairer. He was working twelve hours a day for only a hundred baht!!

While with Nom I began to get involved in Thai life. Sometimes I gave a gift to the Buddha, a gesture that Thai people appreciate very much. Once we met a monk and Nom asked him to give her a lottery number, but she didn't win. Another time she took me to a movie to see a film about ghosts. She is fond of films about ghosts and believes in them, as do many Thais.

In Phuket, after the tsunami, the government sent a team of monks from Bangkok to lay twine around the beach in order to block the souls of those drowned in the sea from returning as ghosts. Apart from Buddhism, Thais have a magical and childlike vision of the world.

I could not wait to relate my experiences to Amor, even if she did not show much interest in my stories. Of course she had never accepted my departure. I had written her a long email where I tried to involve her in my experiences. I explained that the people here are very strange and not like us. They live in a world of their own. They laugh continually. Often when you get near a group of Thais, they will be laughing about something. If, for example, a worker does something wrong on the job, he starts laughing. I thought that I had arrived in a nation of idiots. Then I realized that it's a real philosophy of life, because smiling and laughing is good for your health. You too have to smile, or they get worried. They will ask, "What's wrong with you?"

They have a relatively high rate of homicide—better you smile too. Yet the total number of crimes is lower than in Denmark. In other words, it's better not to upset them, but if you don't get them really angry, they are more correct than us.

Thais have very strong nationalistic feelings, to such a degree that if you are unfortunate to get into a fight with one of them you will probably end up fighting ten. I have really given up trying to understand them. On the one hand they are prudish—they even bathe and swim in the sea while dressed—and don't like exhibitionism, but then you will see them walking around draped in gold ornaments. They seem to dislike vulgarity; they will not even use rude words in public and are almost aristocratic in their manners. But then they will openly shove their fingers up their noses in public as a matter of course.

Nom's parents demanded that I marry her because I was living full time in their house with their daughter. I agreed, although already married in Denmark, because here marriage is a simple ceremony that you can easily annul. The parents, however, wanted money too. The Thai tradition requires that the groom offer a sum of money to the family for the bride. There is some negotiation on the value of the gift—it's is a sort of exchange of goods. The value of the gift is the value of the child that is given as property of the family. I asked for a discount because she had been in prison. We agreed upon about 900 euros. There were no public officials but just a simple ceremony in which the parents married us. They also gave me a receipt. After all, here, with the same simplicity you can marry or divorce.

Of course I avoided telling Amor that I was married a second time. On the phone, she asked when I would return. I told her that I would come back soon and it would be so nice to see each other again.

I spend much time alone in my room, where Nom brings me food to eat. I love my idleness and my space. I need my space! We are strange animals to the Thai people. They can live comfortably, even with ten in a room. They move in small spaces and that space includes dogs, motorbikes, stalls and boiling pots. They are not bothered by contact with many of their own. They are not like Westerners, who often prefer to take elevators alone.

I was beginning to practice Thai habits. I spent hours in the hammock yawning and scratching myself. In Thailand, those obsessed by work and business are mostly of Chinese origin. The average Thai lives a cult of relaxation. If he wins a fortune in the lottery and then loses it, he returns to sleep in his hammock, as if nothing had happened. For the Buddhist, suffering and sacrifice are to be avoided like the plague, while for the Christians they are a means to attain salvation. For the Buddhist life is a colossal trial, the secret being to move as little as possible. The less you move, the less you make mistakes. That's why Thais do not move too much. Thai people, today, are not too different from Thais of 2,500 years ago.

The Thais have not advanced very much culturally compared with the West, having no famous scientists, writers or artists. What is taught today in Thailand is not much challenged, much as in our medieval times when no one doubted the existence of God or the authority of the Pope. Furthermore their religion here is simpler and does not impose hardships but only a bland liturgy. A normal Thai goes to a temple or may become a monk for a month or a year and then returns to normal Buddhist life. There is no seminary and no long term commitment is required.

One day, while we were relaxing in a hammock, news came that Nom's brother had died in a motorcycle accident. He was the youngest son, only seventeen, the former tire repairer and the best-loved of the family. For the family members it was a painful shock.

We organized a big ceremony for him. The body was washed, scented and laid out on a mattress where everyone, both friends and relatives, could come to spray him with water to bless the departing soul. They also put a coin in his mouth, to pay for his trip to the great beyond. Imagine that this was not a free service! I bought the things he liked, such as CDs, some T-shirts and Thai boxer shorts. We furnished his room with these things to encourage him to return for the last time, according to their belief. The mother also cooked dishes that he liked. Then all of these things were taken to the temple.

Monks, friends and relatives, all made a lot of noise, intent on playing cards and having fun. This was not due to lack of respect, but to cheer up the family. There was no reason to be sad. The cycle of death and rebirth will slowly bring about a state of perfect peace.

There was a real feast lasting several days, allowing time for distant relatives to come and pay respects to the boy. There was also a strange incident. A cat, passing near the little altar, suddenly stopped and humped his back almost as if he had sensed the presence of the deceased. Many were convinced that the boy returned to be there among them, until, from behind a box, out ran a rat.

By this time I was living like a Thai. I ate Thai food sitting cross-legged on the floor. I took sticky rice, a specialty of the northeast, with my hands, as they do. I slept on a mat on the floor as a Thai would. I even thanked with joined hands like a Thai and I spoke Thai as well. I had learned to live with all kinds of insects, clouds of flies that took turns with flying ants, beetles and insects of the earth, platoons of fleas and ticks, wasps and hornets which emerged from every crevice. I tried ant egg soup. But I refused to eat *yam khung ten* (a 'dancing shrimp' salad). Yam khung ten consists of live small shrimps poured into a small box with a lid. They are covered with chilli, lemon juice, other spices and they mix these all together. Some shrimp jump out! Nom takes the box, opens it and makes sure that the shrimps are still jumping a little. Then she closes the box again and shakes it. She says that in this way they are better. Now she waits a few minutes and then begins to eat them. When she sticks the spoon in her mouth, some of the shrimp jump out falling from her mouth because they are still alive. They continue to jump even when they are in her mouth! If you look inside the box, it looks like a prison riot.

One morning I woke up with a desire for spaghetti. But there were no Italian restaurants nearby. Now I had never cooked anything in my life so I went to buy some uncooked spaghetti in the supermarket and started tinkering in the kitchen. By dint of trying I managed to dish up something edible. Some Thais started to taste the pasta still raw.

Nom's family has a little place where they cook some Thai food for passing clients and where you can also buy detergent, toothbrushes and pens, so we also added spaghetti to the menu.

Now when I came back from shopping, the kids would run toward me to see if I brought any spaghetti. I instructed the members of the family to cook according to my recipe. I also called back to Denmark and asked Amor to get me some new recipes—she found several recipes in a cookbook and sent them to me. I tried several improvisations and now even the mayor comes here to try it sometimes.

This restaurant is also Nom's house. If you enter a room at any time of day, you will always find someone sleeping or eating on the floor. They eat, drink, sleep, grow up, get married, have children and watch television all in the same place where they do business.

Amor supervises all phases of my cooking over the phone as I explain to her every detail of my new experience. "Dear, we have plenty of waiters here," I tell her. "There are more waiters than people at the table." One waiter is assigned only to open the doors for customers. In Europe one person does the job of three, but in Thailand three people do the work of one! They have another conception of work, another way of thinking and looking at things. Work, in Thai language, must be sanuk, which literally means to have a good time—in Thailand, if work is not *sanuk* a Thai will often try to avoid it. The origin of the concept of work as fun may be from Thailand's rural past, when they went together happily to work in the fields or at least to try to make the work more bearable. They are far from our vision of work, which we understand as a serious moment and perhaps even a sacrifice.

I am in the kitchen to direct the work and sometimes I must rebuke the cook, who lets her sweat drip into the sauce. But you have to do so in a kind way. Any strong reprimand could be understood as a declaration of war.

When I become really frustrated with all these people, I sometimes retire to my room to meditate. I cannot tolerate too many hours in the midst of people who eat all the time. Now the restaurant/tavern operates by itself. I don't touch a grain of rice because a foreigner cannot work here. If the police find you bringing a dish to a table, you will go to jail as a criminal, just as if you were challenging their national security. They enter your name into the computer as an "undesirable person" and for the next 99 years—this is established precisely—you cannot set foot in Thailand. Despite seeming to be full of kindness, smiles and polite greetings, if you make a mistake here, they have no concept of forgiveness and mete out stiff punishments up to the death penalty. In practice here I treasure public relations. It is important for my presence as a representative of international cuisine.

They do not call me by name here but call me 'farang' instead, which means something like 'pale face'. This is to remind me that I come from another planet—it's what they call all Western foreigners. But it isn't a matter of racial hatred. There is no reason why a Christian should hate a Buddhist or a Muslim and vice versa. Hatred arises when one feels invaded or threatened. It also comes about if one fears that their culture can be penetrated or contaminated. But the Thais rarely run this risk. They strongly defend their culture and they make sure, with their laws, that an alien cannot infiltrate or damage it. Their proverbial tolerance is sometimes quite apparent. For example, a tourist who suns herself topless wouldn't bother Thais because they just consider her to be from an inferior culture, much like the dog that pees on the street. But you'll never see a Thai woman with her breasts exposed.

One day I'll leave without much explanation, because Nom would not understand. She has been taught that there is nothing better than the country where she lives. Even in their schools interest in the West is not promoted, because it is considered less spiritually evolved. In the end, I'm glad that Nom can exist with her innocent habits and her munching of locusts. The unknown, adventure, research, discovery, solitude and the risk of leaving the group to take a new path are all concepts unsuitable to Thai culture. Buddhism suggests looking for serenity within ourselves and nowhere else. But I am not a Buddhist and I consider the Thai experience just a transitional phase in my life. I do not rule out the possibility of having lost my head. Maybe I'm the product of a civilization in a daze or a state of mental confusion! They, after all, are well into their own ways.

One day I felt that I was acting like a real worm. So I decided to confess to Amor that I had another relationship. I also told Nom and she exhibited a fairly primitive jealousy. She tried to stab me. Fortunately for me, the fact that she had a criminal record came to my aid. In addition it is not reprehensible for a Thai to have two or more women: one official wife and one as a lover. So she calmed down. Now Nom is happy because the business is going well and with the money earned we bought the land and the place where the restaurant is located. She has become a real businesswoman who runs the whole show.

I have written a long email to Amor in which I talked about my new marriage. Amor sent a reply to me saying that she was also playing a new role in Denmark. A very beautiful moment for her is when she comes home after being with her new lover and begins to write to me—in this way she can rise high above conventional behaviour.

Basically everything that we've each done should separate us. Yet, on the phone, we talk as if nothing had changed or as if we lived in the same house or even as if we had seen each other just ten minutes before. Sometimes we fight. And then she reminds me that I am a polygamist, and that in Denmark a prison is waiting for me!

A Psychological Perspective

He immerses himself in unfamiliar cultures and ways of life, without intermediaries or safety nets, deeply motivated by his spirit of exploration and discovery. He is an adventurer, an explorer—truly one of that rare breed, a lone traveller. But at the same time, untypically, he keeps a sentimental relationship alive from a distance, a relationship which represents his emotional need and the desire for a stable reference point.

9

From Italy to South Africa
I felt at home nowhere

Enrico, from Trieste:

I feel at home nowhere, but this is the nature of us sailors. Other people cannot understand us. I boarded a ship at the age of eighteen. Then it was the only way of seeing the world, either the sea or travel by airplane. But in Italy in the sixties, how many people could find work on a plane? Perhaps five hundred people.

The downside of the sea is that you are away for a long time. When you went back home you felt an immense happiness, but already after a few weeks the desire to leave returned. It's in a seaman's blood. Today a young man would not want to do this work willingly—or maybe just for one season. Once sailors made good wages; these days, however, they are paid the same as in a factory. Now, as an old man, I love to find some of my past friends and fellow adventurers.

Now the cities in the world are all the same. The downtown shops are the same in Moscow as in New York or Tokyo. Maybe my subconscious does not have a reference point. I have no link to Trieste, even though I was born there.

I had an unusual childhood. My father went down with a ship during World War II; it was torpedoed by a British submarine. He survived, while most of the crew on board died. He had seen horrible sights; fellow sailors who could not get out of the porthole to save themselves. My father started drinking and then later he went off his head. Mercifully, God took him when I was eleven years old. This solved many problems because he had tried many desperate things—he even tried to kill me and my mother. Many of them, after returning from the war, were no longer normal, especially those who had survived a sinking ship. I also had an uncle who survived similarly and came back a bit crazy. Today they don't talk about these people. Even the Americans and Japanese had a whole generation of disoriented people. We all know about the Vietnam war generation; television showed it. After a war, every country has some mentally wounded people and some just went off their heads.

Where I lived many people joined the Navy, therefore I followed in my father's footsteps. In 1950, the Italian merchant marine was one of the biggest in Europe; it employed 180,000 people. By 2006, there were only 5,000 workers employed in this trade.

After the First World War, in Trieste, there were the dockers, and there was an employment agency to recruit them. Today this work still exists, but it is off the books. Many people from northern Europe, during the winter, came to work in Trieste because in their countries it was too cold to work; even the animals stayed inside. They would come down by train from Austria, Czechoslovakia or other countries in the north, and end up in Trieste. At the end of the 'fifties, in the merchant navy, the staff was only Italian, and to protect their jobs they didn't allow foreigners on board. Today, however, eighty percent of the crews, especially on cruise ships, are made up of immigrants.

The Italian ships once had a crew of a few men. The owner would try to save on everything; he would even allow sick people on board, with the hope that, if they got worse, they would be covered by seamen's insurance. The crew earned 84,000 Lire a month in 1969. We Trieste workers got 250,000 Lire and the captain got 500,000 Lire a month. I sailed for Texaco. In 1964 the number of Italian ships began to diminish because the Italian owners, to save on taxes, pretended to sell the ships and after they bought them back again, for example under Liberian or Panamanian flags. This continued until the 'eighties. Then the ships' owners started to hire foreign staff.

On 5 June 1967, the year there was a war in Israel, we departed from Bari. We had to go to Port Said, passing through the Suez Canal, and we were to circumnavigate Africa from east to west, clockwise, stopping in various ports to download. The ship had been hired by Lloyd Triestino, which had a large fleet. But that same evening, at 16:00, a telegram from the Ministry of Merchant Marine arrived. At that time there was also a special Marine Ministry. The telegram said, "All ships under the Italian flag must return immediately and wait for further orders from their owners." The ship was loaded to the max. Everything had been prepared in order to discharge in ports from east to west, from

Mogadishu to Mombasa, Beira, Lorenzo Marco, Macuto and then in Durban, South Africa, and also other high-traffic ports such as Port Elizabeth, where they made cars.

Not being able to pass through the Suez Canal we had to go around Africa counter-clockwise. We had to download in reverse, starting from the bottom. Impossible! We had to offload the entire ship and then reload it. It would cost too much, so we did a double tour of Africa: counter-clockwise without stopping to download, then we resumed the original planned itinerary from east to west. The bunker fuel was sufficient. It was better to fill up in Italy, which at that time refined more than it needed for domestic consumption. Many foreign ships stopped in Augusta, in the province of Syracuse, to get some fuel at an affordable price. After circumnavigating Africa clockwise, we inverted the route and began to unload. In Mogadishu there was no port; there were only wooden boats to take the goods ashore. After the war, as a sop, Italy was given the trusteeship of Somalia for ten years. We only had socks left to wear in 1945 and we were investing money in Somalia to make roads. Then I returned there in 1969 and stayed a month because we could not download. The monsoon had begun to blow and when the monsoon hit, the boats could not approach. We only had the ship's powerful service boat, which, piloted very carefully, was able to take us ashore. One crew member stayed three days on land. Then the monsoon started up and, being unable to return, he delayed our departure. For this delay, Lloyd Triestino threw him out with a "dismissed by ship owner" on his employment record. With this stamp in a seaman's book, nobody would take you on board again.

At that time Mogadishu was clean, tidy and liveable. I recall the pricelist in Lire of the brothel in Mogadishu near the Southern Cross, a famous hotel: "blo-blo job 150 Lire. A blo-blo job with drink for 250 Lire. Fuck 250. Ass no have." In another African port, I cannot remember the name, we had to take women on board because prostitution was prohibited. I remember one girl who did not want to get off the ship. She wanted to take her daughter for treatment at the next port, where there was a religious mission that offered specific therapies. The baby had an incurable disease.

Mozambique was still a Portuguese colony then; the capital was Maputo. Beira was a beautiful small town where we were going to load for export. Then there was the civil war. From Mozambique to Rhodesia, now Zimbabwe, there was only one railway line carrying iron ore. And there were ships connecting the colonies to the mother country.

When you arrived with a ship in South Africa you were confronted by a sign written in all languages, including Italian, which reminded you about the prohibition to mate with women of colour, under penalty of imprisonment. Two of our colleagues in Lloyd Triestino spent two months in prison for banging a black girl. In Mozambique, on the contrary, there was freedom, despite its border with South Africa.

The Portuguese left Angola and Mozambique in the same period. As a result, civil war broke out, officially between different tribes, but there were Communist groups, well-subsidized from Russia, sowing discord. In Mozambique, the whites were better off than the blacks, but everyone enjoyed the same rights. Living was cheap, and there was a lot of infrastructure left by the Portuguese. The war then turned a liveable country into a hell. They destroyed everything; they even dismantled the railroad to use the iron. Now they are trying to rebuild again. Mozambique has the potential to become a tourist attraction, while at that time only the rich people from South Africa were going there. The sea has a tide of five meters for the same gravitational reasons as the sea in the English Channel. In a place like that, the beaches are not that great. A tide changes in six hours and twelve minutes; it's the same all over the world. We, together with the ship, went up and down one and half meters. The quays are very high, like those of Le Havre and Southampton, in the English Channel, just because of the tide. So you can imagine the cranes pulling the goods up and down and the dockers handling the goods.

Between one company and another I often stopped in South Africa. I was there when the Americans went to the moon. I embarked on a great new Japanese ship given to the Americans by the Japanese as war reparation, but we had nineteen days of detention, having sustained some severe damage. There was no television in Cape Town. Every two hours the local newspaper came out with a special edition, with a photo of Armstrong walking on the moon. Cape Town was the only place in the world where they did not want television, in order not to open the eyes of blacks. All communication was controlled.

They don't speak much about South Africa, as a tourist attraction. For example, East London, Port Elizabeth, were very liveable, beautiful places. East London was traversed by a stream almost always dry, with an estuary. The city, temperate and green, was on both sides of the stream. The sea water is cold and there is a current of five knots—almost ten kilometers per hour. There are beautiful bays, although there is a strong surf and dangerous tides.

Some supporters of apartheid wanted to divide South Africa into many republics. Some would be white and some black. It would be a confederation, with the army, foreign policy and the economy in the hands of whites. East London was to be the capital of one of these black States.

Cape Agulhas, not the Cape of Good Hope, is the most southerly point in Africa. The weather changes rapidly there; in three hours the sea temperature can vary by fifteen degrees. On board we had charts printed as early as 1889 and there was a report of a sighting of an iceberg in November 1891.

In Namibia, which was called South West Africa, there is Walvis Bay, a port where they speak German. A place of unique sadness! Despite being a tropical area there is a very cold current from the south Atlantic—it's always foggy and cold. On August 15, I had a photo taken and I was wearing a coat. And even though it was also winter there was a terrible stench of fish meal. All of the unwanted fish were processed into fishmeal.

There was no police control; in fact we had several thefts. There were some watchmen, the security guards, and yet they stole some of our load. The thieves were using suits stolen from the sailors and they loaded up piles of lead. Walvis Bay was the railroad terminal in South Africa. Tourists go there, because from there you can travel to the Kalahari Desert. And then they die, especially Germans. It's not a desert that you can cross.

One of the subsequent ports, the one in Liberia, is not nice. It was founded by American Negroes, who came back to Africa to establish a free nation for blacks—Liberia means 'free nation'. But from the first day of its founding, there has been only misery and violence. The city of Monrovia was not bad; kind of tropical. But everything was destroyed by those corrupt, good-for-nothing revolutionaries!

Many of my shipmates sought adventure. There was one who had a broken heart and was trying to forget his past on board ship. For some of them it was a way to turn their backs on the world. There was also a village idiot on board; the crew was his family.

I suspected that one of the sailors was a wanted man. He came from the French Foreign Legion where he had probably changed his name. In some ports he did not get off the ship. He was a nihilist, without homeland or family, a little touchy and quick to flare up but could also be one of the most polite and helpful sailors. He stood aside most of the time. When he had to communicate it seemed he had some difficulties in finding the right words. The captain had a soft spot for him. Then, when we arrived at Tristan da Cunha he stayed there and did not return to the ship.

Tristan da Cunha is the most isolated and distant place in the world. There are roughly 300 inhabitants. It is 2,300 km from the already isolated and out of the way St. Helena and halfway between Cape Town and Argentina, in the Atlantic Ocean. They speak a mixture of English and Camoglin dialect; that's from Camogli, a little town in Italy, in the Liguria region. At the end of the nineteenth century a ship with a crew from Camogli sank and some of the crew who survived the shipwreck stayed there. In fact the island's hospital is called Camogli Hospital. How they found women is a mystery.

However, the inhabitants don't like to be treated like Martians from outer space. Of course tourism does not exist in Tristan da Cunha, and it's the same on St. Helena Island, which has 4,800 inhabitants and about a dozen doctors and nurses. In St. Helena, as in Tristan da Cunha, people know everything about each other. I had an affair with a girl named Virginia, a fishermen's daughter. She was only 19 and I was 36, but she was taller than me. She looked older because she wore glasses. The last day I put a lot of gifts for her on the table—stuff that I had accumulated in the various ports we'd visited and which I gave to the women I met—perfume, a painting set, a necklace and some clothes. She burst into tears. She said she had not been with me to be paid, while I was trying to explain to her that I was not even remotely trying to pay her.

The truth is that she wanted to come away with me. But I was a sailor and I was not allowed to let her on board. Usually a seaman, when he lands in a port, is just interested in looking for an easy sexual liaison. As soon as we arrived in a port, we inquired immediately about where the brothels were. I tried to get away from her in a proper way. I promised that I would write, but it was impossible to stay in touch. Ships with cargo and passengers came from England only three times a year, and even the mail arrived only three times a year. Now, however, there is the internet. When I returned to St. Helena two years later, I went looking for her. Her parents were crying because their daughter had gone to Europe, had not come back, and had not sent any news.

In St. Helena, people live isolated from the world. There is no crime, there are no locks on the doors, everyone trusts everyone else. When the young people move away, for example to London to go to university, it's a shock for them. There are some who don't return, they discover the world. And there are some who flee back home, traumatized by their experience in this new world. Take a girl from St. Helena arriving in London: if a stranger in a car stops and says, "Come on, let's go for a ride," she will probably get into the car. It should be normal between human beings but unfortunately the world is no longer normal. And that is difficult to understand for someone who grew up in St. Helena.

I was traveling to South Africa when apartheid was still in effect. To buy a South African Rand cost a dollar and a half. The whites enjoyed a high standard of living then. The blacks did all of the shit labour, the work that you did not want to do. You gave them a pot of soup and they did everything for you. If you did not like his way of working, you gave him a beating. On a double-decker bus, the upstairs was for blacks. If you walked along a sidewalk and there was a Negro, he had to get off the sidewalk. Now, when a black man catches a white man, he not only robs him, he cuts him to pieces. All the downtown area is black now—evil black.

There used to be an area called 'white by night', where blacks could not walk around at night. But now all the institutions have passed into black hands—the army, the police, the media. They have not yet resorted to expropriation of private property, but now if a white has no work, he cannot find it. For blacks, however, there is all kinds of work. This transition has been run by Nelson Mandela. He managed to liberate people who had been in chains for generations and prevent these people from causing a massacre. We whites were armed to the teeth at that time. We would have lost but we would have made them pay a heavy price in blood. Instead, nothing happened.

In neighbouring Namibia for example, it was normal that farms, factories, homes and property were savagely attacked by blacks. After that the white police recovered survivors and took them away on a truck. The international community was absolutely silent!

Now being robbed in South Africa is normal. I experienced a carjacking, or car theft, twice, at the traffic lights with a gun pointed at my temple. In Johannesburg they have produced a flame thrower which is controlled from under the car seat. You press a button next to the pedals and the assailant is cooked to perfection. It costs 35 dollars. Although this system is criticized, it's installed in many cars. Many whites are fleeing the country, and the blacks are killing one another. The most bloody struggles are between tribes. They are not like the American blacks; they have no cultural background. They squabble among themselves. If you want be good to somebody in Africa, you might think it's sufficient to donate some money to help them. Instead you have to go there personally—if you send a dollar for someone to get a vaccination, maybe instead he will drink a bottle of whiskey. African society is primitive. Then there is the tribe headman, who does what he pleases. He has absolute privilege, the right to life and death over everyone.

The South Africa of today is not the same one in which I lived, but it is still the place to which I am more connected. It was in my mind when traveling, a place I considered to be home, to be my surroundings, where my friends were. I remember once, when I went out of Johannesburg to go hunting, eighty percent of the streets were not paved. You went twenty kilometers and you could find lions. Now it is different. Before I would ride around on a horse and could spend three days without seeing anyone. I covered miles and miles. I had a porter who brought me a tent and I arrived at a camp completely set up. It's out there that you fell in love with this Africa, with these immense spaces. The porter would say, "Bwana, yes sir, Jumbo Bwana; greetings sir." I shot some animals and they cooked them for you. There were servants... All of these things are my fabulous recollections of thirty years ago. I entered the plains on horseback with a rifle tucked alongside. It was like the time of Karen Blixen who wrote *Out of Africa*; there were many adventurers going to Africa then. With relatively little money, they built farms. At that time there was a real longing for Africa.

In the camp there were only huts and inside a bed covered by a mosquito net. I entered with my shoes on and undressed under the net. There you could hear the lions roaring, but they were roaring twenty meters from the camp. It was very different from now, when people are going out on safari and staying in luxury lodges. It's the same thing if you go to Kruger National Park, 350 kilometers long, on the border with Mozambique. The first time I went, there were huts made of mud. Now they are made of stone and come equipped with a bath and a toilet bowl, whereas before there was a hole and I was always afraid that a spider would bite me on my butt.

Now with my Italian retired sailor's pension, I live in Cape Town. I stay with an English governess, a former nun. Before, she was in a convent but she had a man younger than her, who drowned while they were on a canoe trip. Then, to recover or to avoid being arrested, she moved to South Africa.

I live here as an old pensioner. Now, in South Africa, the lives of the whites of a certain age are choreographed. They live their lives without interfering in black society. Nature will provide a way to eliminate them eventually. Here at least I can always find a bit of my old South Africa. The important thing is not to be caught in the firing line of a projectile.

A Psychological Perspective

Here the choice is not of a country but of the sea, which offers a detachment from the world and its problems. The sailor can forget the life he flees, but may still retain the desire to drop anchor, to find a port. Enrico is able to touch people and places, but only through the eyes of one who knows that he will soon depart. His perspective is that of a distant observer, never deeply involved, who stops over for a few days and then goes away. He does not live with the negative aspects of a place, the difficulties of adaptation. It is difficult to determine how much the protagonist searches for authenticity, or how much resentment he feels towards life. Surely, though, there is in him a love for adventure that can only be lived fully when one is free from bonds.

10

From Sweden to Yemen
Goodbye to the Mommy State

A Swedish engineer, age 43:

My enjoyment was getting up at dawn on Sunday, with temperatures of minus 20 degrees, and going to make a big hole in the ice on the river to catch fish. In Sweden you're part of a great system where you're just a number. It's all arranged for you. When you stop working, they buy the coffin for you, but they do not just give you the money because you may spend it on drink—they give you a voucher for the coffin. If you have a window shutter repaired by a private individual, you know that someone will tell the police, because you were supposed to call a company that would then pay taxes. The neighbours watch you, to see how much you earn and whether you pay your taxes. At the end of the month you only have enough money left for cigarettes and getting drunk.

The state will think of everything for you, but avoids giving you anything extra. The tax system taxes you so much that at times it is better to work fewer hours, or you pay so much tax that in the end you find yourself with no more money. What's the point of working hard if, in the end, everyone has the same kind of life?

In the evening, after five, it's desolate! Exit work and go where? The only refuge is your house or the bar. On the street there are the usual few drunks! Only on Saturday night everyone goes wild—you see them in the bars, all excited. You know that they are drunk. Otherwise they are just repressed curmudgeons. Sometimes they lose control, smash everything and then the damage is compensated by insurance.

I remember some of my friends were like angels during the week—then on Saturday evening you didn't recognize them. We would go around the city with bottles of whiskey; as we met a few women, we invited them for a drink. Alcohol, in Sweden, has always been the easiest way to approach people. Then we would go on to someone's house to get totally drunk.

Eventually this reality was beginning to bore me. One day I heard that there was a company that had a contract in Yemen and I applied to be sent out there as an electrical engineer.

I knew almost nothing about Yemen except for a few tales I had heard. The first time I went there it was all home and work. I cooked for myself alone. I had a small room divided into two parts—on one side I ate, on the other I slept and I had a bath in a corner. That was it. I didn't pay the rent for a year; you do not pay monthly but at the end of your stay, when you leave. One dinar was three and a half dollars; now it is not worth anything and it's been renamed the riyal.

From the loud-speakers I heard Muslim prayers being called five times a day. I stayed a year there without having any social relationships—women were always at a distance. It gave me a strange feeling, because in Sweden I was always in the midst of women. A Swiss worker, who's already been here for eight years, has fallen in love with one of these women, converted to Islam and then married her. I almost envied him. We worked on high voltage lines that were carrying the electricity from the north to the south of the country—a very long distance!

In the evening, in the only decent Palestinian place, there was a show with belly dancing. There were some girls from Syria or from Cairo; very good dancers. I fell head over heels in love with one dancer and went every evening to see her. She danced with a sensuality which aroused strong emotions in me. I've also waited for her at the exit of the nightclub but I could not speak with her. She was always escorted and kept under control by some dubious looking characters. Sometimes, given the lack of women, the employees of our company went with some prostitutes, but they had to do everything in secret. Once they put a small girl into the trunk of the car and brought her to the yard.

We often went in Bahrain or Abu Dhabi in the UAE. It takes less than an hour by plane. I have a passion for pearls, so I went to see how they fish them out of the sea in Bahrain. They wear little glasses and dive free-style, half-naked, using stones for ballast. A pearl is a grain of sand that enters the oyster shell and, being a foreign body, is covered with a substance the oyster uses to encase it; that's the way the pearl is born. Obviously it isn't perfectly round.

It will be graded afterwards. There you can still find the dhows, those hardwood boats twenty meters long or more.

There was an ambassador from a European state who came with us to Abu Dhabi to look for Philippine girls. He, the sales assistant, other colleagues and I went out together on Thursday evening, because Friday is a religious feast day. Saturday and Sunday are working days, so Thursday was like a Saturday for us. In Abu Dhabi there was a large five star hotel. We went down to the ground floor where there was a jacuzzi, a sauna and the Filipinas—God knows how many! That was our relaxation—massage and bath with hydro-massage. We bathed together with the Filipina girls; after the massage they jumped into the water with us.

In Abu Dhabi I have seen more gold that I will ever see again in my life. Women were dripping with 24 carat gold and the shopping centers are full of gold emporia. The best we have is Ikea. You see so many limousines! And I've not seen a single beggar.

When I arrived in Yemen in 1987, there was more safety. The police controlled everybody. South Yemen was under the protection of Russia, but there were many rich people; in the military, as well as politicians and businessmen. The Russians were there but they did their own business; they had their naval and air bases. The Yemeni air force still flies Russian MIGs.

Many Yemeni students went to Cuba to study and there was a new hospital staffed by Cuban doctors. At first everything was depressing—I left work at two o'clock, I went to the sea and then back home. Once a Yemeni spoke with me for a while and then a policeman came to pull him away, because he feared that I could instill in him some bad ideas about the regime. Another time, in a hotel lobby, I saw a woman seated, dressed all in black. As she saw me looking at her, she raised her robe just a little and showed me that, underneath, she was wearing jeans. It was the signal that she was a prostitute. She nodded and left. She got into a taxi and gave me enough time to take another taxi. The driver followed her, without asking me anything; he seemed to know what was going on. The two taxis took a circuitous route to arrive back at a street just next to the hotel. She entered by a security door, leaving it ajar. I went in and saw a birthday party where there was beer, whiskey, music and private rooms.

The rich have several wives, usually up to four. They came out on Thursday evening, but at that time the wives' faces were not covered. They put the chador on later, when the war began, two years after my arrival in Yemen. After the demise of Communism in Russia, South Yemen was annexed to North Yemen. Every woman was made to wear the chador and alcohol was banned. Now the girls show only their eyes; they even wear gloves. But before that time some were in jeans, even if the women in the traditional families were already covered up.

Our offices were next to the Saudi embassy. Every morning I met a tall woman; all I could see was a black figure with a rectangular hole and two black eyes inside. I approached her and she moved out of the way. She did not speak a word of English and just looked at me. One morning she responded to my greeting; I fantasized that under the veil was a beautiful woman.

Even the poor had their women—our driver earned $200 a month and had three wives despite being poor. After a while he treated me like a brother and invited me into his house. The women and daughters ate on the floor with their fingers; the male children, he and I ate at the table. His name was Ahmed and he had five children in total. He offered me some ghat to chew; it's a plant that, chewing the leaves, gives you energy and resistance to fatigue; a drug that has now been legalized. Here they use it a lot; it's even a status symbol, because it's expensive. Some of them have deformed cheeks because they usually chew this stuff for a couple of hours. They look like they have a tennis ball in their mouth.

All the time I was glancing at the daughters and they seemed sensitive to my interest. I experienced this game of quick glances many times in Yemen; downcast eyes, shame, faint looks. Because sexual repression is so strong, at the end you breathe sex everywhere and you see it in many attitudes. You look at a woman and she just looks down. Everything appears calm, but you never know what that appearance can hide. The Arab world has so many mysteries. Visiting the driver's house, I had many feelings far removed from our Western way of life.

Our contract employee was 40 years old. She was still a beautiful woman, with long black hair down to her bum. She married when she was fifteen, and had seven children. She was Egyptian and spoke English very well. Her husband was a tradesman and she had a love affair with a Muslim professor. They both lived in my building; she was on the second floor and he on the first floor, right next to my apartment. He would enter his apartment and leave the door open.

By the time he put his bag down somewhere she would already be inside. When I heard him coming, I spied through the peephole to watch her following him in. I liked spying; it was one of my few hobbies there.

She risked being stoned when her husband discovered that she had betrayed him. She fled to who knows where and I don't know if they ever caught up with her. I was very sorry because she worked with us; her husband used to accompany her, and came to pick her up every day. In some villages in Yemen adulterous women are still stoned. Or their hair is cropped to the skull and they are expelled. These are the restrictions they live with, in contrast with the quiet life the people seem to have.

Politics does not concern me. Being a privileged person, I can get what I want in this country and as a foreigner I always have an escape route. I can spend as I want, not like in Sweden.

Now you cannot travel individually as you could before. Once you arrive in Sanaa, the capital, you must have a permit from the tourist police to travel inside Yemen. It is issued only if you buy a package tour from an agency in the capital.

Here you seem to step back in time and you forget about the West. The landscapes and architectural styles reflect a lifestyle far removed from Europe. Yemen has an extraordinary artistic and natural wealth; it's a pity that tourism has suffered a big downturn after the terrorist attack on an American ship in 2000. The government has done everything possible to recover a good image for tourists. In Aden, where I live, there is an ancient area named Crater. It was built in the crater of an extinct volcano. Even in the evening, the heat is tremendous! The rocks from a distance look like a furnace. The rock absorbs heat the whole day, which is always over 40 degrees in the summer! The first few months I was there I lost four kilos. It was just like a sauna! There is the sea, with sand and rock—and the desert, the Rub al-Khali, the father of deserts.

I crossed it four times, but always along the coast, with my friend Omar. He married the daughter of a wealthy merchant; she's as ugly as sin. Her father, just to marry her off, is content with Omar, even if he is not an ideal husband. Despite the constant calls of the girl's father to family duties, he cultivates the pleasure of doing nothing and became a loyal companion on my adventures. We are now like two brothers. Before coming here, I did not think that friendship between two men could be so deep. Don't get me wrong. I'm not a homosexual. We open each other's hearts to secrets that we would never tell to a woman. In Western countries there is a shame, almost a fear, of loving a man. It's seen as a sign of loss of virility. In the Arab world, an intimate friendship between men is not seen as something abnormal, but is encouraged. Among men there is more affinity, understanding and complicity. Men have more things in common—you can understand a man better that a woman. In the West there is more rivalry; here there is more cooperation.

Women, after all, live on another planet; beautiful, wonderful but distant from us. And here she has not lost her mystery. In the West the difference between man and woman is becoming more and more purely anatomical. Here I discovered an atmosphere that I had last experienced as child; magic, enchantment, wonder. Dialogue with a woman here is not as important as it is to us in the West. There is no need to tell each other everything. You are affected by certain gestures, certain looks and that can be enough even to ask a woman to marry. When I met my wife, she answered my questions indirectly, through an acquaintance. Even now that we are married, there is always a barrier between us. It does not mean that there is no dialogue. Above all there is mutual respect.

The Arabs, however, are thin-skinned. We Westerners are perhaps too shameless. My direct and frank way, at times, created problems for me. Slowly I felt the need to convert to their religion, because religion here is everything. It's not only about the words of Muhammad, but also a set of lifestyle behaviours. To accept their way of life, their rules, it's necessary also to convert to their religion. And they really believe and practice that religion. Here fundamentalists even went so far as to sabotage a pub, because they are against alcohol.

Now I live like an Arab; I even have two concubines. It is accepted that you can have a wife even for a short period. All in all it's a way to control prostitution and pay more respect to these women, who, in this way, can maintain their own social status and will continue to have it with their next temporary husband.

In my opinion the desert more than anything reflects the Arab character, his hardness, his detachment. I have travelled through the desert several times with Omar, along the coast. From him I learned to love the silence of the desert, the ability to be alone with yourself. Sometimes the trail took us a little inside, where there was absolute silence! You develop a tremendous buzz in your ears, not being accustomed to the sound of silence. There's not even any wind! Everything stops and remains motionless. Even the slightest noise is muffled in this space. It's a silence that excites you and can also deafen you; it's so strong that some people have a traumatic reaction to it. It isolates you from the outside world so that you feel your heart beating, your blood circulating. If you can listen to it, it helps you to feel at peace with yourself. But you have to be guided; some people, isolated from their usual auditory milieu, have had auditory hallucinations, which may even trigger a form of insanity.

Perhaps it's my case, becoming a Muslim! Seriously, you can reach very deep levels of introspection. I saw the dunes moving and watched the sand that the wind carried away. I saw people and water in the distance, but when I arrived there, I found nothing. It was a mirage or refraction, sort of like a mirror. Maybe there is a village at a distance of 100 kilometers but it appears to be very close. Sometimes you see a lake but when you arrive there you find a sand dune. It's a well known scientific phenomenon.

In the desert there are also scorpions but they are not mirages. In the night it's freezing fucking cold! Yet in the day Omar and I have fried an egg on the roof of the Land Rover—70 degrees in the sun! If you put your hand there, it'll burn your skin off. We slept covered up in the Jeep. It was so cold our teeth were chattering! During the day when the sun came out, we had to wear dark glasses because the sand blinds you.

There were so many camels! There was a nearby oasis, the only place with a little life—water, bananas, watermelons and dates! Very good! And the palms! They have the best dates in the world—large and very sweet!

There was a guy living in a house, in the desert near an oasis, with a goat that provided milk. His house was like a cube—about four meters by four. He offered us the famous desert tea, made with a little grass and a lot of sugar, because the grass is bitter. It gives you energy and allows you to recover from the desert. He also offered us coffee—I don't know what the hell they put in it, but it's spicy. It quenches your thirst. You drink coffee all the time and it can make you feel stunned. It's served in tiny cups and as I emptied it, he immediately filled it again, but you don't know how much you drink. And it really is spicy; it warms and cools you at the same time. Same for the tea into which they add fresh mint.

Sometimes it is more than 40 degrees in the shade. Everyone stopped and I decided to go for a quiet walk! After awhile my head started spinning. I leaned against a wall; I could barely walk. The sweat evaporated so quickly that I did not realize I was sweating. You don't feel that damp heat when sweat is clinging to your skin. Here you move with ease because you don't feel the effects of the heat when the air is dry. The desert weakens you without you noticing it. For this reason you see the nomads of the desert wearing all that wool, so as to prevent the evaporation their sweat. Like when you put a bottle of water under the sun wrapped in a wet towel. It stays cool for a long time.

With Omar I learned many secrets about the Arab world. I entered their homes and I found a welcome, a respect, a sweetness that captivates you. But at the same time you have a sense of privacy, as if something is hidden from you. You always feel that there is something unknown, unexplored. It seems like a fairy tale, because their society is so simple.

I also met several rich Arabs. They have huge houses with air conditioning turned so high that it's freezing cold—you have to cover yourself. One Arab I met doesn't even pay for the electricity—he's a top manager of an electric company. In addition to the normal four wives, he has nine concubines and also a fleet of Land Rovers. He goes into the desert to hunt. He's from Kuwait. I remember his daughter's wedding; the celebrations lasted more than a week. I don't know how many goats and sheep they had slaughtered... we ate so much. Rice was the main dish, with little yellow raisins like saffron and other spices that you find only here. And then these pieces of sheep and goat—delicious! They really know how to cook well.

This sense of mystery accompanies me every time I walk with Omar. I like it when we go to the market together. We walk hand in hand. The souk, a typical Arabic market is a mixture of every smell and colour and is full of people! The bazaars are their lives. There are sacks and sacks of rice flour! You don't take a kilo already packed; you serve yourself from huge bags. The scents in the air are unique; they take you back in time. There's red curry powder, then green; it has a strong smell when it is dry, sealed in bags. You see these green, blue, red bags full of spices—cloves, cinnamon and other spices that they even add to coffee and tea. There's a tea ceremony; in each pot over the coals, there's a different flavour.

The pleasure of food, the tastes and the aromas! It's all natural. I eat rice, beans, carrots and goat. I like tomatoes from the oasis; they're beautiful and mature. I catch fish myself. Camel meat has a strange taste, but it's tender. One might think that it's fat, but no, it's spongy, not fat—except for a thin strip that you can cut away. The fat is only on the humps.

The market is full of stray dogs that eat the garbage. There are rats to be wary of, bigger than cats. These markets are full of waste. At the end of the day they come to clean, but during the day you can't imagine. Men and rats! The cats are intimidated and stay away from it.

Now I live in a villa facing the sea. I can go down to the beach; during the day I'm at sea in the boat. I have always loved nature, the great outdoors. Even when I lived in Sweden I loved those streets where you did not come across any cars. Here I have miles and miles of deserted, pristine beaches, where only a few Bedouin are encamped. There is no pollution although there are still a few cars and the caravans in the desert. There is also the island of Socotra, considered to be the Galapagos of the Middle East.

I don't know how much a Westerner can understand this different way of living. It's not easy to learn about the private life of an Arab because he does not discuss it in public. To have women covered from view seems like a good idea to me—even my wife wears the chador. The secrecy enriches the relationship; without secrecy there isn't intimacy. In the West, my lady dressed up to go out of the house. But here my wife makes herself beautiful when she is at home. For me a relationship is more heartfelt when others don't know anything about what happens in your intimate life, and can't even imagine how your partner looks under her dress. Sex in the West is constantly being discussed, made public, slammed in your face, analyzed by experts. They speak too much about it.

All of the psychologists say we should open up, talk, tell your partner everything and that this is the basis of a good relationship. With a woman in Sweden I tended to talk all the time, even about my secrets, but in the end we didn't understand each other anyway. Despite good intentions, my wife and I squabbled continually about everything; we constantly criticized each other. Here I learned in part to hide my feelings, because there is no pressure to interfere, to know everything your partner does. She is not always in the way, having to share everything with you. Women also have their own world that men respect and we do not seek to penetrate it. My wife doesn't spend all of her time with me.

I think that a gay couple has more chance of developing a good understanding because they are the same sex and have the same way of thinking.

A Psychological Perspective

The Swedish expat feels the need for a radical change of life. But in addition to the appeal of plunging into a fairytale world, quite different to Western civilization, he also harbours a disappointment and distrust of women, to the point of preferring a relationship of complicity and intimacy with those of the same sex.

11

From Germany to Thailand
Smiling all the way to the crematory

A German from Wuppertal, retired:

I had a friend; we corresponded often by email. I remember the words he spoke before leaving: "I have few years left to live, and too much money to spend." At 63 he had been able to drop everything. I admired him; I still had a fear of flying. Often he would call me, announcing: "I'm fine... I've found a young girl; she's very serious; twenty-nine years old." He was happy.

I had known him for many years; we had been bosom buddies. One day he wrote that he had gotten married. I was stunned; he had reached the age of 63 without ever having married before!

He paid no attention to his advanced age and described the character of his wife as accommodating, submissive. He had also recovered his youthful energy. He told me he had totally changed his way of living. He had rented a motorbike and went around with his woman on the back, like Fonzie in *Happy Days*. And he was ironic about the life I still led, walking the dog to the park every morning and taking in the odd movie, sometimes with a grandchild!

My wife died several years ago and by now my children all lived their own lives. While my wife was still with me, we had travelled around Europe in a camper. After her death I fell into depression; I woke up every morning with a sense of emptiness. I looked at myself in the mirror; my cheeks seemed to me to be drooping more every day.

Once upon a time I was a male nurse in a hospital. I loved my work; it made me feel needed by people. I was very involved; sometimes I took a sick person to heart. Now all I felt was my own loneliness. It bothered me to see people hurrying around, involved with their work; meanwhile I spent my days bowling with a group of elderly friends.

It's hard to explain. I didn't want another job but at the same time I felt excluded from society. As an old retired man, it gives you discomfort to observe hectic life all around you, to live in a dynamic city.

The years have passed and you are in a crucial stage of your life. You cross a kind of threshold, beyond which you lose your identity, your self-image. Even if you still like beautiful women, you're out of play, you're transparent to them. If you pay a woman a compliment, you look ridiculous. They can laugh at you, or even think you are a maniac. The drama, and perhaps the tragedy, is that, at times, your wishes are still those of a boy, as in my case and in that of my friend Vincent, in Pattaya.

What with my depression and my fear of flying, I fought against my desire and resisted his attempts to convince me to leave with him. Often he used very harsh language in his letters. It was typical of his character to be abrasive at times, even if his intention was just to shake me up, to get me to overcome my apathy. I remember one of his cynical phrases. "The world is immense and you're just focused on your little shit."

In the tone of his emails I felt his zest for life, his enthusiasm, and even boyish plans. I sensed that something had changed him. He seemed so different from the person I knew, as if another person was writing to me. I remembered a fellow who was often depressed, very picky, sometimes pedantic. Even if he did not admit it to himself, there used to lurk within him disappointment for a life thrown away, a general resentment, an anger toward everything and everyone that masked his selfishness. He was a self-made man. He had lived through the economic collapse of his family due to his father's squandering lifestyle and foolish investments. By sacrificing himself he had been able to rebuild their lost wealth.

He restored an old inn and, working hard, he made a considerable fortune by buying several apartments that he rented out. But also a series of calamities had punctuated his life: the death of his brother in a car crash and the long illness of his mother. He had not had any great love affairs, maybe because of a lack of time or due to his difficult character.

Now he had bought a house in the name of his Thai woman, because in Thailand there are restrictions on foreigners owning a house in your own name, even if you are married to a Thai. You can only buy apartments in a condominium.

But one day I received news from his sister: Vincent had died in an accident on his motorbike at dawn, while he was going to the Bangkok-Pattaya Hospital, to get some medication. This happened about two years after his departure. The distraught sister told me that he had transferred all of his considerable wealth to Thailand, and this had now passed permanently on to his wife. She had never accepted that her brother had married a woman so young, someone who was probably interested in his money. And the fact that she had now inherited a considerable fortune tormented her. She insinuated the possibility that they had eliminated him and begged me to overcome my damned fear of flying and to go there, to try to determine what had actually happened to my old friend. How and where he had lived? And above all, what kind of woman had he married?

She was convinced that her brother had hooked up with an unscrupulous adventuress. She had always wondered, after seeing the photo of his wife, why a beautiful young girl had married a fat old man like Vincent. Unfortunately his sister was old and tired and also her husband was seriously ill, so she couldn't make the trip herself.

I could not help but feel a terrible sense of loss at my friend's death and it was this that shook me out of apathy and allowed me to overcome my fear of flying. Beside the desire to leave, to escape from Wuppertal, now I wanted to know something more of what had happened, to follow his tracks, to retrace his two years of happy life. At the airport I was very nervous. But on the flight, I expected worse. I swallowed another of the sedatives that had already relaxed me and I tried to sleep, to forget that I was flying at ten thousand meters, hanging in the sky.

Bangkok seems anything but a tropical paradise. You expect people with garlands of flowers around their necks upon arrival, but instead you find yourself in a smelly, polluted and bustling city; even its architecture is disgusting. Skyscrapers and houses that look like boxes attached to each other without the slightest aesthetic sense. It is difficult even to walk, because of the noise, street vendors, traffic, the stench, buses and smoke. The Thai people seem to have no concept of ecology. They sit down to eat on the ground, next to a manhole covering a stinking sewer.

In this hellish surrounding you find calmness, composure and a constant smile. If you glance at someone, it's quite possible that he smiles at you. Everywhere you go, everywhere you turn, you are inundated with smiles. And you even discover that, behind the apparent chaos, you're in an efficient and organized city, where you can find anything, including the unthinkable. I tried to resist visiting typical tourist places like the Wat Phra Kaew in the Grand Palace or getting on the boat on the Chao Praya River to see the floating market of Damnoen Saduak. So I immediately fled to Pattaya where Vincent had lived, a short way out of the city, in a villa that he had bought for his wife. Pattaya initially revealed itself as another punch in the stomach: traffic, smog, dirty sea, and yet alongside this always a sense of civilization and composure. They take a lot of personal care, not only in their dress, hair and general cleanliness, but also in their behaviour and gestures.

Before searching for my friend's wife, I decided to settle in a little.

Sitting at a bar I observe all kinds of people passing by: the classy lady, then some creature of indeterminate sex and then the "farang". That's what they call Western tourists: usually fat, with a big beer belly, all tattooed and beside him a skinny Thai girl.

A pickup truck passes, packed with stuff to the top. Then someone goes by with a handcart full of puppets. A bike passes by selling ladders—a bicycle full of ladders! A lot of people on scooters, BMWs, Mercedes: an old car mostly belching smoke. Sometimes an elephant passes by. And then there are hundreds of bars, where hundreds of young girls invite the tourist to stop and drink. After some days I was tired of Pattaya, of the noise, loud music, snarled traffic and the continuous parade of characters; the working girls, the deformed and swollen men, overflowing with beer, bacon and laughing loudly in bars, pawing the girls: a real Lourdes of sex! I just could not understand how my friend could end up in a place like this.

I had no idea how to contact his wife. If I had been introduced at that moment, I would not have known what to say. It would have been a formal exchange of words for the occasion. On the other hand, I didn't even know what I had to find out. The task which I had been given by Vincent's sister was too vague. Even if I discovered that his wife was a prostitute, what could I do? The best thing was to speak first with a friend of Vincent's, who might be able to introduce me.

The problem was how to find a friend of Vincent's in Pattaya. There were communities, not only German, but also English, French and Russian. The Germans, British and French each have their own local newspaper, and often group together, probably because they do not integrate easily with Thai customs. While there are rare cases of true friendship between farangs and Thais, there is always a line drawn between the two worlds.

I began to frequent some local places where Germans hung around but none had known Vincent. In fact there are more than two thousand Germans in Pattaya. Vincent had told me about one of our fellow townsman, a certain Frank, who had moved years ago to Nongkai, a Thai town on the border with Laos. He described him as an odd type, one who had made a life of challenge to conformity—a former seminarian and teacher of theology, an entrepreneur, a gambler who had lost almost everything on the tables. It would not be difficult to trace him because there are only a few Germans up there.

So I left Pattaya to go to Nongkai. I saw the other side of Thailand: dense forests and rice-fields, red dirt and village houses, atop wooden pales protruding from cement platforms.

Nongkai is a quiet, clean, orderly town, despite being in the northeast, the poorest region of Thailand, where most of the girls working in the bars come from. There are also some nice shopping centers and the famous Mekong River, with many restaurants where people are smiling out at you, calling to you, greeting you. And it was easy enough to enter a couple of places frequented by foreigners, make contact with some Germans, and track down Vincent's friend. We met at a restaurant along the river: a very impressive one because, on the opposite bank of the river, you could see Laos.

Frank was more or less my age, but didn't show his years: tall, skinny, sporty looking and neurotic, living with a Thai about thirty years old: two children but only by her. We talked about Vincent—he didn't even know he was dead. Ultimately they had met only a few times. He could not tell me much about the relationship between Vincent and his lady. Usually they met each other without the women. This is typical in Thailand; the men often socialize with each other. There are many more things you have in common with a fellow countryman; things that you don't discuss with your Thai woman. Typically she usually does not care about the farang's country, which is the main topic of farang discussion. When I asked Frank if Vincent's wife was a prostitute, he smiled. It is difficult to determine whether or not a woman is a prostitute; certainly they aren't the classic Western prostitutes. He explained to me that the concept of prostitution is very ambivalent in this country. Prostitution is even prohibited. You will hardly find the kind of prostitute who is cold, mechanical and working by the clock. Here, often, they ask you to help them financially because they must support their family. They do not look like professionals. In the bars they listen to you. You can just sit, talk and joke. You drink a few beers and you leave. You have the chance or the illusion of a conquest: of course a conquest that's very easy.

The ladies at the bar look like standardized dolls, laughing constantly like children at whatever bullshit you say, but deep down they are not very interested. Often they are looking for someone to marry them. They can also come to clean up your house, to take care of you. They are fit for everything. Even the paralyzed man can find a nurse.

In short, one ends up no longer understanding anything. Basically, the customer often forgets that it's a financial relationship. These are, then, normal girls, of modest means, mostly waitresses or store clerks, who sometimes see in the farang an opportunity to improve their lives. Furthermore Frank told me that once a friend took him to a large marriage agency in Bangkok, attended mostly by farangs. They had thousands of women on offer; women of all ages with photos and personal data, but there was not one woman of high economic means interested in marrying a farang. They were mostly shop assistants, maids, secretaries who earned around $200 per month.

If the marriage with a farang is highly coveted, it's because Thai men hardly ever marry a woman of low economic status. I asked Frank if, in his opinion, they could have eliminated Vincent, as the amount inherited was pretty big. He didn't know quite what to say. He only recalled a strange episode that could perhaps have given rise to some suspicion. In Thailand they sell lucky amulets, which Thais put a lot of faith into. There are journals that publish only photos of hundreds of these amulets. They come at all prices, although they are mostly expensive and they are usually worn around the neck by a chain. There are amulets which protect you from disease, traffic accidents, snake bites and even from murder.

Frank remembered that Vincent's wife had bought herself a very expensive amulet against road accidents, but she did not try to convince him to buy one for himself. Of course this was not a clue.

After, he said with an ironic smile: "You have to consider that sometimes you are worth more dead than alive, especially when there is a family of hungry people behind and you don't give them economic help." I immediately recalled Vincent's proverbial stinginess. Then Frank gave me the phone number of a mutual friend of Vincent's, in Pattaya.

So I returned to Pattaya. Enroute, two girls on the bus told me their story in halting English. They had come from Petchabun, in the northeast, and they told me, "We're going to Pattaya because there maybe you can meet a farang who has lots of money."

"Where's Pattaya?"

Pattaya is near Bangkok, in the province of Chonburi. They took the bus to Rayong. Thais usually go to the bus station without knowing anything about the bus schedules. They don't know because they don't ask... A German would say, "Better to take this bus at this hour, so that we can arrive at this hour".

So they arrived in Chonburi at four in the morning. They got out and asked, "Is this Pattaya?" And the driver said piteously, "No, it's a further 50 km from here. You have to take another bus and the first one leaves at seven in the morning." Then they had breakfast. You have to realize that, in any place in Thailand, if you turn up at four in the morning there are still kiosks where you can eat and sometimes there is an open market. When traveling at night, the bus stops at several stations. Get off and you will find unexpected life; open shops, restaurants, karaoke parlours and various agencies.

They got on the bus to Pattaya. Timidly they asked the driver when they would arrive in Pattaya and he asked, "North Pattaya, Pattaya center or south Pattaya?" And they thought to themselves, "What do we tell him?"

Pattaya has a length of 5 km and is 2 km wide.

Then they took a shot—"North Pattaya."

The driver looked at them, assessed the situation and asked, "But you go to work?"

"Yes!"

"It's the first time?"

"Yes!"

"Then there are more bars in South Pattaya. I will tell you when to get off."

I got off with them and we went to look for a room. There were plenty of rooms for rent. Each building has a little office with some fellow dozing at his desk who, if necessary, can show you the rooms. We enter a long corridor. Doors and windows are in the corridor, the room is about three meters by three, with a bed in a corner. No furniture; only a mirror! Walls painted in gray, a neon light on one wall and a ceiling fan in the center. It begins to turn and drops down a flurry of dust. From a little door you see the bathroom. There is no sink, but only a shower. "Well, we'll take it."

We went to dinner together. The next day they went into a bar and asked, "Can we come here to work?"

"Okay, okay."

They started to work.

In Germany when you hear the life story of a prostitute, sometimes interviewed with a distorted voice, their back turned to the camera, she says that thugs had beaten and forced her into it. Here it is different. It's always an economic issue that drives them to seek the farang. But it's nothing dramatic—no one has taught them that it should be a drama. They are happy to bring home the money to help the family. Parents often know what's going on and sometimes they themselves send the girls to farangs.

In our country a sex area is a seedy, disreputable place, populated by scum and junkies. Here next to the go-go bar, you find an altar to the Buddha where the girls go to pray, an international library, a bank, a five-star hotel and international restaurants.

A red light area for us has to be squalid and degraded. Prostitutes have to be vulgar and associated with the underworld. Programmed by our Christian culture, we associate sex with degradation. Our whores use foul language. You can see a mile away that they are prostitutes; everything is according to the script equating sex with perdition.

The Thai prostitute often speaks to you about her family. Here religion does not condemn sex. Having a gay in the family is not a tragedy. But pornography is prohibited; sexual contacts are considered strictly private. While in the West, men are almost obsessed with sex, here it's even difficult to see a Thai man turning to look at a beautiful woman. There are also good-natured cartoons poking fun at the sexual obsessions of farangs. In our country you meet seventy year old men who care about the loss of libido. Here the libido does not even know what it is.

Thailand is a puritanical country, the opposite of the sinful and unscrupulous image portrayed by the media. It does not deserve the reputation in the West of being a country for sex. In the West the woman is more seductive; she often radiates seduction, provocation and sensuality. In Thailand the woman is more contained and reserved.

In Pattaya I contacted Alfred, a friend of Vincent's; unmarried, almost bald, with a prominent belly. He lived alone and preferred relationships with no strings attached. He was still choked up about Vincent's death. They had spent much time together and he also knew his wife well.

He explained to me that Vincent's wife was a "bar lady"; he had met her in a bar, so it is possible she had had sexual affairs with other farangs. After she had met Vincent, she stopped working in the bar. He gave her a fixed monthly sum, and every month she sent some money to her parents. Here there is no state pension for all. In Thailand, it is the responsibility of the children to support their parents if they are poor. I didn't ask Alfred if there was any possibility that they were involved in Vincent's death. This seemed to be so far from his mind, and he spoke fine words about her: an honest, kind-hearted woman who really did Vincent a world of good!

One evening Alfred invited Vincent's wife to dinner and introduced me: she was very elegant, slim, physically attractive, even with a certain class, light years away from the modest and simple image that I had drawn from Vincent's descriptions. Evidently the sudden fortune showered on her had also changed her look, so that she had become socially refined. But the more I watched her, the more I found it hard to imagine her as a former prostitute. She was a real lady, with polished manners. When I realized she didn't know that I was her late husband's friend, I begged Alfred to keep his mouth shut. It seemed to me the best way to observe her natural and spontaneous behaviour, beyond pleasantries and formalities usually reserved for a husband's friend. But as we talked, I began to feel strongly attracted to this woman, to the point that I forgot that she was Vincent's widow. I began to think that, after all, she had done nothing wrong and the suggestions of Vincent's sister struck me as completely out of place. I made up my mind that I wanted to rent a villa near the sea. She offered to help me, to accompany me in the car. In a few days we began to fall in love.

I went to live in the villa that Vincent had bought for her. With the inherited money she had bought another villa for her sister, in addition to a building with about seven studios that she rented. She had supported all of her relatives. For one she had opened an internet center. Another relative worked for her in the management of the building. She had built a house for her parents and she sent them money regularly. Strangely, however, she said that she felt alone and did not feel all that much loved by her parents.

Here, if one member of a poor family comes into money, it's hard to keep that money for himself. He becomes responsible for a whole host of needy relatives, who cling like lice. It's a duty which he can't shirk. The family has a great moral authority and is bound together strongly. Families even feel economically involved in the marriage of a daughter with a farang. There is a moral obligation to give financial support not only to parents but also to brothers and sisters. Practically the daughter is never dropped from the family.

Now I can say with certainty. I too, like Vincent, was in love with this woman, her manners, her class, her kindness, the smile that accompanied her every word, every gesture towards me. She was full of solicitude. She arranged the fan, brought me breakfast in bed, went to buy things that I liked without telling me. Without realizing it I had completely taken the place of Vincent. But her character did not match with Vincent's description. She had a confident, determined way of doing everything, and knew how to give orders to everyone, quite apart from the typical attitude of the woman in Thai culture, who always tries to put you at ease. Of course, in that house, I sometimes felt Vincent's presence, but I always found an excuse for myself. After all, I obeyed my feelings and hadn't done anything wrong, since Vincent was now no more. But some of her attitudes were beginning to surprise me; especially the carefree way in which she displayed her wealth and squandered Vincent's money. For example, she entered a shop to buy a lamp, and carried off a bed which she then gave as a present to somebody.

She spent for the sake of spending, to feel rich and magnanimous, as a typical upstart. In worldly matters she was as ignorant as a goat—once she asked if Spain was in Africa. But I was not bothered by her ignorance. I was even astonished by my recovered sexual ability. I must admit that I began to think less about my friend, until one day when I felt his live presence in that house.

In a room I recognized a painting of Vincent's; one he had wanted to take with him to Thailand. He was very fond of it because his grandfather had painted it. It showed a path in the middle of a forest and a lone old fellow walking with a cane. Then I noticed an urn on a sideboard and nearby there was a photo of Vincent, smiling and looking happier than I had ever seen him before. It gave me a chilling feeling when she said that the urn held Vincent's ashes. He had been cremated two days after his death.

From some of her stories, other details could be puzzled out. She often said, with a hint of complacency, that Vincent considered her half-handicapped: "'You driving a car? Let it go. It's not for you.' Now I go around in a Mercedes and if Vincent saw how I was spending his money, he would die a second time of a heart attack." I was stunned. A woman so educated, who suddenly showed such a lack of respect towards her dead husband, ridiculing him. She added that he was stingy. If there was something they needed to buy he could make you cross the entire city to find where it was cheaper. Knowing Vincent, I knew she was telling the truth. She told me that she admired him a lot but had never been in love with him. There was no doubt that his death had done her well. She could dispose of a big fortune at will; no tight-fisted man in the way. When she was working at the bar, she shared a room with two girls. Now she had bought two houses and two cars. Another element aroused some suspicion in me. She had a brother whom she hated but was forced to comply with. Every now and then he knocked on the door for money and she forked it out. She herself called him a thug, a person without scruples, capable of anything.

She had an album with photos of the marriage and funeral. There was a picture in which there were heaps of dollar bills on the table next to the bridal couple. The money was exhibited to the guests. It is a Thai custom to show that the bride has married a rich man. For us there is nothing more vulgar than a show of money. For us money has something dirty about it. However, in all those photos Vincent was smiling, looking young and happy, and that, on balance, reassured me. If there was something in my former friend's woman that was starting to annoy me, it was that she kept talking about money, proposing the purchase of land and villas in co-ownership which of course would be exclusively in her name, because of the impossibility to register any property in my name.

She knew, however, how to pick me up. She had created around me a perfect little world. Whatever I was asking, she found a way to give it to me. She accompanied me everywhere by car, for whatever reason, as if she was my private driver. For a while, I delighted in being treated like a sultan.

Once she caught me watching a beautiful girl. She said that there was nothing wrong with this, that she would allow me to take other women to bed. I was bewildered! I was even free to bring them into the house where we lived! I thought she was joking.

It gave me the feeling that with her everything was possible. Then slowly I began to feel suffocated. I was imprisoned in a kind of gilded garden. In reality, in all that I thought, I did, I said, she was there, omnipresent and omnipotent. Even if I wanted a woman, she would have had to have approved of her. She was a cunning genius, giving you the illusion that everything is possible, but in reality you were totally under her control, in her hands. You have no freedom and nothing that does not belong to her as well, because she manages everything you do. That's why I went with another woman without telling her. I needed to do something only by myself, not under her protection and surveillance. When she discovered that I had betrayed her, she threatened that she would make me pay. She used harsh words. She had a look that exuded hatred. I do not remember any other woman who had shown such a crazy reaction. After a while, as if nothing had happened, she was sweet and helpful again.

One night she showed me a gun that she normally carried in her bag, although in Thailand the possession of weapons is banned. I realized that I was dealing with a woman capable of anything. Certainly the change of her economic condition had gone to her head, allowing her to express a personality repressed for so long. Generally here, women are subservient to men. Men often mistreat them, beat them, get drunk and go with other women, make the women support them, make them pregnant and then abandon them, leaving the women alone with dependent children, without any support.

In addition to the wife, it is often tacitly permitted to have a mistress. But it happens that, sometimes, they cut the man's cock off. I'm serious. Every so often you read about it in the newspapers.

I became more suspicious. I found the key to a drawer that she kept locked and I opened it. As the villa was two-storey, I felt pretty sure that I would hear her coming out of the garage and going up the stairs. I had plenty of time to put everything in order. I found a sea of letters, mostly written by Thais, but mixed in with these there were some letters from farangs.

So Vincent was not the only farang with whom she had had an affair. But I was not so surprised. What struck me was a letter written by her: probably a rough copy. The recipient was not Vincent, a certain Marius. She said: "Dear, I miss you so much, I have only you in my heart, I hope you are well and that your mother recovers soon. If I could be there with you now, I'd take care of her. Thanks for the money you sent me. I already bought the land. When will you send the money to build my house?"

Why did Vincent go to the hospital, exactly at six in the morning, when there is almost no one around, and just a simple nudge with a vehicle can send him to the other world?

Once, I don't remember why, I chided a Thai shop assistant. This time, too, when we got home, she displayed a venom toward me that was out of proportion. Thai people are often on the side of their countrymen. They are very nationalistic. Even when married, in this country, you remain a farang. You don't acquire any rights, even to buy a house in your name, and every three months you have to go to immigration to get a visa.

On another occasion I was discussing something heatedly on the phone with a friend. She tried to rip the phone out of my hands and demanded to know why I was fighting.

All this happened in little more than the two months that I had been with her. With Vincent she had not displayed such behaviour. He had written me that he had found a mild, sweet and submissive woman. Obviously, she had only been playing the role of a sweet and condescending woman; otherwise he would have dumped her. I wonder what she would have had to swallow and suppress all that time they were together. Vincent, among other things, could have quite an arrogant, at times unbearable, character.

Maybe she was harbouring hatred and Vincent did not know. You can never be sure of the feelings of a woman, if she is the economic source of an entire family. She isn't free to express her feelings and she must accept things that maybe she does not want. Your intolerable attitude can increase her hatred—and knowing Vincent, it was possible. Maybe, without realizing it, he had created hate within her that she had kept carefully hidden.

I began to suspect that he had been murdered. But with what proof could I go to the police? None of what I had found was concrete evidence.

And yet, in the same time, I found it difficult to believe that she was a murderess. In spite of her sometimes irascible character, she could also be very generous, worrying about and taking care of her family and even her friends. When I was with her I felt that my suspicions were ridiculous.

But at times when I was thinking by myself, my suspicions would return. I could not go on in this way, caught between two opposing states of mind. I risked going mad. One morning, without warning, I gathered my things and left. There was nothing more I could do.

In my opinion, a man falling in love loses the ability to think clearly. An elderly man who feels marginalized in his own country, perhaps with a failed marriage behind him, becomes an easy prey. The newspapers splash sensational stories about sex tourists but ignore the many cases of men, often elderly, who are lured by what appears to be true love. The reason is simple: sexual intercourse is on offer for a handful of dollars. A sentimental relationship can provide the lady with accommodation for life. It becomes a natural, as well as a moral, duty to help your girl, who invites you into her home to get to know the parents, as a guarantee of seriousness.

They act like we did, in our country, 60 years ago: home, church and family—in this case, home, temple and family. Or rather, home, family and brothel. We Westerners like to redeem prostitutes. There are farangs who send money to support them, or marry them, as though it was something out of the movie *Pretty Woman*.

The tale of the woman forced into prostitution and then saved by Prince Charming, is big business for this country, as are the sex districts. Patpong, an entire area of prostitutes in Bangkok, is also a great marriage agency. There are thousands of Thai girls who receive marriage proposals and financial support to leave prostitution. But sometimes they remain working in bars and maintain romantic relationships with several different guys.

Of course there are also successful marriages. But why is it that a high percentage of these begin in the brothel? The secret is simple. They often don't look like prostitutes but rather like simple girls, attached to the family. Even the half-naked girls dancing in bars have lazy attitudes, not appearing all that seductive. The attachment to the family is the great lure of Thai women. If you ask one of the girls in the bar, "what do you look for in a man?"

most of them will not tell you: I want a handsome man, intelligent, educated, sporty, with a sense of humour, and so on. She will tell you: "Chai dee" which literally means 'a generous heart', and in practice means someone who will support her and the family. However, in their culture, the husband has a secondary role after the blood relatives, especially if the husband is a farang. They have a strong bond to the group and to a national identity. For them the farang is culturally different and difficult to integrate into their world, and is often admitted mainly for economic benefit.

But also, if you are a farang, they handle you with kid gloves. Before making you feel uncomfortable, they will think about it over and over. You will hardly ever see arrogant or aggressive behaviour. And it is just this respect that we sometimes mistake for excessive shyness.

For Thai people it is normal take care of someone, to make somebody comfortable, to serve and be served. We Westerners have a complex about being too servile. It seems to us to be demeaning. The Thai people are servile but far from submissive. Everywhere you go, you're often surrounded by attention and care, and feel the touch of humanity. It is fundamental to Buddhist education, to alleviate human indifference, mistrust among people and the cynicism of existence. The massage is not just toning your muscles. It's a way of infusing relief, putting you at ease. If you insist on watching a woman, it's possible that she will smile at you, will try to avoid making you feel the discomfort of rejection, but you shouldn't assume that she is available. It's her education. If they were in our country, they would be shocked by the coldness of the people; meanwhile in our eyes their kindness can appear too obsequious. So the prostitute will not be cold and mechanical; she will try in some way to make you feel like a person. For this reason the Westerner is left dazzled.

The modern Thai language has three different expressions of wives: *Mia Luang, mia noi* and *mia ciao*. *Mia Luang* is for the 'official wife', *mia noi* is the mistress, and *mia ciao* is the wife to rent, who, while not having any recognized status, is still included. You pay the bar and you go with her not only for sex. For example you may go for two days to an island, to restaurants, and so on. It's like taking a rental car. There are all types and all prices. She can also stand for hours to take care of you, massage you, wash your back and apply scented oils.

Whether or not this is the best way to cheat you is a different kettle of fish.

I have lived here now for three years. I've seen all types and have many stories to tell. A friend of mine has a curious job in an agency. He writes and translates the letters between farang and Thai girls: hundreds of letters. They are more or less a copy of the letter I found in Vincent's wife's house. The old story is: "I can't wait to take care of you. When will you send more money?"

Personally I appreciate Thai culture, the education, the correct ways, the respect that you find less and less in Western countries today, but sometimes it's difficult to understand what they are really thinking. Their faces can all look the same: a smiling mask.

There are frequent cases of farang deaths. Cremation occurs quickly and, when it comes to a farang with few family connections, the autopsies are perhaps a little less thorough. There are often several incidents in a month of suicides, accidents and other strange deaths that arouse my suspicion. The bodies are burned, and the prospect of negative publicity disappears with the smoke.

I have a photo of Vincent, one that he had sent me from Pattaya. He is on his bike stripped to the waist, wearing orange Bermuda shorts. She is hugging him from behind, with a straw hat and flowered sarong. Their laughter is explosive. It's almost as though you can hear it; a joke or something very funny. I am comforted to think that he spent two full and happy years as he appears in the photo. Knowing him as I did for many years, I think that he was never as happy as then. And, after all, his money has saved a family from poverty!

Pattaya is a city unique in the East, invented exclusively for the farang, and born during the war in Vietnam. It's not the real Thailand. The American military came to Pattaya for rest and recreation during the war. Only 40 years ago it was a small fishing village. Now it is like Disneyland or Las Vegas. There are amusements of all kinds. Pattaya is selling you a dream, an illusion. It is the carnival of love. Sometimes the farang is not presentable. You see him and his girl walking hand in hand. He takes the girl to a restaurant. She smiles at him, pours the beer. She listens to him. And he ends up believing.

Now I live here, in a skyscraper, on the thirtieth floor. Mosquitoes never get that high, except for some that come up in the lift.

I have changed my view of Pattaya. The atmosphere is less tense and neurotic than in Europe and you can find every comfort at a cheaper price than in your own country. There are international restaurants, medical centers and health centers of European standard. Also you can find the same facilities as at home: the foreign newspapers the same day, which are printed from the Internet, DW international TV, cappuccino, bratwurst and croissants at any time. The Thai people work hard to ensure you have all of the amenities of your home country.

There are also quiet beaches if just you go a little further. Sometimes I go to the island of Ko Lan, about 40 minutes by boat from Pattaya. There I rent a motorbike and I go on to a lonely beach with clear sea, white sand, some bungalows and little monkeys in the trees.

I like hot weather and outdoor life. Here it is eternal summer. And I don't feel, like in Wuppertal, my loneliness in a hectic city where everybody is working and no one has time. Pattaya is a tourist town all year round. You can see people doing anything, sitting at the bar or lying on the beach, all of the time. Everywhere you go you can chat with someone and pass the time of day. Now I have more friends here than I had in all my life in Germany.

Pattaya, is, after all, the graveyard of the elephants.

A Psychological Perspective

Unfortunately, the body ages much faster than the spirit, the desires and the will to live. The elderly person, in our culture, is often considered to have had his day, and may be ridiculed if he behaves as a youth. He is sometimes forced to suppress or mask his impulses. If he pays attention to a young woman he may be branded as a depraved old man. If he goes to a disco with a young crowd he will be viewed with suspicion. There is no wonder that Vincent, removed from his home environment, zooms around on a bike 'like Fonzie'. And there is no surprise that he ends up as prey to a ruthless woman.

12

From England to Ethiopia
Escaping from my own mind

A man from London:

I had an antique shop in the Kings Road and fortunately my family was rich. So, at the age of forty, I asked myself, "Why should I continue working?" At the bank I had more than half a million pounds in addition to various rented properties. And my mother's house was worth another 450,000 pounds.

After her death, I left everything in her house as it was when she was alive. I didn't have the courage to empty it and I didn't want to sell or rent her house either. Sometimes I went there and went around the rooms, looking at her photos, opening the closet, caressing her clothes. I didn't move anything; the drawers were in perfect order, the same as she had left them; her overcoat and her scarf were still hanging on hangers. Everything in that house was like a museum. And I would talk with my mother there... I kept the pantry in order and bought the coffee that only I drank. Yes, I know, it's not normal, but I was very fond of my mother.

Meanwhile, I stopped working and I rented out the antique shop. At 43 I was alone in the world, with a considerable income and a vintage Jaguar that I almost always kept in the garage, because in the city it's easier to use a small car. I woke up at noon; I had brunch in a nearby restaurant; I went for a walk, then I came back home and rested again. Later I had a coffee or tea, and sometimes a massage in a nearby massage parlour. In the evening I phoned some friends to decide how to spend the night. I couldn't wish for more.

I don't know what the hell happened to me. When I worked, I had a lot of friends, I went to parties and events. But then, after having left work, I found myself more and more lonely. While everybody was kept busy or engaged in work, I was the only one who had nothing to do all day, waiting for the evening to call my friends. I was drinking everything, from precious brandy to lousy spirits, wandering from one pub to another or I stayed in the house all day, watching TV. Every day there was the usual string of people killed, calamities, dramatic accidents! I had the same sensation as when I played a videogame, as if I had just knocked down all those dead people on the screen. I did not give a damn! Once I'm dead, all the world will be dead with me!

I don't know why, but strange fears and bad thoughts invaded my mind. I could not control them; they were stronger than me. They were like birds flying freely in my head. Perhaps it was because I spent too much time alone during the day. The slightest problem gave rise to anxiety, like getting sick, or losing my friends.

I became depressed and ended up going to a shrink. The sessions with the psychologist had become the only regular event of my day but then, eventually, the conversation languished around the usual arguments. I laid down on the couch, relating everything that had passed through my mind, even idiotic thoughts that you can only say on the psychologist's couch. That's how Dr. Stenghel, after about fifty sessions, told me in a determined tone that I had to radically change my life, rather than to repeat ad nauseam those endless sessions

"You are like a moth running non-stop around the same streetlight. You must find the strength to fly away, to begin a new life," he repeated. Fine words! Probably he didn't want me under his feet anymore, now that he had given me up for lost. He suggested I make a journey to a country in the third world, to face and experience some far away realities, to help people who have nothing, who live on the edge of decay. I had to get rid of my empty days, without a glimmer or shred of a project for the future. I answered him saying that nowadays, thanks to internet, it is possible to keep in touch with distant worlds; to get to know the remotest of cities and the least explored areas of the planet. "You can learn everything there is to know about all the cities of the world," he said, "but not their sickly smells, their mosquitos, beggars; the stressfulness of moving from A to B; the never-ending wait at the airport, the problems with your luggage, the queues at the customs, the rush to make it in time; the times you stammer out your request to the waitress and she pisses you off because she doesn't speak your language; the hotel room that regularly lacks home comforts. Then you miss your books, your CDs, your DVDs." According to him I could no longer limit my life to drinking brandy, to polishing my Jaguar, to watching

TV, to evenings spent in the pub. I needed a powerful experience, something that would slam the truth of existence in my face. I had to turn everything that belonged to me upside down, cut with one stroke all the threads that bound me to my mother, to my things, to my memories.

You can imagine how much I wanted to finish up among beggars, away from my Jaguar and my mother's house! All this was insane. It was like throwing myself into the Thames without knowing how to swim. Yet Stenghel's words penetrated into me. "I'm proposing an escape, a clean break from yourself, like letting out a bird that has lived many years in a cage. Your brain is the most powerful weapon existing. It can become an infernal machine, your own prison of torture. At the same time it can give you incredible power."

Now that my mother had gone, I was tormented by guilt. I had often left her alone, especially towards the end when she needed me more. The day she died, I entered the room where she lay motionless and I found the windows open. She was wearing a light dress. Immediately I closed the windows to prevent her from catching a chill, then covered her with a blanket and chided the housekeeper who had opened the window. Since childhood I have always suffered for my mother's loneliness. I remember the pain I felt when, in the morning from the window, I saw her walking alone in our park. I would do anything to make her feel less lonely. But I did not succeed; I couldn't do it. I could not replace my father. But I could not bear even the idea of seeing her with another man, other than my father. She did not make a new life for herself and had bestowed upon me all her love, all her loneliness and all her money.

I remember one particular day! It was about 11 in the morning and I was already on maybe my 6th or 7th beer. The television was turned on but I caught only scattered sentences that drifted in and mixed with my usual floating, idiotic thoughts. I got up and I went to the toilet. I was in front of the bowl, watching my out-of-proportion stomach and my thin legs, without being able to unload my bladder, when the phone rang. I heard Stenghel's professional voice; he asked why I had missed a session without informing him by telephone. I said, "I'm very sorry, sir, but I don't know what's happening to me. My mind is in utter confusion. I can't free myself from it." He kept silent for a while, then said, "There is a frightful being very near to you, from whom you will never be free. It's the most mysterious being that exists. You will never be able to know him. That creature is you!"

The idea of a clean break has matured slowly in my mind because at that point I was in a tunnel with no way out. But I had to make a superhuman effort, particularly since the psychologist now threatened to abandon me to my fate. So one day, like an automaton and under the influence of a strong dose of assorted drugs, I mechanically gathered together all of my mother's dear objects, deposited them in the cellar and then assigned an agency to rent the house. I've pretty much passed the rental income on to Dr. Stenghel. After my departure, I began new sessions with him by telephone, by email and bank, so that he could follow me to the ends of the earth.

I spent a day driving the Jaguar around London. I had to separate myself from everything—from myself, from my mother, from my past, and head off to an unknown destination suggested by a stranger, even if he was an expert on the problems of the soul. While I was aware of my insanity, when you cannot hold the reins by yourself, you end up handing them over to the first person you feel you can trust a little. But I didn't know where all this would lead me.

I thought of Ethiopia for the climate. Addis Ababa enjoys spring-like weather and mild temperatures all year round, because it is close to the Equator and 2,200 meters above sea level. It was a distant, different country, yet where people are more similar to us in their features, compared with other Africans. As a boy I was a fan of prehistory and remembered that in Ethiopia they had found the remains of a human ancestor, a skeleton dating back millions of years, preserved in a museum in Addis Ababa. I could at least revive the memories of school, visiting the place considered a cradle of civilization—the Rift Valley, where they say there are the tablets of the Ten Commandments.

Of course, I had a preconceived image of Africa: miserable, poor, desperate and degraded. An image of Ethiopia seen on television as a child was still etched in my mind: lepers with legs swollen like logs, infected with plague and infested with worms. People who were dying without assistance. I remember a man bleeding because leprosy had eroded his foot and one eye, with live wounds covered with flies. He was almost a skeleton covered with skin. And he was still alive! Life struggles against death even when there's nothing that can be done to save it. And people threw money at him from a distance.

To be a tourist in Ethiopia is not easy and a guide is highly recommended. In Addis Ababa it's better to move around cautiously—it's a chaotic metropolis with over two million inhabitants. I wandered inside the market like a convalescent released from a hospital. I had the feeling that at any moment something strange and unpredictable might happen to me, as if everything I could see could somehow reach out and touch, contaminate, invade me. I had just arrived and I already wanted to get back on the plane and leave. What did I have in common with all these Africans? I was so pale, stiff and ridiculous—always watching, on the alert, even for the insects buzzing around me. But in Africa you can't put a barrier between yourself and others. You are immediately recognized because you're white; that, for them, is synonymous with rolling in money. You have their eyes constantly fixed on you. You're almost assaulted by people, by vendors, by the scenes around you, by the bodies, the smells, the strong light and the colours.

Despite my discomfort and my indefinable fear, I was struck by their vitality, their energy, that sea of life, in which everybody's hugging, greeting and handshaking. The market is their world, the paramount meeting place, particularly for the women who live their lives more in seclusion—for them it's a great occasion to share in everyday public life. It's the biggest outdoor market in all of Africa—you can find everything there: crafts, handmade products, sandals made from recycled tires, gold jewelry, pots and pans, cattle trucks, people without legs on filthy, stinking wheelbarrows, brought there by friends and relatives. I washed myself all of the time; I smelled the smell of death.

When I left the hotel, I took a taxi and once inside I quickly closed the door, because groups of kids would run after me and tug my pants. The hotel security men carried long sticks and sometimes the kids escaped with a broken head! When I walked around the city the kids ran after me in droves.

I had nightmares about getting sick. If I were seriously ill, I would have to sneak out on the first plane. Now the situation has improved; they have built hospitals and some outpatient departments. But at that time, for a medical specialist, it was better to go to Djibouti where there is a very well equipped French hospital. There is a very slow rail link, more than 450 miles long, linking Addis Ababa to this largest port on the Red Sea—with people constantly loading and unloading the train with plants, animals, timber, sacks of flour. All the while children relieved themselves with impunity in the middle of the train compartment. Most of the Ethiopian goods produced for export use this line. There are people with sticks, controlling the messy, chaotic crowds flowing around the stations.

At first I lived in the hotel. There were small, seedy hotels which served also as bars and brothels. I immediately opted for the high end—the Sheraton, a haven of luxury, of ostentatious, brash wealth, surrounded by a depressed town, between the exhaust fumes of dilapidated cars, ramshackle homes and families on the street. There was waste everywhere and shantytowns without water or light, near to squares with a few Italian colonial buildings. Then I rented an apartment in the south of Addis Ababa, where there are residential neighbourhoods.

And from a distance I confided all to the psychologist, while he renovated his cottage. I often complained, "What should I do? They ask me a lot of questions! They keep asking me what I am doing in their country. I feel as though I am spied on and under surveillance." Stenghel reminded me to keep my temper, to become involved in the scene quietly, to talk freely about myself and not to be ashamed of my anxiety and depressed state of mind, even if they took me for a being from outer space. How could a person be depressed who had everything in life? They found it incomprehensible that I suffered from depression, despite having everything—freedom and money. And moreover I had come to Ethiopia to cure myself. They asked if my condition was contagious.

"Enter the villages and homes. Look around you. See how they live. Don't be on the defensive," Stenghel insisted. "Let yourself be carried away by the people you meet, by the events of life, even those that you would prefer not to see, those disgusting sights that turn your stomach. The more you close the world out, the more your paranoia will grow."

When I arrived I knew nothing of the political situation, nor of internal security. It was certainly not appropriate to ask Dr. Stenghel, whose therapeutic method seemed to include endangering the lives of his patients. Ethiopia is a federal democratic country in which the most populous ethnic group prevails. There are more than seventy ethnic groups with different languages. The official religion is Christian Orthodox, the one with the symbol of the double cross. The contradiction, however, is that almost half of the people are Muslim. But the Ethiopian government has never accepted the Muslims and has been fighting them since ancient times. There is a peaceful coexistence at present, although in recent years Muslims have become more observant and you see women completely covered, something the Ethiopians themselves were not used to seeing.

My mother taught me to avoid the dangers of life. When we went to the sea, she did not let me swim one meter into the water. She was so terrified that I could drown that I never learned to swim. I was also taught to not to let myself be involved in difficult situations, to keep other people at bay, to look at life from behind glass and through books. Her secret weapon was etiquette, that 'proper' way of doing things, which erects a formal curtain between you and others. During my life, according to my psychologist's diagnosis, I had developed an overly suspicious attitude towards others as well as an exaggerated fear towards the risks of life. Dr. Stenghel tried to destroy my defenses in a forceful way—he didn't use subtle language. He was a kind of Nazi SS officer disguised as a psychologist. I can almost see him, in his leather swivel chair with his habitual pipe and cashmere jacket; behind him towered two African elephant ivory tusks. More than once I had the suspicion that he was using me for some obscure experiment or that he wanted to get rid of me by increasing his fee, then shipping me off to Africa where I would be contaminated by one of the many diseases—salmonellosis, cholera, typhoid, hepatitis, leprosy, tuberculosis, meningitis.

Despite everything, I was still determined to follow his advice to the end. I know very well that to put your life in another person's hands can be pure folly, but it can also be a liberation. I no longer had to torture myself; "What do I do? Why do I do it? What do I want?" To make choices, to take initiatives had become a torture for me.

"You're experiencing a phase of total passivity and escape from yourself. It doesn't matter—go on. It's what you need. You can even die. But be aware of everything happening to you!" He had actually said, "you may die!" Maybe he was joking but I touched wood and then got all of the vaccines. I stuffed myself with drugs. I often ate spicy food, it was the only natural remedy against diarrhea. Anything in contact with water can cause intestinal trouble, so you should always tell people to wash fruit with purified water because they usually don't do it. For them it's normal to use the tap water, which is not drinkable.

There were also con artists who would try to cajole a bit of money from you with little gimmicks. Stenghel said, "let them do it. Let them take away a little bit of money from you, as I do. Don't see them as enemies."

Here it's normal to chat with the first person you meet on the street. After a few minutes he might treat you as his inseparable friend and then you discover that he is just waiting for the right moment to ask you for some money. He begins to allude to family problems—a father, a son, a wife with some nasty disease—to tell you that he has no money for medicines and you, as a stinking-rich white man and his close friend, with money coming out of your ears, cannot hold back. But when I complained to Stenghel about the hypocritical friendship of Africans, he replied that it was just my defense mechanisms creating the usual wall of distrust.

After several days in my state of futility, I met my interpreter and guide, Wobit, a very simple and beautiful Ethiopian woman. One day she took me to her house, a fine villa. Her father, though, was a beast! Awesome! Even the children feared him. Tall, brown, hair like Africans of Eritrean origin—but funny! The brothers introduced me to eating *ingera*, the bread that looks like an animal hide. Instead, it's an elastic bread, more like a sponge. Then spicy chicken and other dishes. They offered me a delicious wine, *tej*, made with honey. Then Wobit took me to see a beautiful place outside Addis Ababa, where the brothers went hunting. Ethiopia has unique scenery!

The father had dairy cows from Switzerland, which had made him rich, but they do not live long because of the climate. They only have time to produce calves; meanwhile those born here live longer. Of course I thought immediately that I would meet the same fate as the Swiss cows, that I too would not survive the trauma of change, the many absurdities which assailed me every day.

Whenever I visited Wobit, I was introduced into a parlour, with two braziers in the middle, where the coffee was prepared. Wobit nestled on a stool, in the presence of siblings, father, mother and several friends, put the coffee, already ground in a pestle, on one of the braziers and on the other brazier she put grains of incense. She poured the boiling water into the *gebena*, the coffee maker made of clay, and she added roasted coffee. We sipped from small cups without handles, which burned my fingers. The cups were filled continuously until evening. The coffee would become weaker and weaker, due to the addition of water and its simmering in the *gebena*.

Despite the discomfort of feeling out of tune, and disconnected from these people, despite seemingly having been beamed down from another, different, more modern and dynamic world, I felt relaxed being part of that great family. Drinking coffee in the middle of the house represented a moment of detachment from the outside world, of union, of community. I also began to see that there was a way to exorcize my fears and loneliness. I compared the situation to when I sipped coffee alone at home, watching the TV.

Wobit and I also went to Lalibela, a small village of underground, rock-hewn churches, declared a UNESCO World Heritage site. You breathe a very strong sense of religiosity, of mysticism, of detachment from the world. You can almost feel a divine presence. People are simple and there are neither banks, nor tourist offices. Thanks to Wobit and her brother Nagasi I started feeling a little more at ease.

I've known the modern Addis Ababa, the sights frequented by foreigners, the most sophisticated shops on Churchill Avenue, the international as well as local restaurants, where you eat with your fingers from a communal dish. Addis Ababa is not only about poverty and depression. With money you can almost delude yourself into thinking you are living in a European city—just being chauffeured around in a car with tinted windows and without venturing into the remote, degraded and disreputable areas. However, still motivated by Stenghel, I walked alone in the city. I sat at the bar, talking with everyone and regularly received the usual requests for help. But if you gave some money to someone, you attracted others. When I was eating in an outdoor restaurant, there were beggars looking at me and hoping I would give them something, like you would give to dogs. When I was inside the restaurant, they looked at me through the window, making signs and waiting for me to come out.

After two months there I knew more people in Addis Ababa than I did in London in my entire life. The Ethiopians are wary of strangers, but if you gain their confidence, they open themselves up to you. One person introduces you to ten others. Here relationships are stronger, both among relatives and friends. The children, as they become adults, always maintain a high regard, and even awe, of parents and even neighbours feel responsible for the behaviour of other children. They do nothing other than exchange visits. It's just customary to turn up at the house of relatives and friends at all hours. An Englishman would invite you out of pure formality, but then you risk traumatising him if you really appear at his home. They have the habit of presenting themselves unannounced at your house, while you eat, or are in the bathroom. The visits are real raids that often prevent you from continuing to do what you were doing. And if you send them to hell, they will consider you a pathological case, of suffering from a nervous disorder. For me it was totally inconceivable, the primitive behaviour of a people who don't have any sense of intimacy, and are unable to establish a boundary between themselves and others. They are also able to make an appointment with you for today and present themselves tomorrow. I then learned that having somebody tell visitors that you are not there is considered an offense, a lack of respect.

Sometimes even a guy I met in a bar, with whom I had just exchanged a few words and to whom I had mentioned the area where I lived, would turn up at my home. Maybe he had stalked me or, asking around, had managed to track me down. For me it was an attack on my person. I remember my grandfather, when he heard a knock at the door, shouting, "who's there?" in a menacing tone, to warn the intruder, even before entering, that he was disturbing him. Even with Nagasi I was rude. Once I asked him, "what the hell did you come here for?" Obviously, in all of this, there was no support from Stenghel, who said that there was absolutely nothing wrong, that the enemies were just in my head. I had to change my head and not my surroundings, which were fine as they were.

Basically there isn't a real reason for Ethiopians to visit each other, except to come and have a chat. Here debate is vital—meeting for a chat or gossip is their favourite pastime. Sometimes I also recognized that their unannounced, sudden visits were forcing me out of my paranoia. Nagasi often brought me honey wine, which I was crazy for. He had studied in London and we used to hang around together. Addis Ababa is full of bars where you can sit for hours chatting. I rediscovered the habit of long conversations that I had when I was a student. Here there are only a few books but many conversations. Wherever you go, you see Ethiopians discussing everything. In Africa oral culture has always had a greater value than written.

Wobit was fascinated by my tales of English life, the sense of loneliness and anonymity! In London, when I met my neighbour who I had known for a lifetime, we would talk about the weather and the dead leaves in the garden. Even with my secretary, who had worked for me for years, we were careful not to touch on anything too personal. Wobit, on the other hand, always had to visit relatives or friends—a moral obligation that you cannot escape in Ethiopia. There was always a sick uncle, a birthday, a wedding, a cousin's return from America, a funeral. And if you don't present yourself, they were offended.

She, then, as a woman, had more tasks. She did everything possible for everybody, not only for her family but also for friends and now also for me. She was concerned about my well-being and whatever I needed. At the same time she was a strong, independent woman, who did not mince her words, even when it came to her family members. As a joke we said that we would exchange our houses. I would give her my home in the Kennington district in London, and she would give me her villa outside Addis Ababa. Faithfully following Stenghel's advice, I spoke about myself sincerely, without hiding my flaws. I told her I could not stand all of those Africans who were watching me. I pleaded with her not to take me into the midst of so many people. I was also annoyed that she would stop in the street to talk with some acquaintance.

My precarious psychic condition continued to affect my ability to think clearly. When I met Alf, a Norwegian and self-professed palaeontologist, I do not know what prompted me to follow him, just when, in Stenghel's words, I was becoming better adjusted and beginning to establish the correct relationships with people. Alf had dropped out just like me. Perhaps that was the first reason for my attraction to him, and the other that he was completely crazy and different from me. I met him in the Addis Ababa Museum, in front of the skeleton of that famous hominid called Lucy, dated more than three million years old, which I had heard so much about.

He was 71, thin, with two bright eyes, but one always half-closed. In 1987, he had had a terrible accident and was in a coma for over a year. The first few days after he awoke from the coma, he wandered around the house as if he had emerged from a remote age. He had come, from a state of purely vegetative, unconscious life, back to human consciousness. It seems that this event triggered a strange change within him! Now he was interested in the human brain, in the birth of the first man and the development of man's awareness—an event that scientists still cannot place in history and that Alf strangely associated with awakening from a coma. Then he had a sudden impulse to drop everything and to go right to Ethiopia. There, according to his abstruse calculations, the first hominid had appeared, already equipped with a little common sense and savvy provided by that mysterious, diabolical cranial organ that we call a brain, that is also the root cause of all our tribulations.

He maintained a clear but distant memory of his life before the coma—the walks with the dog, the office, his friends, his home on the fjord. He was divorced and worked as an accountant at the Municipality of Oslo. And then one day he had a collision with a German truck, which came too slowly out of a bend. I told him, "It must be wonderful to emerge from unconsciousness and rediscover your imagination and the beauty of nature."

"And death!" he answered.

I could not help thinking about the meaning of his words. He was right. The first man discovered at the same time two opposite things that animals aren't aware of; the wonder of creation and death. Alf knew all the dates of the fossils, locations, hypotheses, theories. Sometimes he was a bit confused. He had brief memory lapses, as if for a few seconds a switch in his brain was turned off. He had lived like a mole, inside a dark office, where he knew only stamps and calculators. And one day he took a backpack and went away. Now he was a new man, the classic rebel from the middle class, a little fanatic, who loves to travel the world with little in his pocket. The trip, the camp, the movement from one place to another were his habitat, his new philosophy of life.

He seemed to be sent by Dr. Stenghel to redeem me. But what was true about him? When you're away from your country, you can invent what you want; nobody can verify what you say. There isn't a home that's a reflection of you, neither is there your study, your library, your office, your friends who call you. And anyway he didn't speak too much about his private life before the coma. But he had the charm of those who defend their ideas to the hilt, and the talent to involve you in crazy pursuits, making you believe that they are normal.

For several years he swept back and forth across Ethiopia. He explained to me that other bones, belonging to a biped of about six million years ago, had recently been found in the Rift Valley. Many theories on the evolution of man were being upended. In fact the oldest specimens known until then were dated to only three million years old. He was convinced that the first human beings had appeared in Ethiopia. He made statements like, "Ethiopia is the only country in the world where you can feel in touch with your ancestors." He wanted to end his days here, among the ancestors of man, without enduring old age, medicines, hospitals, the evenings sitting on the veranda watching the ships passing in the fjord.

Wherever he went, he searched in the most remote places, looking for who-knows-what. Once he found a bone dating, according to him, several million years, but did not know if it was the finger of the right hand of a hominid, or a chicken bone.

We made several trips together; I followed him like a bloodhound. It was a challenge to me and also a gamble that pleased Stenghel, who said that I was making great strides, considering the retiring life I had led before. We went into places where you had to hack through the vines to penetrate and you had to watch the branches held onto, because there might be snakes. When I showed the smallest sign of lack of resolve, Alf reproved me, called me a sissy, a spoilt big baby. How could I put myself in the hands of a lunatic adventurer, in the precarious condition I was in? I had no choice, aside from telling Stenghel and his experiments to go to hell, taking the next plane out and adding another failure to my life.

We were at the hot spring near the Wenchi Crater Lake. At certain points you could almost imagine that you were in the Scottish highlands or at Loch Ness, but then you turn around and, instead of a farmer in a kilt, you see a warrior, with tattooed gums, red head and a spear in his hand, maybe also a mobile phone hanging from his neck. And the strange thing is that he looks nice too, unlike some repulsive sights you see in industrialized countries, with their fat bellies covered in tattoos.

Alf brought Zema, his guardian angel, with him. She took care of him, anticipating his needs. She handled everything, providing supplies, food, placing traps. She dressed in very chaste clothes, like all Ethiopian women—hand-woven shawls that covered her entire body. Alf once managed to force her to put on an unlikely skirt of leopard skins. He had also made a bow with palm branches and arrows of cane.

Zema was the right woman for Alf, able to humour him and, if necessary, assist and cure him, although he seemed quite unaware of his venerable old age. It was so sweet to see them walking in the jungle hand in hand. Zema had only one fixation. She wanted a son by Alf at all costs and hounded him for one. She desperately wanted this, as a salvation, the great event of her life; at forty she was playing her last trump card.

We traveled by jeep, and erected the tents for the night in front of a fire. I often thought about Wobit and Nagasi and I missed them. We were at Lake Tana, the source of the Blue Nile, which, uniting together with the White Nile from further north in Sudan, gives rise to the famous River Nile. There is a narrow, deep gorge where the waters of Tana form a waterfall. The noise is terrifying; you feel the tyranny of nature. This, I believe, is the charm of Africa. Nature here is more alive, stronger than man; for this reason the Africans are indolent and fatalistic. They know that they will never prevail. Sometimes my teeth were chattering and I stammered incoherent words as though I had a fever.

Every evening Alf went into the tent and I saw his shadow by the light of the fire. He threw himself down next to Zema and invariably she began to caress him. She wanted a son above all else. I heard Alf's voice saying, "not tonight, please; leave me alone," but she insisted. She spoke to his penis, "Look here, it looks like a young boy!" And in the end you could hear the moans of intercourse. I saw the shadow of her rise and fall as he lay motionless, as if under a spell. This was repeated regularly every evening; the caresses seemed to make him drunk and confused. He always devoured double portions of meat. He emerged from the tent with sunken eyes, no expression—you could see that he was worn out, not by Africa, but by an African woman.

He continued to have moments of absence and loss of memory. He was pleased with his manhood but worried that she wanted a child at any cost. In Africa, offspring are everything, providing defense and continuity in village life. Not being able to have a child is a curse. Voluntary celibacy is considered an affront to the family, the community. Even a single child is not enough and could not provide guarantees, as the child could die.

In the mornings, Alf came out of his tent violently shaking his boots, in case some scorpion had crawled in. I slept fully clothed, and emerged from my tent as I had entered, just a little more smelly. Before heading off, he drew a circle around the tent with a stick so that he could check, on his return, if some snake had insinuated itself inside the tent. He knew a different treatment for each type of animal bite. He sprayed the tent flaps with a repellent liquid for animals as well as insects.

To make matters worse, Alf was the antithesis of modern man and had no interest in take advantage of modern comforts. Probably as result of his coma, he enjoyed feeling like a primitive man, moving through the jungle using tricks typical of prehistoric men, or paramilitary maniacs. We ate roasted squirrels almost every day. He prepared nooses which hung from sticks of wood, like the rings along a fishing rod that guides the line. A squirrel would slip inside to play and, trying to get out on the other side, would slide from the branch and hang himself. In reality, even the tribal people didn't survive with such devices. At the market you could source all of the basic elements for the kitchen. But Alf was not a normal man—he was a close relative of the Neanderthals. He took worms from a small hole in the ground and threw them into a container of drinking water where the worms washed themselves. After a few minutes he ate them raw. He cut cactus and chewed the pulp to extract juice, which he then spat into a pot where he was cooking insects that he had stripped of wings and hairy legs. He said that it was necessary to boil them well because there can be parasites on the hard skin; he then mixed them with herbs found on the spot.

I desperately called the psychologist by satellite phone, as I often did even from the middle of the jungle. He told me he could not speak because he was in a restaurant and they were serving him roast beef! I complained to Alf, "What I'm doing is absurd and senseless. I don't know why I'm here anymore." Alf was silent for awhile and then said something that seemed directed at himself. "We are all laboratory animals, crazy little mice." Then Alf put lizards in foil and gave them to me. He tried to console me by advising that lizards are cold-blooded and therefore don't have viruses, unlike beef steak. That day not even one squirrel had hung himself in the trap.

From the jungle we passed into the savannah and I realized that there was a lack of water there. "We don't need it," Alf declared. And so, at dawn, we found ourselves crawling on our knees in the grass, like three mutilated zombies, to soak our pants with dew so that we could then wring them out to get water. Although I phoned Stenghel every day to ask for help and understanding, I knew what his answer would be. It was always the same, like the blade of a guillotine; "Let everything happen to you. Don't hinder anything. Be receptive and treasure everything that happens to you. Just be aware."

Sometimes Alf's jeep seemed to be coming apart, as we raced at more than a hundred kilometers an hour on dirt roads, to shake off rhinos or to avoid a possible assault by bandits. The sun visors were peeling off, the windows down. I knocked my head against the roof at each hole; I felt my stomach coming up to my throat. It was raining and the mud splashed on the windshield. He was past 71 and drove recklessly, as if nothing was the matter and he couldn't see a damned thing. He nearly missed turning into the curves. Finally I insisted that he stop and I told him, "We not driving any further, even if you beg me in Chinese." Only after I convinced him to let me drive did the race resume.

I had never felt this way before, to be a true man, able to face up to a crazy old fellow of 71. I didn't realize I could be so brave. As Stenghel said, I was recovering my self-esteem. I started to consider myself a tough guy, a primitive fighting animal and not a mollusc or a big baby dragging himself from one pub to another. I had grown up spoiled, over-protected, afraid of the smallest danger. Therefore, even if Alf had a severe case of senile dementia, following him unconditionally was a real-life education for me. When I think about it, Alf had also come from a sedentary and lower middle-class background. Both of us had lived a little apart from the world, but now I still wonder what strange mechanism during the coma had caused such a reversal of his personality. More than once I thought, "I'm going around in Africa with a fugitive!" Basically, when you think about it, what would be the first objective of a fugitive other than to create a new identity, new interests and a new reason for living?

Once he was unusually talkative. He spoke to me in a way he had never spoken before, like a man who had returned suddenly from his past and he said things that really made me think. He spoke in general, but I suspected he was referring to himself, as though his past, kept hidden until then, was suddenly emerging like a flood. "Usually people's lives run on the same track, until something unexpected occurs. You are a clerk all your life; nothing happens. And then it all happens quickly. You meet a woman, leave your wife, get a divorce, marry the other one, then she leaves you, your friend dies, the automatic watering system fails, you run out to buy a new timer, you crash your car and you find yourself in a coma in a hospital room. Everything escapes your control. You are no longer the same. For years you have lived in a false refuge. Man is not born to hide in a cave, to live a flat and sedentary life. He is not a domestic animal, as they would have us believe. He is the most aggressive animal ever to appear on this planet, born to fight for power, for the conquest of territory. And his structure has not changed since he appeared millions of years ago. Our brain is the product of a struggle for survival. You cannot keep it in mothballs or in front of Windows on a computer screen; it ends up devouring itself. You're a little big man designed to challenge the universe. Do not forget it! That's your destiny."

There was something delusional in his eyes but there was also a magnetic and strangely striking analogy between his conclusions and those of my psychologist. He had chosen this path and left the reassuring life of the bourgeois after his coma. I gave my thanks to Dr. Stenghel.

We were also in Sudan, on the border. Zema had gone into a shrine to ask for the grace to have a child. In one village, three men attacked and kicked us because we peeked inside some windows. These morons! They said that we were looking at the women inside their houses. We didn't even know there were women in those houses.

Sudan is a fundamentalist Islamic country, except for some areas where there is a sort of anarchy and they do as they want; the military, the politicians, the corrupt gangs. In a village in southern Ethiopia, where the Dorzie live, there are round, windowless houses with pointed roofs. They walk around almost naked. They make scarves, hats and other things for tourists; for 15 Birr, less than two dollars, you can take away a beautiful object. These houses are very high, made of mud, cow dung and other natural crap. And as they grow older, they dry out and shrink lower. We entered one of those houses used as a restaurant and sitting on the ground we ate with our fingers an unrecognizable food, barely edible. Without any reason, Alf left a stratospheric tip.

Alf turned onto a track that climbed up a hill. We drove for a mile, uphill, with the jeep bouncing and we found ourselves in front of the fence of a house overlooking the valley, the savannah and a lake, on which pink flamingos fluttered. At a distance, we saw a half-naked man and woman. He, David, was a Jewish former veterinarian from Queens, New York; he cultivated the soil, the acacias and bred animals. She, Masa, was covered only with decorations, necklaces of beads on her forehead, neck and hands. They lived well, all the time half-naked, in the midst of animals. There were animals everywhere; even inside the home there was a sort of cow-goat with big horns, a nyala. And dogs, cats, monkeys, wild boars, antelopes called klipspringers, which always live in pairs. David wore riding boots. Stocky and strong, he spoke of his animals, their names, their habits, their ailments, with the love of a mother. In America, he had left his own house and an obedient wife who did the income-tax returns for him every year. His love for animals was suffocated there, in Queens. He loved to observe them in their wild environment. A lady with a little dog which suffered from colds was not for him.

Alf brought David something that was typical of American middle-class man—a replacement head for his Remington electric razor. David had an advanced water system; he collected rainwater from the roof. In Ethiopia it rains an average of one meter a year. He collected 100,000 gallons of water per year on a roof of less than 100 square feet. Taking advantage of the slope, he had built a collection tank on the roof of the house, so that the water flowed by gravity without the use of pumps. He filtered the water through several layers of sand. It could be recycled because it washed itself, with the accumulated dirt being removed as the water circulated back in the opposite direction. Then he disinfected the water using an ultraviolet light. He had also prepared an ultraviolet sterilization system for instruments he used for veterinary purposes.

His hobby was amateur radio. He had an antenna with a rotor and a bunch of postcards, confirming links with many different countries. The cards arrived in Addis Ababa *poste restante* and Alf brought them to him. For light he used 12-volt bulbs, like car headlights, attached to batteries, which, during the day, were charged by solar panels. He had set up four square feet of such panels, that produced two kilowatt-hours per day. His aim was to provide as much electricity as possible and always to have ice available for his essential Four Roses whiskey. We unloaded four cases that had fit exactly under the seat of the Jeep, all material that Alf delivered to David. I didn't even know the cases were on board; they were very heavy. One night, almost as if dreaming, I had the impression that Alf and David were whispering in Hebrew and fumbling with electronic things. It seemed like a Mossad operation.

I couldn't figure out why David had left America. He was very evasive, but showed a keen interest in me. Once he wanted me to wear a certain African costume. I had to undergo an initiation ritual. I was blindfolded and covered with a sticky concoction. He himself combed my hair.

Alf and I accompanied David around the villages to visit the animals. We were welcomed like Hollywood stars. Usually we sat next to the elders or the head of the tribe as a sign of high regard. Of course eating with our fingers was a must—raw meat dipped in chilli pepper. For David and Alf this was normal. Around a low table, they grabbed the food from a big pot and they shoved it into their mouths. I could not avoid also eating with my fingers from a communal dish, but it made me sick.

I participated in their festivals and dance—always group dances. You feel you belong to their community. Here dance is a social ritual, a way to feel united, part of the group. I had to rediscover everything—words and gestures. They express themselves much more with body language, laughing at everything. My seriousness fell like a mask; I discovered that the world is not so serious and should not be taken seriously.

David told me, "Solitude here is an unknown dimension. The Africans have their own rituals. Meanwhile today, in America, you risk facing everything in solitude. We live our suffering in solitude, as though it's something that's come down on us like a curse, something alien to hide from others. We refuse and we are afraid of mystery. For us everything is scientific. But how would life be without mystery? If God came here to tell us what's right to do, everybody would obey just out of fear and the world would be boring. I think that God does well to keep himself hidden and leave us in this mysterious world." Instead we know nothing of ourselves. We move in stories that do not belong to us. We cling to our memories, our fears, our habits, like shipwrecked beings cling to a rope thrown from the ship. Only when you accept the pain are you a man. Human existence is an adventure, a drama, and as such should be lived, but with the right to get insurance before embarking if it serves to give you courage." Accept suffering? What did he mean? I felt there was a strange analogy with what Stenghel had said.

I listened to him, but I could not get the idea out of my head that there was something that he wasn't telling me. One evening he began to pay me compliments; it was rather embarrassing to be courted by a man. He said, "I like your way of speaking." Yet it took me a long time to realize that he was a faggot.

We got drunk. At that moment I just let everything happen naturally, maybe because I was pretty tipsy or the situation itself was out of this world. I didn't consider it a gay experience, but just something different. Of course I was eager to report to Stenghel what had happened to me. When he heard that I had had a homosexual relationship, he seemed to gloat. By now I had no doubts—I had ended up in the hands of a sadistic psychologist.

Then Alf and I pushed farther south, where we confronted more distrust from people we met. They could not even understand our guide. It's like travelling back in time when you move away from Addis Ababa. You see old customs practised, such as deforming their lips and tongues and tattooing their gums. They also pierce their tongues, like the new fashion in the West. And then there are the superstitions that date back to distant times. Everything in Ethiopia smacks of ancient civilization—the historical remains, religious rites, unexplored areas, the villages where they have never seen a white man, where their lifestyle has been the same for hundreds of years and where the elderly still have power over the community. Ethiopia is virtually a nation of villages. In Ethiopia, the foreigner is kept out of all the political intrigues. There is a form of ethnic federalism applauded by the West, despite all the corruption and dictatorship.

When Alf and I returned to Addis Ababa, we each went our own way. I left him for a while to his prehistoric manias. It was the period during which all citizens of Eritrean origin were expelled. They loaded them onto trucks and left them on the border with Eritrea, just as you unload rubbish. People received an expulsion order and within a few hours had to leave everything behind—their homes, possessions, habits, friends, work. I don't know how they ended up. The International Convention for Human Rights condemned it, but, for Ethiopia, the international community didn't lift a finger. It was a shock for me when I went to visit Wobit and learned that she had been expelled from Ethiopia with her entire family, because of their Eritrean origin. They had just disappeared, as if they had never existed; I learned nothing more about them. I only know that they had been stripped of everything; cancelled as human beings. I think they felt themselves to be Ethiopians. Basically here the concept of national identity is rather vague—Ethiopians and Eritreans have continuously mixed and belong to the same race and culture. Wobit's father had come to Ethiopia when he was ten years old; he had always lived here and had also worked at Ethiopian Airlines. He had worked his whole life here and married here.

Alf did not have a fixed address. I decided to look for Zema who went to Mass every day in Addis Ababa. I found her, sad and disconsolate—not only was she not pregnant, but Alf had returned to Oslo and didn't want anything more to do with her. When she phoned, he remained silent on the phone. I made her give me the number and called him myself. I recognized his voice.

"Hello, this is Alex," I heard a groan.

"I'm Alex," I repeated.

"Who are you?"

"It's me, Alex..." I had no response. "Hello! Hello Alf? Are you there?" There was silence again. "Do you remember me?"

"No."

"You were not in Ethiopia two months ago?"

"No."

"You've never been to Ethiopia?"

"No."

"But are you not Alf?"

"Yes."

"Have you forgotten everything? Are you okay?"

"Who are you?"

"It's me, Alex."

There was nothing more to do. The conversation could go on forever. I called another time and spoke with his brother—Alf had Alzheimer's disease; he was finished. He had forgotten everything—Zema, excursions into the jungle, squirrels, lizards in foil. His mind had gone, regressed to the flat, motionless stage of total detachment from everything, as in a coma; no tomorrow, no ups and downs, every day unchanging. He had returned to the vegetal condition to which, perhaps in his subconscious, he aspired.

So there were no more Wobit, or Nagasi, or Alf. I began to think about going back to London. Addis Ababa once again seemed strange and far away and had an air of expectation, of passivity, of abandonment, of letting things go. It is that dark African evil that you cannot unravel; reflected in the many faces like Wobit and Nagasi, all with the same big eyes. I missed their warmth. I tried to find something of them in every Ethiopian I met. But I saw around me only resignation, African fatalism. Suffering begins the moment you are born. You cannot do anything about it. In the West we would start a revolution if the lights go out for a quarter of an hour, whereas here they do not complain if they have a dozen flies crawling around their eyes. You see the Africans sleeping rough outside; you think of your city with clean streets, efficient services, nice cars, dynamic people. You feel superior; you would like to get on your high horse, to start pontificating, you would like to change them, educate them, to impose your culture. But I had come here to learn.

Zema came to visit me; she brought me food. She did not speak but was a reassuring presence which I could rely on. I wondered, after all, if Alf and I were interchangeable for her. It would be enough to give her what she was looking for at the end; a son and economic security. I had never considered the possibility of bringing a child into the world. One evening I had a brainwave—I would make Zema pregnant; I would look after her and our son and stop paying Stenghel! Why not? Life goes on, and both of us lacked continuity, offspring, a purpose for living. The child would grow up in the midst of the community, raised by everyone.

I told her about my intention in the same way that you talk about buying a wardrobe. Perhaps I would take her to my heart, but this was not important now. It usually begins with a courtship, a romance, an engagement. She is the woman of your life and your son is the culmination of a dream of love. At that time, however, I saw her simply as a female who could give birth to a small caveman like Alf, capable of surviving in the wild world. I do not know if I was starting to think like an African or had totally stopped thinking entirely.

For a while I had to shuttle between London and Addis Ababa in order to look after my business interests. I could continue to play the role of explorer, to live for adventures or extreme situations and make do with my credit cards—a special jeep, a rescue helicopter... Instead, I preferred the reality of Africans.

Recently I've decided to live here permanently. Ethiopia has helped me to stop gazing at my navel all of the time. Being here means receiving a continuous call for help, and not paying my psychologist any more! Here you have the feeling of unlimited power. Your economic power is multiplied by a hundred and you feel you can do whatever you want. I choose to help people, because it's good for me and because I can see in front of me the immediate effects of what I do. I want to rip people from the jaws of death; there are street children who have no health care whatsoever.

In England, I do not know if we suffer, if we're happy or if we are torturing ourselves inside our four walls. And I do not give a damn. In London I was anaesthetized; I lived like a fish in a refrigerator. Ethiopia has made a very strong impact on me. The barriers that were between me and life, between me and other people, do not exist here. There are no veils. You also see the evil that is part of life—you see it to the end. Ethiopia is a country of extremes, of great passions and terrible cruelty. I saw women who eat only after the man has finished, and only if some food is left. Or men who even travel thirty miles on foot to visit a friend or their loved ones.

Religion here is very powerful. You feel the weight of its authority, like a hood.

I hate talking about humanitarian aid. I cannot say I didn't sleep at night, thinking about the poor blacks who do not eat. I came here just to solve my own problems. I supported paying for various medical expeditions, with a plane landing in many villages to conduct cataract operations. They complete twenty operations a day and then fly on to another village to do the same. The humanitarian organization I work with is completely apolitical. In reality, since there are many Muslims in Ethiopia, there is the risk of being considered pro-American, but that's a risk that does not prevent me from making my choices. Now I live with danger. Just imagine how I was before, when it was hard for me to stick my nose out of the house. As Alf said, our mind is structured for survival. When we remove one danger, we invent another one. I lived in the quiet of my apartment, watching television between a beer and a nap. And yet in my mind I had created all sorts of disasters, monsters, ghosts, dangers and tragedies.

My relocation to Africa has been, in some way, the final departure from my mother, the point at which I have grown up, become independent and can face the world alone. But I am not healed completely, although I do not really know what it means to be healed.

As Stenghel had said, "You can even die but not be cured."

A Psychological Perspective

His isolation from others, his obsessive introspection, accentuates his anxieties and fears. As Alf tells him, "Our brain is the product of a struggle for survival. You cannot keep it in mothballs... it ends up devouring itself." In this case, breaking out of his shell, the radical departure from his culture and habits, changes his mental perspective, allowing him to escape from a narrow and egomaniacal view of life.

13

From Italy to Laos
Only a communist really appreciates capitalism

Giancarlo, from Milan, age 32:

I had a discotheque in Milan with a partner. We earned money discreetly, even if we had many fish to fry. All night you have to deal with hundreds of hot heads, all excited by the blaring music.

There is a law that says 'If you give a drink to someone who is drunk or who is sixteen, you go straight to jail for three years, and your business will be closed down'. And if I give you a drink and you pass your glass to your friend who is sixteen and he gets drunk, I will be responsible, not you. In the meantime, ecstasy has arrived in the form of various little pills. I would have been responsible for any drug trafficking that took place in my club—I have to be responsible for ten thousand idiots who take drugs in Milan? Me?

One day a customer punches me, opens the drawer and tries to escape with the day's takings. I grab his arm, he falls down and drops the money. Then the bouncer comes, kicks him out of the club and closes the door.

The thief begins to bang on the door. He wants revenge. We call the police, who arrive after the thief has already disappeared. They wanted to close the club for fifteen days due to problems with public order. But wasn't it me who was punched and almost robbed? It seems that the bouncer had no authority to kick him out. He is not a public official, the law does not recognise the role of the bouncer. When you hire him, it must be just as a courtesy service, to accompany clients to the table, to the bathroom, but he cannot throw them out.

Another day, the municipal police come and ask us about our licenses. "Do you have a license to sell alcoholic drinks? Fine. But you also need permission to stay here to sell them."

"Excuse me, I asked for the liquor license because I wanted to sell drinks."

"Yes, but you did not ask for permission to stand here and sell them."

The law requires, in addition to the license that states where liquor will be sold, also a certificate authorizing you to stay exactly in that place to sell them. As well as a health department authorisation, which we already had! The outcome? They had to close the club to draw up a report about us, which resulted in a fine and then a court case. It's a criminal offense not to have that piece of paper.

The police generously agreed to allow us to close the discotheque spontaneously, by ourselves and in a short time. So in that event, no report, no fine, no forced closure and no court case! The end of ten years of work! To be truthful, the seating capacity was the only questionable thing about our business, as we were located in a basement. There is a limit imposed on this, not to exceed a certain number of persons admitted, proportionate to the number of escape routes available in case of fire. But nobody, really, could give a damn about that.

I had to start all over again. I had both the will and the rage to react, but I could not find an outlet for either. I found every job opportunity to be an insult for someone over thirty like me, an electronics graduate and computer expert, with an excellent knowledge of English at native speaker level and now also an expert in public relations and management. One of the most interesting tasks on offer was moving slabs of aluminum from one place to another, using a forklift truck. In Milan, the great, rich, industrial center of Italy, the salaries offered were between 800 and 900 euros per month, plus restaurant vouchers. Rent and condominium expenses, excluding bills, were already more than 500 euros a month.

The selection of temporary employment at agencies rely on girls who have no idea who you are and are not interested in finding out. Once, in one of these pseudo-interviews, I pretended to know the Greenlandic, Vietnamese, Mongolian and Afghan languages. She did not flinch—she filled out the application form and inserted it into a file. If it had been true, you would think that it would be interesting to look into this human resource a little more closely. But they are not wrong. For a salary of 800 euros per month, what can you expect?

I lived in the typical Milanese environment. After eight o'clock in the evening, there seemed to be a curfew on the street—all human life was concentrated in some bar: two old guys holding football coupons, some poor schmuck getting drunk and a bunch of bored teenagers. My girlfriend called me every night but we didn't have much to say to each other; our call was just a mutual duty, a continuation of inertia, a lack of courage. Ultimately the marriage, the future home in a residential district, my entrepreneurial activities, the milieu of upper Milan, summed up the whole of our life plan, a perfect picture that we had built together in our minds.

Once a piece of this construction broke off—specifically my job—everything collapsed, like dominoes. She had seen in me a social statement, a character driven by ambition. Now for her, I was no longer the same person. She kept repeating, "I don't recognize you. You look resigned. You have lost your fighting spirit." At first she remained very close to me, but then she started to distance herself. It was good to end the relationship.

"Shall we meet again, remain friends?" A clean break was the best solution; it helped me to forget her.

When you get up in the morning you have in front of you the desolation of your neighbourhood, of that call that never comes, of your call in vain. I waited, just waited for something to happen. I spent all of my time in my home. Where to go? What's in a suburb of Milan? You spend time thinking about what to do, but you can't do shit. Do you stay at home watching television or go to the bar to play billiards? You escape from the void, from that day that never comes, from the boredom of the same faces, from those silences made of nothing to say. Then the idea comes to you as a liberation: to see other places, other people, other mentalities. Before leaving, I started to feel a vague sense of lightness and freedom.

I tried to look at my situation from all sides. I wondered if the lack of a job was the real cause of my discontent. I began to think, "My brother, the lucky one with a regular, responsible, well paid job in a large insurance company; is he really so lucky? All in all I have in front of me new things to discover, while he has a settled life, always predictable. He gets up in the morning (it is still dark), he goes out and he gets in line with other cars (with their lights on). It's not an overwhelming line-up, but tiresome if you do it every day. Then he parks the car (it is still dark) and takes the subway, which goes underground. He enters his office where he spends his day in a dimly-lit environment; there is a window onto a courtyard, from which he sees drizzle falling on the glass. When he comes out at about 5:30 it is getting dark again, so he returns home after dark; he gets into his car, turns on the headlights and joins the line again with all the other cars.

This is repeated every day and it's not that kind of darkness in which you see the snow illuminated by the moon, with a backdrop of mountains and sky. It's that useless dark, which brings out the blues of a grey city, like something out of a film about drug addicts. And even if you start your day with a delicious coffee, it will not change the day's outcome."

I said to myself, "If that's the alternative, I'll play my life like a roll of the dice or a video game. I will blow those bloody dollars I saved, no matter what happens. At least I will try an adventure in a different country." The important thing is to escape this state of passivity, returning home in the evening and just sitting in front of the TV like a zombie. In practice you let circumstances decide your life for you. You become fatalistic. To hell with my middle-class dreams!

My father and mother tried until the end to make me give up. They viewed my idea, of going out and splashing all my money around the world, with horror. In their minds I had to save it up, in anticipation of an uncertain future, to buy a house and raise a family. Sooner or later I would have to marry and have children. The best solution, according to them, would have been a good psychiatrist, but I tried to reassure them, saying that I would not throw my money away, that I was not going in search of an eternal holiday.

In reality I left without a clear idea about my future. How did I end up in Laos? I hardly knew it even existed. I knew vaguely that it was a place for tramps. I was in Thailand for several months, where they are very well organized in terms of tourism, and I decided to cross the border into Laos and renew my visa. To stay in Thailand I needed to renew my visa every 90 days.

With a shared taxi from the border, after about 20 kilometers, I arrived here in Vientiane, the capital. I found accommodation in a small, ancient, half decayed hotel, the River Hotel, which sits right on the banks of the Mekong River, this huge river which winds through almost all of Asia. From the balcony I saw, in the distance, the other side of the river which is Thailand and I watched some Lao people walking along the banks under an umbrella or entering fully dressed into the river. As we have the goal of tanning, they have the goal of remaining a cadaverous white.

I could scarcely believe that I was in the capital of Laos. Although I was in the center, it felt like a small town, rather than a capital city. Everywhere there was a sea of bicycles, scooters, driven by girls and boys of indefinable age, all looking young and the same, and some *tuk-tuks*, all of which squealed especially when braking. A tuk-tuk is a three-wheeler van with an open side which acts as a taxi, where the passengers sit behind. Then, little by little, you realize that you're not in a remote village with rural people and goats. You are, in fact, in an international environment full of young foreigners. You see refined little places, French, Indian, Italian restaurants, or Asian restaurants, where, after taking off your shoes, you enter a room with low tables and mattresses and sit cross-legged.

There are places for everyone, even the chic, contrasting with the general poverty. There is also a different type of tourism, which is more intellectual and less mass-oriented, compared with Thailand. And you feel an air of sophistication, with a certain French atmosphere, from baguettes, the patisseries, some colonial-style houses and cosy spots, very authentic and formal. Then, just round the corner, you go into a local market and find the opposite, especially when it rains—mud, flies, leaks and dirt.

I like the sleepy atmosphere of Vientiane, which results, in my opinion, from the union of Buddhism and Communism. You stroll around among the temples and don't notice the time passing. Nobody is in a hurry. You can go into a store and find the shopkeeper sleeping blissfully. You can spend a long time waiting for something indefinable, perhaps a person, a bus or for it to stop raining, or you can just sit in pubs and chat for hours, without haste, without looking at your watch. There is a saying in Southeast Asia: "The Vietnamese plant the rice, the Cambodians watch it grow and the Laos listen to it grow". Here it is a pleasure to drink their Beer Lao in a glass with plenty of ice, or their locally produced coffee, served in huge mugs. They have no need to envy Brazilian coffee.

Who knows why, in Milan, after half an hour in one place doing nothing, I was bored. We have this Christian guilt about sloth. Here I'm getting close to the Buddhist philosophy—to let the world flow around me. Sometimes I remember, in Italy, phoning some friend and suggesting, "Shall we meet tonight?"

"No, I'm tired."

"Tomorrow?"

"Impossible; on Wednesday I finish work late."

"When?"

"I don't know; I'm expecting someone to come to change the tiles. Saturday at seven—is it ok for you?"

I might say, "But this is only Monday!"

The fact is that, in Milan, if one does not have an agenda full of meetings and your phone does not ring every ten minutes, you feel like a failure.

Initially, in Laos, I was struck by the phenomenon of stalking. Once a transvestite smiled at me on a tuk-tuk. But here everybody smiles at you, so I did not pay particular attention. I got out of the tuk-tuk and walked to the hotel. In the evening I heard a knock at the door. I opened and found myself facing the transvestite who I had seen in the tuk-tuk, and the security man asked me, "Do you want him?" I answered politely, "No, thank you!"

I started to meet up with a Frenchman who I couldn't quite pigeon-hole: half-bald, with grey hair falling over his shoulders and pseudo-intellectual glasses. When he spoke, he jumped from one subject to another. He had an absent-minded look, always forgetting something; his bag, sunglasses, cigarettes—all the while demonstrating an incredible memory for some bullshit somebody had said three days earlier.

He had the ability to filter and listen only to the things that interested him, which was almost nothing, and he rode around on a bicycle with at least two days' stubble. Once he took me to his home—one of those magnificent mansions once built by the French, which was now crumbling to ruin. You entered via a porch, all mouldy from damp, which was occupied by a lady with a sewing machine. You passed through a little main door made of a metal net, the sort that you see on chicken coops, and you climbed a narrow, creaking staircase. Then through a door carved with elephants in bas-relief. Inside there was an apartment with parquet floors, worn shiny in some places. The dining room had stained glass windows from which one could see the Mekong. Everything from chairs to furniture, paintings, walls, seemed to be very expensive and decorated with style. At one time it must have been the home of some French VIP.

Gilbert—that was his name—spoke of working in a vague sort of way. He bought and resold homes, cars, even groceries. He had his finger in almost every pie. One positive thing was that he knew all of Laos, better than a tour guide. I asked him why he lived in Laos. He replied that he had always preferred communist countries.

"I live here because, now, only in a communist country, capitalism is really appreciated. I have never seen such passion and admiration for luxury and money as you see in communist countries. Consider that Laos, having lived all of those years behind the communist façade, is now opening up to the West and to foreign investment. Year after year, Laos is approaching the Western model. Right up on the banks of the Mekong, here in Vientiane, they are building a big complex with a large hotel and shopping center, with Chinese capital. Underneath from this slow, sleepy atmosphere, there is a feeling of excitement and of new things being born. Once, I remember, you could not even close the door of a hotel room. While you were under the shower, you felt a Kalashnikov pointing at your ass. When you wanted to move from one city to another, you went to the police and their command warned the head office station in your destination city. So when you arrived, you had to present yourself promptly to the new police command."

One evening Gilbert took me to an underground place. We entered an apartment. But it was actually a dimly lit nightclub, with flashing lights, like Christmas lights. It consisted of a large, empty room, with plastic chairs on the sides, two clapped-out sofas and a few bored country girls, sitting cross-legged. They turned on the music as we entered. There were no customers, but just some obsequious waiters, who were also a little intrusive. It looked like a pathetic attempt to imitate a luxury nightclub.

Another time he took me to a village where everyone came out of their huts to greet him. He had a gift for everyone—chocolate, a pendant, some wine. Then we entered a large room with a roof of banana leaves, completely empty. There was not a stick of furniture. They all sat cross-legged on the floor around us. He began to interrogate them one by one with the aid of an interpreter; we were told simple stories of common life, of poverty, of daily family problems. It was as if everybody spoke at once, as if they could not talk about themselves without involving the family, friends or others.

One of them had asked for a loan because he had to finish building his house and there was a person responsible for collecting the money. Here everyone gives a small amount of money to those who need it, with very low interest. It has never happened that someone didn't return the money. He would be despised and banned from the village.

Amid all the Lao people Gilbert seemed to play the role of a primary school teacher. They raised their hands, all demurely, before speaking. I didn't know if he was gratified to be the center of attention or if he was doing it out of charity or if there was another, hidden, motive.

In the meantime I met Susan, an American girl. In the evening I got into the habit of strolling along the Mekong, filled with stands where they cook local low-priced specialties, served on candlelit tables. The feeling is unique because it is not something specifically for tourists. It's their real way of life. Sitting at a nearby table there was a pretty girl with huge sunglasses with a green plastic frame, and a mass of curly hair. She looked at me and smiled.

I thought she was crazy. In fact she was. We started to live together the same evening with the excuse of splitting the cost of the room, as is usual among travellers. The first time we made love it was with the background of a TV broadcast of military parades.

Sometimes, late at night, she turned on the CD player and started dancing by herself. Once she went out onto the balcony, dancing completely naked. She travels the world playing the clarinet and selling chains and necklaces to other tourists. She always wears amphibian boots and a sea of necklaces and rings. She looks like a tomboy and then spends hours caring for her hands. Physically, she looks like a dark-skinned Indian and she was a native of Oklahoma. These are the only things I could find out about her. We didn't talk too much...

I had never had such a relationship before; however, we understood one another. She never asks anything about me or my past. In turn, I have no idea what hell of a mess she is dragging behind herself and I don't want to find out.

We live in the city, in a shack, slightly more decent than the others. In the evening there is plenty of life because not everyone has a bath, so you see people moving around with towels and coming back looking like freshly-shelled eggs. Although it seems like a slum, it is not scary. As each person looks at you, a smile appears. Honesty and morality here are very important, as well as consideration for others. For example, wearing a miniskirt is frowned upon, and would be pointed at.

People are more naïve and simple but not stupid. They are very hospitable, especially if you buy something to eat. Once they invited us to drink a beverage of a yellowish colour. Susan and I gladly accepted, eager to immerse ourselves in their world. Then we noticed that the liquid came from a vessel with a sexual organ inside it. It had belonged to a tiger! Seeing the astonishment on our faces, they tried to reassure us, telling us that the drink would give us great energy and vitality.

When we went to buy something in the market, we came back with bags full of fruit, vegetables, meat, spices, all of which we had paid a pittance for. No chemical preservatives are used here. Some foods had an aroma that I had previously not experienced; for example, spinach or apples, even the ugliest ones in the market. As you drive by on a motorcycle, you can smell this aroma even fifty metres away. The chickens are not pumped full of hormones. There are no large-scale farms; everyone has his own small-holding. You may well meet someone who raises goats, not for trade, but only for his personal use.

What I call 'the atmosphere of black and white films' comes back to life here. Especially when I go around on a scooter, among many other scooters, I feel like I am in an Italian movie of 50 years ago. The discos and pubs are full of Laotians every evening, even on weekdays. With only the cost of a beer you can spend the evening dancing. Since it is mandatory to close at eleven o'clock at night, the places are filled quickly and so there is no need to stay out 'til three in the morning for fun. There is also a sense of new things that are being born. I read in the local newspaper in English that, in a few months, they will install two ATMs. This, for them, is news.

I unmasked Gilbert one evening, when he invited me and two other friends to dinner at his house. We talked about many things and he bombarded us with questions. The topic was Laos, but there was also talk of other countries. In the end we exchanged our personal travel experiences, nothing special or compromising and once in awhile he got up to go to the bathroom.

Then I went into the bathroom and I noticed something very strange that shocked me. There was a box attached to the wall that did not match the stylish decoration, and two lights on the sides of the mirror. Switching on the lights, I switched the central light off by mistake and I was in the dark. From a crack in the box on the wall I could see some light. I approached and I heard a quiet buzz coming from inside.

I tried to lift the lid, as much as the lock allowed and I could glimpse a hole that linked directly through to the room where we were conversing. I returned to the room. On the wall shared with the bathroom, there was a huge picture and under it a couch. I sat down and pretending to stretch one arm; I slipped my hand under the picture and moved it slightly. I saw a microphone.

At that point I started to sweat bullets. I could no longer understand who the hell this Frenchman was and why he had to record our conversations. Was there was some blackmail behind it? Or was he a spy? It was all very fishy!

Despite opening up to tourism, Laos has a constant fear of spies. Just a few days ago, a man dressed in civilian clothes came to my apartment and wanted to see my passport. He left without saying a word. This attention was probably due to my frequent visits to Laos. Maybe one day they'll come back to cross-examine me after a world-wide search to find out more about me.

With a cool head I tried to reconstruct our conversation. More than anything else, we had talked about our travel experiences. Maybe in a country like Laos, a trivial thing, spoken unwittingly or naively, can become compromising and can be used against you. The situation grew more and more tense and insane in my imagination. I was on the point of exploding and making a scene, tearing the picture down to unmask him in front of everyone. Then I changed my mind. I didn't know his friends very well—after all, they could be accomplices.

After that we all got up to leave. Once everyone else had gone, I ran back up the stairs and pounded on his door violently. When Gilbert opened the door, I confronted him, "Why have you recorded our conversations? Who the hell are you?" He quietly let me come in, sit down and wait. Then he reappeared with some tapes and a dozen notebooks full of notes, erasures, sentences written and rewritten.

"I'm a writer. I collect material from life, from the people I meet. I've got piles of tapes. I listen to them over and over again and then I write my books."

Except that he had never had a book published. He lived in Lyon with an aunt and a dog, but he couldn't stand to remain too long in his country. To stay abroad, he had done various odd jobs, including a cook and a piano bar singer. He explained to me that he was seeking the truth, the natural, spontaneous narrative. In the end, he was very convincing, despite his eccentricity and unusual personality.

That evening he was far more open and told me about his private affairs. Normally he is tight-lipped and reserved; perhaps he simply wanted to reassure me. He confided in me that he was in love with a Laotian girl and that he'd paid a hefty fine after he'd spent two nights with her. That was why he'd decided to marry her. Here a Westerner cannot co-habit with a Laotian woman unless he's married to her. In every area there is either a policeman or rather a village headman, and when he gets to hear that you are sleeping with a Laotian woman, he immediately comes looking for you.

Now Gilbert and I are firm friends, even though we rarely see one another. He is often traveling in search of new ideas for his book. Recently he wrote me an Email from the Philippines. He is in Guimaras, where he met German friends who he first met last year. He says that it's always raining, so even the fucking mosquitoes are growing exponentially.

When he has to write in his notebook, he shuts himself in the bathroom; as the walls are all white, it makes it easy to find the mozzies and to strike them down with an electric fly swatter that is his faithful companion on every trip!

I felt that Susan had a bourgeois past, and that somehow we could have been a couple like many others, with a home, children who go to school and take drugs. One morning we woke up and we started making plans. I needed to enclose her, not let her get away. I had a fear inside me of losing her. Perhaps she understood—and then she disappeared.

I searched for her all over Vientiane, fearing that she had definitely left Laos. After a week I found her seated on the ground between two stalls at the market. She came back with me. I realized then that I must not try to hold her. I also understood that life is like a flowing river; you cannot trace its future course. The river goes wherever it wants, depending on the levees, on the ground, on the surrounding conditions.

We went to visit Luang Prabang, the old capital, 250 kilometers away from Vientiane. It's a place of importance in terms of world heritage, listed by UNESCO, but we had the unfortunate idea of taking the bus to go there. You can go there by plane, but they fly some sort of small plane which does not inspire much confidence. The best approach is to swallow the yellow pills, which are sold at the bus stop. The bus plods along roads which are straight for only five meters; all curves, climbs and descents. Someone vomits and the smell makes the vomiting contagious. I almost wanted to get off the bus in the middle of nowhere. There was no air conditioning. The driver hit and killed a cow, so there followed a long negotiation with the owner for compensation. And since the one who causes the damage must pay and he keeps the remains, we helped the driver to load the corpse onto the roof, from which the cow promptly fell down after a few curves. So in the end the cow had to be loaded inside.

Now I've been living here over a year and a half. I have made several friends, both Laotian and from other foreign countries who work here. And now I'm considering to open a business. In Laos there is a commission for foreign investments. After reviewing and accepting your project, they follow up with you in all the other steps. A law, just to encourage foreign investments, says that the capital and installations belonging to the foreign investor cannot be confiscated. There is a bureaucracy to go through and permits to obtain, but you can do it. They have a system of "one office". Once your project is accepted, you get all the licenses, permits and various things from a single office. Most of the activities will include the participation of Laotian investors. My final goal would be to settle permanently in a communist country, to manage an independent business on my own, with peace of mind.

Since I share a room with Susan, I got into the habit of sleeping on the floor. As she sleeps there, like so many Laotians, eventually I got used to it too. It's good for your back. Now Susan brings me breakfast in bed—in fact on the floor. And a few days ago she asked me, "Why don't we open a shop selling art objects?"

The only drawback in Laos is health care. Here it is better not to have any health problems. The best thing they can care for is malaria, but when it comes to surgery, it's better to run away. The hospitals are sometimes empty, also because there is no equipment. According to them, the hospital is not needed. They say that if you don't die as a child, eating spicy food with your hands, you will never die. Fortunately Thailand is just a few steps from here, with hospitals on a Western level, but of course you have to pay. In the evening, watching Thailand across the river, we can see more lights there than here, although the capital city is on this side and on the other side there is just open country. Once we entered a pharmacy. We woke up a little girl who was asleep, leaning against the counter. I had a cough and she gave me codeine, a medicine difficult to obtain a prescription for in Italy, which does not cure the cough but shuts it down. Since I knew about it, I said, "This is too strong. Don't you have anything else?"

Then she gave me some simple candies and she went back to sleep.

A Psychological Perspective

Some young people adopt the philosophy of just packing their bags and leaving, if they cannot find an outlet for their ambitions. With little hope for the future, they stick to the present. Giancarlo's tendency to procrastination grows, and his willingness to take on big projects decreases, in tandem with his growing desire to take from life what is available immediately, without waiting for a future that offers few guarantees.

Probably the failure of his business triggered some latent potential already within him. His life thus evolves from a bourgeois vision, based on security, possessions and savings, toward a philosophy of having everything at once and forgetting about tomorrow. Unconsciously he was never all that convinced of the traditional plan of life that was prefabricated in his mind, despite the fact that he describes it as perfect.

14

From Russia to China and Switzerland
The world is my home

A woman from Vladivostok, age 31:

At one time they used to teach us that Russia was the happiest place in the world, and that in America people sometimes went without food. But we couldn't tell if it was the truth or not, because we'd never gone out of our country. At that time, only 'special' persons were allowed to travel. And so we believed we were happy.

My mother told me that, when I used to wake up, I would ask her where my father was. I would tell her to go and look for him; but I can't remember any of this now. He had left us and I kept asking about him. I was a difficult child. I always fought with my classmates—they assumed I was a little retarded. My teacher used to let me sit by her, to keep me quiet. But later I improved.

I have always wanted to be the first in everything—at kindergarten, at dancing, at school, in the family. If I came second, I wasn't happy about it. Only first place mattered to me, otherwise I would get angry; I would cry. That's the way I was. I've always wanted the best for myself; the best clothes, the best shoes. And my mother would reprimand me, saying: "Why are you like that? We're not a wealthy family! What's so special about you?" She would sometimes beat me, but it never got her anywhere. I was very young and it just wouldn't sink in.

Before, life in Vladivostok was very different from life in Moscow. Where I come from, a lot of people work on board ship, and this gave them the opportunity to buy fine clothes and quality items in foreign countries. The father of a friend of mine was a sailor, and every time he returned home, he would bring us gifts, from Singapore or from Malaysia, for example. And we'd be thrilled. He would tell us stories about other cities, and he'd have a stock of postcards with him.

At Moscow Airport, when they made the announcement for passengers to board the plane for Vladivostok, it was evident that the best and most fashionably dressed travellers were those bound there, because before, it was only in Vladivostok that you could buy expensive clothes. Everything is changing now in Vladivostok. Nothing ever changed before. New blocks of flats have been built, and new shops. During the Soviet regime, there was no necessity for things to change. Now lots of people come to Vladivostok looking for work, for drugs and for prostitutes. The people here aren't happy about the fact that a lot of 'undesirables' have come to stay. Crime is rife, and we don't like that either. We used to do business with other countries, but we never acquired their bad habits.

If you happen to be a tourist, I would take you first to Svetlanskaya Street. We have the port and the town center where everyone loves to stroll, especially at weekends. Youngsters love to play the guitar, drink beer and get into brawls. Then, let me take you to where I live. It's just fifteen minutes from the beach; you can walk along the shore. There's a long road that runs beside the ocean, and most of the time there are high waves there. It's not a sandy beach but there are bars there—you can eat, drink and watch the waves crashing into the shore through the windows. Now that I live far away I miss the great expanse of ocean I was used to since my childhood; everything seems small to me in Europe.

Further to the south, there's the large island called Russky Island; a twenty minute journey by boat. It's very big, and there are some fine spots to visit there! Before, it was off limits because it was a military zone, but I used to go there with my mother and stepfather, because they had a permit. It had a Research Centre, a fine-looking place and very clean. Nowadays anyone can go there; and it isn't that clean any more.

We have lots of Chinese in Vladivostok, now. They come in their huge buses to Svetlanskaya Street, which used to be called Lenin Street. Vladivostok doesn't have that many tourist spots. Well, actually, if I think about it, there are some fine places, like the highest point in town. From there you have a view of the whole of Vladivostok. It's particularly beautiful in the evening, when the lights are on. We call this place the 'Funicular', because you get there by a funicular, or cable railway. Even today, if you happen to meet a man, he'll take you up there, especially at night time.

We could also pay a visit to the Kamchatka, since I have a friend there who's invited me. It's a plane journey of a little over two hours from Vladivostok. There's a television compere who's been everywhere on the globe, and he reckons Kamchatka to be the most beautiful place in the world. We call it the Switzerland of Russia, because of its fine mountains where you can go skiing. There are also hot springs where you can sit in the warm water. There is snow everywhere and forests with tall trees.

Lots of Japanese also come to Vladivostok. They like Russian girls. There are plenty of marriage bureaus, and many Japanese men are out to get a Russian wife. But if they marry, they'll go back and live in Japan. Once I met a couple of Japanese men. We went out with a girlfriend of mine to a night club, and they didn't know how to order their food because they didn't speak Russian. My friend had worked in Japan, and she could speak a little Japanese. She helped them out and they were so pleased. "How nice it is to have a girl to help us!" They took us out for a drink and a meal, then we went on a brief tour of the city. They bought us lots of gifts. We met up again the next day, and they came to my flat; my mother cooked for them and we took photos, too.

I had my first proper relationship with a man when I was seventeen, when I went on my first trip out. My stepfather bought me the tickets for a week's cruise. This man was a sailor from Vladivostok, and worked on a ship. I told him I was twenty-one. Afterwards, he really and truly fell in love with me. At the time, he drove a fine looking yellow car, and was allowed to travel to any country in the world. Every time he came back from a voyage, he would buy me clothes. I was seventeen and he twenty-five. I can't say now that I loved him. Well, maybe I did... I was very young and very foolish. But later I lost my mind over a 60 year old man who was a waiter and was also ugly. Except I did not find him ugly. My mother was worried and took me to see a psychologist who said, "It is all your father's fault since he left you and now you are looking for a father." But that waiter was also gay and when I realized it I wept for two days.

I had Europe on my mind: Switzerland, Spain, Italy, France. For us in Vladivostok, a European, a foreigner, is always a novelty. A Frenchman touring the world on his bicycle turned up in Vladivostok. He was in the papers with his photo on the front page, but then they stole his bicycle.

Westerners sometimes arrive on military ships, and stay for only a few days. Often they are military men themselves. They go to the night clubs and stroll about in their white uniforms and the girls can't wait to talk to them. "Can we have a photo taken together?" If you're a Westerner, people will go out of their way to make contact with you. They are used to seeing ships coming and going, and they have the feeling that there is always something wonderful beyond the ocean.

When I was sixteen, an American ship, the *Rubin Jane*, came into port. I was at school in 1989; after school, I would go and buy ice cream and cakes. Once, I had ordered too much and when I asked for the bill, I discovered I didn't have enough money. There was an American standing behind me, but I was so shy about it that I couldn't open my mouth to speak, and I was about to cry when he said, "Okay, I'll pay for you." My English was pathetic. Then he began to talk to me. I apologized and thanked him, and he asked me where we could meet. We fixed a date at a kiosk on the beach. He came along, and we went on seeing each other for several days, as friends, not exactly as lovers, as I was too young. And we kept in touch. He wrote me several letters and my stepfather wrote back for me.

When I went to China to buy clothes to sell, I took on a man who acted as my guide, and I paid him, because nobody there speaks English. Once they realise you're Russian, they ask you if you need help. One of them once said to me, "I'll help you free of charge." Every time I went there, he would do everything for me, buy me flowers, souvenirs. I asked him, "Is it true that you have restaurants where they serve dog?" And he said, "Of course." Then I asked him if he had eaten any himself, and he replied, "Of course." I asked him what dog tasted like, and he said, "Delicious!" I told him that for us Russians, the very idea of eating dog is horrifying; and he replied, "But it's absolutely delicious!"

The Chinese border is relatively close—a six-hour bus ride. At the border, there isn't exactly what you could call a Russian town; more of a village, Gradekova. It has several hotels now, whereas before there was only one, and a run-down one at that. If you arrive towards evening, you spend the night in Gradekova; then, the following morning you enter China by train—barely a two-hour journey. When in China, every now and then you hear someone say "Hello!" If you ask for information, half a dozen people gather round you. They look at you as if you're a superstar. And yet no one understands what you are saying, and they all laugh.

The thing that struck me most three years ago, in 2002, was the utter chaos. Everywhere hordes of people and traffic—cars motorbikes, bicycles—deafening noise, hotels where they don't even make up the beds. Once I asked the maid if she would change the sheets. "Not to worry," she said, "they've been slept in by Russians." I didn't give a damn who'd slept in them!

In some hotels they would ask me from what hour to what hour I needed the room. And when I left, another guest would take my place. Of course, they didn't change the sheets. I always carried spare sheets with me. In some hotels there was a tap but no water. The bathroom, at the end of the corridor, was often out of order. In winter, when it was very cold, you could poo in the corridor, because the following morning it would be shovelled up by the cleaning staff. In the meantime it had frozen solid and didn't smell.

At the restaurant, there were always two or three waiters watching to see how I managed with my chopsticks. You've got to learn the odd word of Chinese, though, or else you don't get to eat. I usually pointed to someone in the vicinity who was eating ravioli. But that's not good enough for them. You've got to specify how much ravioli you want, and they ask you in Chinese. You reply by counting on your fingers, and wait for the order to arrive. After a while, they come back and ask you what you want inside your ravioli. They don't understand, even when you make gestures. Once, I tried in a thousand different ways to ask for the bill. Then I opened my wallet and asked "How much?" And they went on laughing.

Sooner or later, everyone gets hit by the "Chinese syndrome". If you don't adapt to their way of using their brain, you risk turning schizoid and killing them all after your first week there. Then everywhere and anywhere there's always someone hawking and spitting. But anyway, I like Chinese food and you get a generous portion. Not like Switzerland, where you're served a mere sample. No one leaves their plate empty; there's always something left on it. However, I don't believe they throw anything away. Every time I went to eat, I imagined I was being served someone else's leftovers.

The Chinese are hard workers. Some even set up their beds inside their shops, which stay open twenty-four hours a day. They know how to do business. They can do anything—build, clean, sell. Not like us lazy Russians. The Russians object: "Why do they come to our country?" I personally think it's a good thing. They sell products dirt cheap; they are there at the market even when it's freezing cold. There are poor people amongst us who cannot afford to buy from the supermarkets, whereas they can shop at the Chinese market. Old people too. But selling cheaply, for Russians, means that the goods are not up to standard!

When I finished my studies, I began working at the Institute of Marine Biology—for a pittance! I earned no more than a hundred dollars a month. So I took on two jobs at once: the Institute; then to China to buy clothes to sell. At that time it was common for girls to work, let's say, in Japan, or in other countries abroad, as dancers or in other occupations. They'd come home with stacks of money. I was envious of all those girls who met rich men on their holidays. Once a girlfriend of mine said, "There's an opportunity to work as a dancer in a club in Hong Kong."

"Are you sure it's dancing only? We're not going to end up as prostitutes, are we? People buying and selling us?"

"Don't worry, now, because this agency takes on only professional dancers. If you want to come, you must tell me straight away, as we are leaving the day after tomorrow."

I spent a sleepless night. I'd been given just one day to think it over. My mother worked all night on my costume. And so I left for Hong Kong. My stepfather was so angry with me. "You are a scientist," he said, "and you must stay and work in Russia. You can't go and be a dancer!" And so I cried, but I left all the same.

I didn't like living in Hong Kong; I cried every single day and was terribly lonely. No one wanted to be friends with me, only colleagues. As always, there was very little money, even if more than in Russia. But then I realised that if I wanted to earn more, I'd have to start going with men, otherwise I'd have to live on a mere five hundred dollars a month. At the end of one of our shows, a Swiss man asked me if I wanted to go with him. But at that time I thought, "Oh, to go with a man I don't know!"

My boss said I was to go with our clients. I said no. Once, my mother rang him from Russia, complaining that he was forcing me to go with them. And so I thought: "If I go with this Swiss here, he'll ask me, 'Why don't you go with the others?'"

The Swiss, whose name was Jerry, suggested we meet after the show, or better still, the following day; that way, nobody would get to know about it. I said to him: "If you want, you can have lots of girls; and I can help you choose."

"No, I want you and you only."

"I'm sorry, but I can't."

"Okay, so what do you want to do?"

"I'd like to go to the zoo and see the pandas."

It's a large park with tropical plants and birds. And so we went there, and had lunch together, too. Then he said to me, "Now what would you like?"

"I want to see the precipice and gorge where Thelma and Louise committed suicide." I meant it as a joke, of course, but he answered, "Okay, let's go and get our visas." I thought he was joking too. Instead, he succeeded somehow in getting me a visa straight away, and within four days, we were on a plane to Los Angeles. Not only was he an industrialist, but also important. Perhaps I shouldn't have placed my trust in him so readily, seeing as I hardly knew him; but I felt instinctively that I could.

From Los Angeles we went to Salt Lake City, in Utah, the Mormon city. Jerry was informed on everything. He explained to me that, at one time, the Mormons were allowed to have several wives. One of the founders had had thirty wives and sixty-six children, and the hotels they stayed in always provided a large bed with several pillows. And yet they put you in prison if they catch you having oral sex! We then hired a car and spent a night in Bluff, in a motel in the desert. In the morning, there wasn't a soul about, and we went and had breakfast at a self-service place. You paid by placing the exact sum shown on the price tags, in a basket.

Then we went on to Mexican Hut, where they shot the final scene of the film *Thelma and Louise*. A road full of sharp bends takes you up to a sort of plateau, off the edge of which the two drove into the gorge below. What a sensation! What an emotional impact! I closed my eyes and imagined myself diving off the edge, just like Thelma and Louise! Jerry told me of another place in the States where they go to commit suicide: the Brooklyn Bridge. You find people there walking up and down the Bridge, on the lookout for would-be suicides; and if a 'suspect' car stops, they approach it with the intention of dissuading its driver from going through with it. Anyway, before proceeding to commit suicide, it's a good idea not to leave your engine running. One man who changed his mind at the last minute found they'd stolen his car.

Jerry afterwards went back to Switzerland, and I returned to Vladivostok. He'd insisted on taking me back to Switzerland with him, but I'd said no; I don't know why. We'd had a good time together. Perhaps I saw him as being too old for me. More like a father figure and this was not good. I'd simply left him my address in Russia: 355/12 Russkaya Street. And that was all. Goodbye, and that's it.

I resumed work at the Institute. Then, in January, I received a letter from Switzerland. He'd written me: "Where are you and how are you? I want to know what's happened to you, how you are getting on." Round about that time, I'd started using Internet, and so we were able to be in touch more often.

I kept a dog. I loved her an awful lot, but she got cancer. That nearly killed me, and I simply wasn't able to imagine my life without my dog. And so he would ask me how I was, and I would reply, "Oh, I am so unhappy because I think my dog is going to die, and I don't want her to die. I shan't be able to live without her." Each time, he would find the right words to comfort me. Then he said: "Perhaps you need some money for your dog." And he sent me some. Then I went to the vet's and had two operations done on her. First one, then the other. I bought stacks of medicines; I tried everything, but to no avail; eventually she died. I went through a bad spell—I wasn't eating, I shut myself up in my bedroom, I simply wanted to die. I stopped going to work. My parents wept and said, "What can we do for our daughter?" And this man kept calling me, asking me how I was.

"I'm very ill. I think I'm going to die." He wrote me some lovely letters. He said he understood how I felt. He wrote, saying, "Can I buy you tickets for Switzerland?" My parents, too, encouraged me to go, because they saw how dejected I was. And so off I went.

Switzerland is a beautiful place, very clean, and people smile at each other, even if they're complete strangers. In the lift, too. And they talk spontaneously, even if they don't know each other. We'd go out and I'd talk to everyone I met. Jerry would ask me if I knew them. "No, I don't know him." But for me it came natural to talk. He was jealous. He would say, "They say hello to you because they can tell you're a foreigner." "But I say hello because *they* say hello." In Russia, too, you don't talk to people you don't know; you talk only among friends and certainly not to strangers in the lift unless you need to ask something. In Switzerland it's "Hey, how are you? How are you doing? Okay. See you. Bye!"

He took me everywhere; to the mountains, to Geneva, to Lugano. Everywhere was spotlessly clean. In Switzerland, everybody lives comfortably—people, animals, birds. And what I like in particular are the flowers on every single balcony of every single house. I like the mounted police, too; I'd never seen them before. In Russia we have people who are gay, and gay clubs; but we don't publicise them. In Zurich, two men have no problem kissing in public.

Everybody spoke German and I was shy. And so he said to me, "You mustn't be shy; you've got to say, 'I'm sorry, but I don't understand German. Can you speak English, please?'" I once tried this out in a supermarket where I'd gone on my own. I began speaking English; but, although everyone speaks English, you've got to tell them first that you don't speak German. Everybody is really kind, even when you're asking for information.

I loved all those swans, too. Beautiful! And each day I would buy bread and go and feed them at the lake. We paid a visit to his sister's place—her house is simply beautiful. She is married and has two children. She looks after the house and the garden. She cooks well and made pancakes specially for me, and a cake, too. Then I felt cold and she lit the fire for me; when I had a bout of coughing, she prepared a medicinal drink—just like my mother. Then her husband told me that they had been together for forty years. "Well, it stands to reason," I said. "With a wife like yours, you can stick together for ever."

"No, with a husband like mine!" she retorted. I was on the verge of crying. What a lovely, perfect family! She also said that, with or without my Swiss boyfriend, I would always be welcome in their house; "I think of you as a daughter." They tended to my every need, and were genuinely concerned for my wellbeing. If I wasn't okay, they couldn't even get to sleep, especially my boyfriend's brother-in-law.

My man's flat, too, is lovely and very clean. He's very much on the ball. One of the rooms is set aside for his office. There's the computer, his desk, a table with photos of me on it, the odd box, newspapers, Playboy. All very neat and clean and tidy.

I don't know if I could ever again have a moment so perfect in my life as when Jerry asked me to let my mother come to live with us also.

I was used to filling up my suitcase, putting everything inside, even some winter clothes when going to the tropics. With Jerry I never pack suitcases when we go off somewhere. For him it's all so easy. He says: "Where's the problem? You go to the airport and simply catch a plane." We buy our clothes when we land. Each time, we buy everything from scratch, even including toothbrushes, toothpaste, scissors and shaving cream. He likes to travel with ease, moving from one city to another like from one district to another in the same city. The world is his home. He says, "we are citizens of the world". We like to feel like foreigners and tenants of the world at the same time. Just to look at a train or a plane is our passion. Usually we avoid the tourist marathons, such as visiting ten monuments in one day or crossing the desert by bike. We like to wander aimlessly and indolently through the cities of the world, to spend the time just to look at the people, to sit at the cafe, to chat with everyone from street vendors to hotel porters, to the various characters that we meet everywhere, in airports, in hotels, in restaurants.

Jerry is an uncommon man, a little strange, but I love him so much. He likes to dress me, to buy suits for me. We spend much time window shopping. He enjoys making me wear unusual, funny or overly sexy suits, because he likes when other men look at me with desire.

We went to Tuba City in Arizona to see the footprints of dinosaurs that date back seventy million years. They are to be found on the Native American Reservation of the Navajo tribe. You simply ask one of the members of the tribe, and he'll act as a guide. You have to ask him nicely, though.

The first real tiffs with Jerry began at Dubai. We risked missing the plane because I'd wanted to buy a pair of beach sandals and suntan cream. And that annoyed Jerry to no end. "Where do you think you're going? The moon? Couldn't you have bought them on the spot? Seeing as you've got little or no experience of travelling, why don't you listen to someone who's travelled the world and has far more experience than you?" We quarrelled because the evening we arrived, he didn't want to dine out, and made do with an ice cream; whereas I wanted to go to a good restaurant. Travelling for me is an occasion, like Christmas or the New Year—a solemn event to immortalise and save for posterity. And so I just couldn't accept the fact that he had no appetite that day.

I wanted us to do everything together, like having breakfast in the morning, and going down together to the hotel dining room. That day it was forty-five degrees in Dubai. A scorching heat! Our driver said, "It's not too hot today; the other day it was fifty-four degrees." Then he stopped the car, picked a few dates from the trees on the roadside, and gave them to us. Delicious! In the hotel foyer, behind the reception desk, there was a huge aquarium with sharks in it. Then we went into town. A vendor of fresh orange juice, a Pakistani, informed us that it was early yet. The bazaar comes to life in the evening. So we went off to the beach. The water was clean and very warm. You didn't have time to sweat: it simply evaporated off your skin there and then. Basically, it's a kind of heat that's bearable, that's if it doesn't kill you!

Every single shop is staffed by Asians. The Arabs don't work. You can pick out an Arab family straight away—lots of fat kids trundling along with video games or professionally wrapped expensive boutique items, and in the rear, a human form draped in black: the woman. And leading the caravan, a man with a white robe in striking contrast to his dark body hair!

Even the buses carry only Asian passengers, no Arabs. There are shops of every kind: top-notch boutiques, jewellers selling diamonds, sapphires, emeralds and other precious stones, and gold of a deep yellow, bordering on red; all your top fashion designers—Armani, Versace, Valentino. And everywhere glass skyscrapers, either completed or under construction. It's one big race to be top, to produce the biggest, the most handsomely designed and, most important of all, the most expensive skyscraper. I felt I was living inside a fairy tale or a children's book. We saw the 'Burj Al Arab', a sail-shaped hotel, the tallest in the world at over 300 metres with 60 floors! It is on a tiny island connected by a bridge. Each suite is on two floors—335 square metres per suite! And there is a reception desk on every floor. Now they are building artificial islands in the sea for villas and condos that represent the five continents. They say that the island shaped like the U.S.A. was bought by Michael Jackson for 32 billion dollars (or perhaps it was millions, I don't know…).

Jerry was a perfect guide. He explained to me that in the Emirates there are no drug addicts, criminals or outcasts. The foreigner can be neither poor nor a misfit—he has to be perfect. He cannot interfere with the life of the Arab in any way.

At the hotel restaurant I was wearing a tight-fitting black, semi-transparent suit with a long slit up the side. I was far too sexy. An Arab couple was sitting next to me and Jerry. In order to eat she had to brush aside her chador and try to get her spoon up to her mouth beneath it.

There are religious restrictions and prohibitions, particularly for the women, but in our hotel, as foreigners, we could do whatever we wanted, including drinking alcohol. After all, for them you are an infidel, a sinner. Since they are all Muslims, it is also considered a sin to carry wine to the table. But because the waiter has to work for a living, he is exonerated from having this considered as a sin. At the same time the Arab wants to be part of the international 'jet set' of sinners. From this year, 2007, there will be Formula One racing in Dubai, but those scantily clad 'grid girls' that you always see at the conclusion of the race congratulating the drivers will be absent, and there will not even be champagne for the winners. Maybe they will shower them with Coca Cola.

Then, in the evening, we hit town again, this time in a hired car. Almost immediately, we had a run-in with an Arab. We were cruising along, when, suddenly, a huge car shot out from a side street. We didn't hit it because we were doing a mere 30 kph. Jerry gives him this look, as if to say, "what an idiot!" We started off and the Arab began following us. He kept on overtaking and stopping in front of us. Once, he even got out of the car. We backed away and drove off... with him following us. "Look at him," said Jerry, "he's barely five foot tall, with his white frock, high shoes and a table cloth on his head. If I whack him across the face, he'll go round and round like a spinning top for a quarter of an hour."

Jerry was in the habit of going to the pool every day and swimming for four hours. He could have lifted him up with one hand. We wondered why it was that he was so cocksure of himself. He must have been carrying a weapon. We took the tunnel that goes underneath the Creek, the narrow strip of water that divides the new city from the old. And we finally managed to shake him off.

That evening I quarrelled with Jerry. He wanted to stay in our room and read a book. How can you retire to your room at nine in the evening to read a book when you've just arrived in Dubai? I got very angry because I wanted us to wait together till midnight and see in the new day, which happened to be my birthday! But he went on reading, and I went out and slammed the door.

I began walking about the hotel like a lost idiot. I had gone out without my makeup, and very casually dressed: jeans and a pair of gym shoes. I wanted to cry. I was seated in the foyer ignoring the usual complement of ogling males, when a waiter came up to me and said, "His Excellency the Sheik invites you to his table." There and then I imagined a courtesy invitation to some celebration, a birthday, perhaps, or a wedding. And without asking questions, I followed the waiter into the hotel tea room. It was almost totally in the dark, very dimly lit in fact, so much so that I tripped on the edge of a carpet.

There were six men seated upon cushions around a low table, soft lighting, red fabric covering the walls and unobtrusive Arab background music. As I approached, the Sheik sent the men away with a snap of his fingers. At almost the same moment, several waiters entered the room, carrying trays of strawberries, cherries and Champagne. I thought at once that I had been taken for a prostitute. I started to inform him of the misunderstanding when, with the gallant air of a gentleman, he came out with a rather shocking revelation. He had been following me all day long because he wanted to invite me and my man to a cocktail party in his villa. So he was the man in the limousine! He said he had noticed me at the restaurant in the hotel and had got his chauffeur to follow me. He was a good-looking man of about 30, tall, dark, with moustache and glasses.

He apologized for this somewhat eccentric behaviour. He wasn't in the habit of following women, but for me he was prepared to give virtually anything I wanted, just to have me even for a single night. He asked me the way a child asks for a sweet. He had a truly hypnotic gaze and had succeeded in rousing my curiosity. I followed him, more than anything because I wanted to get my own back on Jerry. After all, I was being offered an evening with intriguing prospects, as opposed to what that idiot who had already gone to bed could offer.

He parked his car between two villas. One was his and the other belonged to his brother. They had erected a black plastic curtain in the middle, so that one could not see the wives of the other. And so the Sheik took me into his house: It had an imposing entrance hall with two staircases, one to the left and one to the right—all in pink marble! A gold and crystal chandelier in the centre, an indoor and an outdoor swimming pool! He led me into a room, along the length and breadth of which stretched a massive wardrobe filled exclusively with women's clothes, of all sizes. It was the entire season's collection—bathing costumes, dressing gowns, lingerie. He admitted to being a fashion freak. He attended the shows of all the major fashion designers, and would buy the clothes he most liked.

He said that one of his passions was to clothe a woman. All the clothes I wanted would be mine, on condition, though, that I dressed and undressed in front of him. He was very ceremonious towards me, as if he considered me an object of value. Rather than in my clothes he was interested in my naked body. But I didn't object to the idea of being an object of pure contemplation, and so I began to undress. He wanted me to wear some articles of clothing that had just arrived. I also had to take off my knickers, because a pair of close-fitting pants could be worn only with tights. While he was watching me, quite unable to hide the fact that he was hankering after me, I was gazing into his eyes. They were the only feature about him that really interested me. I felt that his eyes not only gave away an intense desire, but the fact also that he was keeping it very much in check.

Jerry also had taken the time to observe my body with such interest. Of course he had shown desire and excitement, but without any degree of obsession, or the kind of ecstatic, morbid contemplation which characterized the Arab. When I realized that I was beginning to get excited, I decided to get dressed quickly and return to my hotel. He didn't insist, and like the perfect gentleman that he appeared to be, he accompanied me back to my hotel.

Before going out, I asked him if I could see his other wives; he just smiled. My question was for him totally absurd. As we went back to my hotel in his limousine, I asked again about his wives. He explained to me that while they considered a Western woman as a status symbol; the 'true' wife is at home. To sum up his way of thinking, he can take the liberty of stepping into our world but he does not allow you to enter his.

At one point he suddenly stopped the limousine in an isolated place and he kissed me, with a speed that did not give me time to think. I could almost not break away; then he started to undress me and kiss me everywhere. Then I looked at the clock and was frightened.

There, in front of my hotel, right at the entrance, was Jerry, all worked up. He had seen me step out of the limousine. It was about three in the morning. He made such a scene, first in front of the Arab, then in our hotel room, and also he slapped me. I told him the whole story; then we made love.

We celebrated my birthday in a romantic under-water restaurant that we reached by submarine.

Now that I am thirty-one, if I had to go back in time and live my past life over again, I wouldn't be happy, I'm sure. I'm not the person I was anymore, because I have enjoyed a better existence. But still, I wouldn't want to change one single moment of my life, like when we went to pick berries by our country house. We made jam and also froze them for winter. When I was young, I was immensely happy and carefree.

A Psychological Perspective

The motivation for her to leave her country does not merely revolve around a need for a better standard of living, but rather a desire to discover a world long forbidden and often fantasized. The rich man she meets fulfills a childhood dream of waiting for a father who never arrived. Behind the dream of a powerful man, there is also a need for boundless love.

15

From Italy to Siberia
A second chance at life

A man from Turin, age 46:

I had read about isolated, icebound villages in remote places, without electricity, lost in enormous spaces into which no one would, or would want, to enter. Some geologists, as late as the 1982 expedition to Siberia, found a family who knew nothing about the fall of the Czars or the birth of the Communist Party. I was wondering how they could survive their impoverished condition, with a temperature between minus ten and minus forty degrees. I could understand survival in a hot country, where you can sleep outside and eat the fruit that falls from trees. When I proclaimed to my friends that I wanted to move to Siberia, they thought I was crazy.

During the time of the Czars criminals were banished there; even Stalin did the same thing. In addition to criminals, also intellectuals, artists with revolutionary ideas and educated people were sent out there as well. These same exiles would later contribute to the civilizing of Siberian cities.

I left my home, in the province of Turin, Italy, because I had become a bum. I didn't eat, I didn't go out and I had lost my will to live. My wife and my son had been killed in a car accident, and a few months after that I had discovered that my wife had been having an affair with another man for years, and everyone knew it but me. Maybe even my son knew it, but I will never know that now. Wanting to know the truth, I tried to meet her lover, but when I phoned to talk to him, the person who answered the phone said that he was away. Later he moved away and I could no longer find or keep track of him.

If I could have awakened without remembering anything, I would thankfully have done so immediately. I longed to erase the memories, to start from scratch in a place where no one knew me. Since my life had lost any value, I felt that I could conquer any danger now. I subconsciously looked for extreme situations, challenging the limits of human endurance, which could distract me from the obsessive thoughts that were giving me no respite. So, perhaps because of some reminiscences from school days, Siberia aroused in me a certain attraction.

When you are burdened with a family, you often think, "If I die, what they will do without me?" You are constantly aware of things that could endanger them. Because of this you feel obligated to return home and you abhor any kind of risk. You become a clenched-tooth coward, defending the safety and serenity of your family. While I lived for my wife and my son, I was never adventurous, but merely a methodical man, too limited within, and by, my finite world. Although I was well off and lacked for nothing, home, family and work became the complete focus of my life. I was an engineer in a construction equipment company, respected and appreciated for my work.

It was now the end of October, 2000. I was at the Moscow train station waiting for the Trans-Siberian train, which left every Friday at ten minutes to midnight going all the way to Vladivostok, near Japan. The train crosses all of Siberia and covers more than nine thousand kilometers in about a week. Generally Russians don't like the Trans-Siberian train because they consider it uncomfortable and used only by people who don't have the money to fly. There is also a story that once the train was stopped and the passengers robbed. Today, however, things have changed and there are private coaches for tourist groups, with the quality of a four star hotel. The train also boasts a nutritionist, who chooses local products at each stage of the trip to prepare food on board.

I wanted to lose myself in a train that rolled thousands and thousands of miles from Europe to Asia. I wanted to be lost for days and days, traveling across the vast Russian steppe, with the feeling of leaving everything behind me, not knowing or caring where I was going. I wished to lose the story of my life in the great spaces of Asia and to be dissolved in its snow. "My wife should see me now!" I thought. She often kidded me because, for vacation, I would rent the same house with parking, in the same locality, two months in advance. "Woe to change!" she teasingly quipped. "You won't even try a new beach. Unless you knew the bartender, what would you do if the coffee has a different flavour?"

There were two different routes to Vladivostok. The shortest route passed through Mongolia to the south and the other one crossed the whole of Siberia. I explored the cars of the train that passed through Mongolia. There were rather luxurious first class Chinese carriages, some even featuring mobile showers. In the end I opted for the more Spartan Russian coaches, because I wanted to see the real Siberia. Tickets could be purchased for first, second or third class. Third class was overcrowded and was probably used only by people making short journeys. It was inconceivable to think of anyone making it all the way to Vladivostok in those conditions. Second class had compartments with four beds but I chose the first class compartment with just two beds. In my mental state, I preferred not to have too many people around me. I purchased a ticket only to Irkutsk since I didn't know if I would, or could, continue past that. Irkutsk is located right in the heart of Siberia, just a few kilometers from Lake Baikal, about four days' travel from Moscow.

While on the train the time is always Moscow time and the dining car follows that schedule even seven time zones away. You might have dinner at three in the morning after having lunched at eight in the evening. All long distance rail systems in Russia use Moscow time all of the time, though local trains do use local time. I didn't give a damn what time it was, as I ate when I was hungry and stared out of the window the rest of the time, while the train crossed the vast, uninhabited and inhospitable expanse of land.

The landscape of birch trees and hills covered with snow seemed to be in a constant never-ending loop. It was like seeing everything blurred and out of focus in front of my eyes, yet hauntingly, in the foreground, hovered an image of my wife. I suppose if I had taken a rocket and had landed on Mars, it would have been the same. I tried to uncover the real her; I wanted to know why she had done what she did. The absurd thing is that I had never noticed anything wrong. For me, our relationship seemed wonderful and she appeared to be happy with me. Could it be possible that she had only pretended all along? I just could not understand. Had I lived a life of illusion, a false reality? She was now gone and without even an explanation; I started to despise her. I began to hate a dead person!

I pictured myself back home, catching her with her lover, imagining what I would say at that moment, forming a sort of soliloquy in my mind. And then I saw my son and we talked, just as if he was next to me. I mentally repeated to myself the speeches I was forming and without realizing it I became estranged from everything, excitement overtook me and I reproached him. Abruptly I awakened and stood, paralyzed, gazing out at the vast nothingness. In the distant background I heard the sound of a Russian radio, reminding me that I was now out of my country, far from a past that was still alive, yet which seemed as if it had never existed, like many of the images that flowed by the train's fast-moving windows.

In the train's saloon there were people of various nationalities. In any other frame of mind I might have made lots of friends, as we had many days to spend together. Despite my intention to remain aloof, a Hungarian musician about my age spoke to me, sensing that something was tormenting me. In making conversation I told him that my ticket was only to Irkutsk, but that I was going on to Siberia because I was thinking of living there. He looked at me as if he were looking at a UFO. "Take special care of anyone who approaches you," he said. "There is a lot of crime there and also many drug addicts who need money to buy heroin."

I had not even thought about the crime issue, which surprised me since at any other time I would have taken proper precautions. The 'old' me would have done detailed research on the hotels, restaurants, prices, itineraries, risks, and places that were more or less safe. And this indifference to everything gave me an odd and unusual sense of freedom from care. The weight of problems, precautions, the things had to be done had always been a burden on my shoulders, but not now. Now there was just me and the train, hurtling at high speed through inhospitable and almost uninhabited lands.

People were selling a lot of things, both within the train and on the platforms where the train stopped. I bought some food from a local vendor, which was cheaper and more genuine than that in the dining car or in official shops. Vendors entered on one stop and left on the next, and waited for the next train back. They sold practically everything, every time. "They give a bribe to the head man on the train," the Hungarian told me.

We encountered a railroad engineer strolling through the train, selling glasses to earn a supplement to his salary, which was very low compared to those who worked in private companies. The musician explained to me that it was normal to meet college graduates who had arranged to do menial work for the same purpose. I asked him if he thought that the situation in Russia was better now or before the dissolution of the USSR. In response he cited an illuminating example. "Caged animals in zoos," he said, "have plenty to eat and a safe place to sleep. They even have sex, yet they are sad because they are bored and trapped—and that's communism. Instead, in the jungle, they risk being killed daily and have to kill to survive; but they are free. The law of the jungle is like capitalism. There is nothing as bloody as life in the jungle but the animals want to be there, because they have to be free."

Apart from some sporadic conversation, I spent most of my time looking out of the window. Sometimes scenes of misery and abandoned tenements would mar the countryside, and, if I could have, I would have stayed on that train without stopping anymore. Even the idea of getting out and looking for a hotel in Irkutsk was beginning to weigh on me. I was an external observer of all that was passing by and around me. On the train there was also somebody selling his personal objects, such as bracelets, necklaces and other family things and this also depressed me for some reason.

A few hours before reaching Irkutsk I met a man named Boris in the dining car. He too was getting off at Irkutsk and he seemed very interested in the fact that I was Italian. Using the alphabet, he began to list all the Italian characters he knew, from Berlusconi to Celentano. He had gotten on the train at Yekaterinburg, near the Ural Mountains, which marked the border between Europe and Asia. He dreamed of getting out of Russia too, because, being of Polish origin, and with the fall of communism, people had become a bit racist toward him. He was a frail little man, about 50 years old, of dark complexion. He puzzled over the fact that there was nobody waiting for me in Irkutsk, and that I didn't know where I was going. He was probably thinking that I was just a little crazy, but what would he have thought if I had told him that I was running away from my entire previous life? Proclaiming that nothing in life happens by chance, he assured me that I had chosen the right place. Something subconsciously had brought me there and maybe one day I would find what I was looking for. So in that moment I thought, "will Siberia give me the answer to what it was that I was looking for?" But in dwelling on it more, the concept seemed to me to be absurd.

Boris offered to take me with him to the village where he lived and stay as long as I wanted or needed, until I found better accommodation. His persistence felt a bit too forceful, and he didn't seem entirely sincere. He could have taken me anywhere, robbed or even killed me, but at that moment I was only a passive observer of my own life and quite unable to take any initiative. And so I accepted his proposal.

We rented a Jeep with driver and the 250 kilometer journey from Irkutsk to his village seemed interminable. While Boris did his best to distract me, I forced myself to hide my irritation, despite the fact that he was smiling all of the time and flashing his yellow teeth. He pointed out some elderly women with rags wrapped around their faces, selling hot tea, hot potatoes, home-made cakes and pies along the road. "They are called *babushka*," he said, "and they spend all day on the road in the cold, thinking themselves successful when they have scraped together even a little money. In the beginning of autumn they also sell apples, berries and cucumbers. People buy them to take home; they are cheaper than in the city. Some people from the city drive some distance out especially to buy these things." It became apparent that he had appointed himself as my personal servant, guide and guardian.

I pretended to be interested while Boris was trying to show me 'the sights', even though I was not in the mood and there was little to be seen. Lots of snow, a few factories, one-storied wooden houses with peaked roofs and people lined up in front of some kiosk did not make it into the Michelin Guide of my mind. At an open market and at thirty degrees below zero, there was a man licking an ice cream—at least I think I saw him—that was a strange sight. As we continued our travel, signs of life were becoming much rarer.

Next to a kind of prefab building we noticed some wolf pelts hung up. "They make hats out of the pelts," Boris explained. He went on to say that villages can be attacked at night by packs of wolves. They burrow under fences or jump from rooftops into the stables and slaughter the animals. The inhabitants form armed groups to inspect and protect the surroundings and one time they succeeded in exterminating eighteen wolves in one night. I felt that, since I was by now in Boris's hands anyway, I might as well give him what I thought he was looking for. After confessing to not having a lot of money, I proposed hiring him as a guide, to assure him some profit. He agreed gladly as he had just been dismissed from his last job.

Surrounded by this landscape, of bleached Siberian forest blanketed by endless piles of snow, it seemed that we would never arrive. The word 'Siberia' means sleeping or dormant earth; that which is motionless or immovable. This linguistic interpretation did not give justice to the reality of these bleak surroundings. I imagined it as an abandoned planet, far away from everything, without time or memories. By now the landscape offered nothing interesting to see, because my fatigue took precedence over all other sensory inputs. All I desired in my groggy state was to close my eyes, rest in a warm place and awaken the next day to see that I had already arrived.

When Boris told me that we had reached our destination, I saw some wooden houses and wished only for a room with a cozy warm bed. I was even annoyed by the delay that resulted from the warm welcome that Boris's family gave me. There were introductions to his delicate, small-framed mother, his fat, bleached blonde wife and his intensely freckled son of about fifteen. They all stared at me to the point where I felt like some rare and recently captured wild animal. The fact that the house consisted of only one big room reflected the degree of their poverty. Exposed electrical wires, doors without handles, and a wall with various things hung from it, such as rags, pots, furs and all their clothes, were their house decorations. It was apparent that they cooked, ate, socialized and slept in this one room. A large bed, supported by four tree stumps and consisting of a big board, was where all four of them obviously slept.

At the table, before eating, Boris would say a short prayer such as "Lord, give us the strength to respect your commandments, to act with love... and have pity on our unworthy souls... in the name of Jesus Christ, Amen." I was moved by the sincerity of the recitation.

Next to their house there was an animal shelter and a small tool shack where they found a place for me. There was a bed that barely fit into the room and a small heating stove. The bed was made up of rags and old furs stuffed within a wretched blanket. There were no sheets and under the bed were piled heaps of potatoes and sacks of grain.

Boris invited me for a regenerative bath in the *banya* near his home. (The *banya* is a steam bath created by running water over scorching hot rocks.) For Siberians this is a kind of ritual, sometimes used as a social meeting place. Although I really needed it, I resisted the invitation initially, but when I entered I found it enjoyable. The *banya* is very moist and the temperature of the steam is very hot.

Inside the house, thankfully, it was very warm. Using the *pechka*, a traditional cooking stove, almost any room will warm up quickly. It was hard to believe that the outside temperature was minus thirty. Siberian houses are made of wood, using centuries' old techniques and modern materials are rarely employed. Siberian pine has been found to effectively hold in the heat. Although Boris was always available if I needed anything, I played the role of recluse on my first day, not wanting to talk to anyone.

The desolation of the place had increased my depression, as all I could see from the windows were shabby houses and some scattered, abandoned tools in the snow. The separation from my family and past seemed even greater than ever. I had brought photos with me which detailed everything of my former life—our wedding day, the vacation in Santa Margherita Ligure, my son's First Communion, all of the birthday celebrations, our home and many other small details of my previous life. I was more and more haunted by the memory of my wife, who had always seemed so caring and amiable toward me. I was plagued by the nagging question of how she could possibly have betrayed me as she had. There was a wall of death before me that I couldn't break down! The images of people, drawn by the newspaper announcement, who came to my house and stripped it of its once-loved memories, now formed a dreadful parade in my mind. One took away a chair, another a bed or a lamp; some took knickknacks, one the TV and others some tables. In my memory, I saw drawers pulled out and the clothes and personal items of my wife and son thrown around or piled on the floor like trash. All our rooms had been completely demolished, seemingly dismembered. I saw myself remaining alone in that empty house that had been a symbol of my happy life for almost fifteen years. Only one chair remained, with the photos and letters that my wife had written to me, from when we first met until tragedy struck.

Now here I was, having fled thousands of miles away, in a cabin in the heart of Siberia, haunted by the photos and letters in my hand. I mentally replayed some of the episodes of my past and tried to interpret them through the light of her betrayal, trying to find maybe a phrase or word or hint of something that I had not noticed. I remembered one time watching a TV movie together, in which a woman had betrayed her husband but had then returned and been reconciled to him. While for me the ending was a happy one, she expressed disappointed and was even upset by the outcome. In retrospect maybe she was identifying with that woman, and plans for leaving me were already brewing in her mind. And to think that for years I had not noticed anything! I found it difficult to stop myself from this destructive replaying of scenes from the past.

Boris commented to me that if you can survive the long dark winters here, you can live in continual peace, because life passes very quietly. On the other hand peace and quiet provide little to do. A significant pastime was to go to buy something like toothpaste on one day, while another day getting the shampoo or the milk or a little fruit. When the residents had to buy something more important, they went 'into town', which was indeed an exciting adventure. Once, just to relieve the boredom, I tried repairing a tractor, although I had previously resisted the urge to do so for some time. The difficulty here is learning to use tools in the cold, while encumbered with gloves that prevent you from working properly. Touching a tool barehanded is unthinkable since the skin will stick to the metal, causing you to suffer a 'cold burn'.

I sensed that I had to leave this place soon, but something was holding me back. But what? Since it was winter and the bulk of the work in the fields takes place from April to September, nobody was doing anything in the village. Nothing can be done from October to March anyway, because the place is blanketed with snow. Everywhere you look is a white desert, dotted only by a few circling crows scouting for food. Sometimes you needed to shovel a path through the snow just to reach your neighbour's house. And sometimes it is just too cold to go outside at all. The cold precludes growing or fixing anything, and you cannot build anything because you can't remain outside the house for more than an hour.

How can anyone utilize a period of six months when he can't do anything? He ends up drinking vodka as a pastime because it's hard to stay inside and do nothing for a long period of time. Often the drinking starts in the morning and continues through to evening, and that despite the fact that after 10 or 15 minutes someone will already be drunk. Sometimes I also drank with them and I noticed some very strange things. Under the alcohol's influence, they become euphoric, raising their voices, bickering with each other about anything, singing robustly although usually not well. They will lie down on the snow or pile themselves on top of each other. With inhibitions removed normal behaviour patterns are challenged. It is not uncommon to see one man's wife in the arms of another. Boris informed me that alcohol is intimately linked to the condition of poverty and the misery it causes. Well-off families are rarely affected by the influence of alcohol and so maintain their integrity. Usually their money buys them big houses and maybe even a car. They have no need to, and don't, abuse alcohol. They cultivate plants, breed animals and travel into town to sell them. But the majority of them live very poorly and drink very heavily. This helps them to deaden the reality that they don't wish to confront.

Boris confided to me that in Siberia there are more women than men, because the men drink more, and more often, so the average male life span rarely exceeds 55 years. Drinking vodka is a national problem. Some in the villages made spirits distilled right in their homes, just as many families in the West make wine. It is called *samogon* and it's much stronger than vodka. Yet, according to my host, this apparently insignificant population, despite its alcohol problems, had produced many outstanding people. An old classmate of Boris's was the grandson of an exiled dissident writer. While at school he was a very clever young man and spoke three languages. Today if you met that same person on the street he is most likely lying on a bench, insensitive to the cold, with a death grip on a bottle of vodka. He had become a strange and lonely person, teased by little street urchins, oblivious to what was happening around him. Personally, I was fascinated by him, despite the fact that most thought him unhinged. What impressed me was not only his loneliness but also his independence from what society thought was playing by the rules. Would I end up like this man? He survived with money sent from his sister living in Germany, and yet despite his homeless appearance his body was still quite intact.

The people of Siberian villages have been subjected to scientific studies of their extraordinary endurance. Some of them have been known to do seemingly impossible things, such as working forty-eight hours straight without rest, water or food or after breaking through the ice on the river, swimming in that same river water at a temperature of minus 30. For short periods of time, they can work in the cold and sleep in the snow. After these heroic feats of endurance, the rest of the time is spent doing little but drinking vodka. And that summarizes their way of life.

Even though the people here come across as crude or rough in their ways and somewhat cold socially, beneath that exterior one often finds a surprising and unexpected gentleness of spirit; a facility for emotions, excitement and exaltation can spring into flower at the sight of an adorable wolf cub, for example. When you look closely, you are almost overwhelmed by their spontaneous, genuine warmth. Regularly, when you enter a home, they bring unrequested tea and make every attempt to put you at ease. One immediately notices their robust physical size and is impressed by their tall, statuesque beauty. Boris's wife and her son attended to me continuously in many small ways, while the grandmother, now suffering from arteriosclerosis, repeatedly advised me to be careful of thieves.

I met Boris's daughter, who lived in Irkutsk, one Irina, who was 25 years old. She lived in one of those low housing blocks for working families. Boris and I went to meet her. I saw her approaching, all dressed up, with high heels in the mud, as if the surrounding squalor did not affect her in the least. She was a bus driver. Russian women have this remarkable ability to do the work of men as well as the men can, while at the same time maintaining their complete femininity. Like apparitions from a ghostly novel, they decorate the bleakest of places with elegance, class and grace. The contrast between the refinement of the women and the rudeness of the men surprises many who come to Siberia.

Irina also exhibited a better than average intelligence and ambition, because she planned to open an import-export business. At only 25 she still had ideals and faith rarely found in older Siberians. She confided in me that her salary was only 310 dollars a month and that she had moved to Irkutsk at seventeen. Having faced difficulties and deprivation at first, the people of her village had always come to her rescue. The people who owned the *banya*, for example, were especially kind to her by offering her regular meals.

She philosophized that, in Russia, there is either poverty or wealth but very little middle class. The country is rich in oil but those riches reside in the hands of a few who transfer the money abroad. Poverty is not only the result of a lack of money but also because many Russians still don't understand the basic rules of capitalism. They expect everything to come from the top down, as it had during communism. For this reason the mafia, black-market and prostitution flourish because they offer the illusion of easy money. I was amazed by her maturity.

Because I was the only one who could relate new and different stories, I was becoming the most well-known character of the village. In the evenings they gathered around me as I told them about things that they had never heard of, or knew about. A girl named Ludmila translated my stories with the help of a dictionary, because hardly anyone spoke English. Since the days were long and considering that there was little to do, I developed into a sort of medieval storyteller who told tales of grand undertakings, of other worlds, distant lands and extraordinary journeys. The West for them is so far removed from their reality that it's almost cloaked by a magical aura.

Each night after a few vodkas I became involved in their lively dances. I was fascinated to see them dancing with uncontrollable energy and bursting with irrepressible merriment. In those moments I tried to understand and capture the Siberian soul. There was something in these Russians that eluded me, especially their ability, in almost any situation, to express strong emotions, an overwhelming charge of energy and a zest for life.

There was a cafe-restaurant near the village, with a huge room where dancing took place every evening. On the wall behind the orchestra there was a portrait of Lenin still hanging, which nobody had removed. Since there was no more Soviet Union or any more empire, and communism was dead here, then why was the portrait still there? I speculated that the nostalgic thoughts and feelings of the elderly had prevented its removal.

One day Boris had an amazing surprise for me, when he took me to a Russian country house. There were people on the threshold of the house who ushered me inside and some women in the kitchen who greeted me. Soon I found myself in front of an old man lying on a bed with his eyes closed. Boris whispered in my ear that he was dying, and then he called the man by name but received no response. But when he told him that an Italian had come to visit him, he made a small movement of his eyes, slowly opening them to stare intently at me. I spoke to him in Italian and his face lit up. He made some effort to sit up in bed, for he too was Italian. He had arrived there during the last war with one of the few Italian regiments in Russia, and had never returned to Italy. He grasped my hands and shook them with all his remaining strength. Though his voice was weak and he spoke with difficulty, he clearly had a Piemontese accent. We talked like old friends for almost two hours and it seemed that he had forgotten that he was about to die.

He described his misadventures during the war with a bit of humour, which is easier to do when the experiences are diluted by the ingredient of time. He related, for example, that when they walked around at temperatures of minus 42 degrees, with the snow up to their knees, they stuffed cardboard or newspapers in their boots. At minus 42 if you have leather shoes made with nails your toes would be crushed. The snow and cold make the leather so hard that after an hour you would have no more feet. Since the grease in the Model 91 rifle, the weapon issued to them, froze, you couldn't shoot it, so that all you carried around was a hunk of useless ice. But the Russian sub-machine gun was made to shoot at those temperatures because it used special grease. Because the Italian trucks had no antifreeze, before they could be used they had to light fires under the truck to thaw them out. Imagine coming under sudden attack and instead of fighting back or retreating, you had to light a fire under your trucks? After the tanks have rolled over you, you could stay warm by the leftover blaze. The Russians were especially trained to fight in those temperatures. They traveled and fought in American-made tanks unloaded in Vladivostok, where they were supplied with gasoline and everything else they needed.

An Italian soldier's coat turned into a crust of ice if it got wet, so you just became embalmed in it. You couldn't even open your coat to take out a fresh rifle magazine. Thousands died in the snow. What few horses and mules they had were shot and then usually eaten. If they couldn't get into a house for shelter at night but had stay outside next to a fire, they were doomed. They could not survive the night at those temperatures so they needed to take over a village every day. When the Germans arrived, they massacred everyone and settled themselves into the homes.

One day they arrived at a village at dusk; the Italian soldiers were really only boys aged between 18 and 20. They approached one of the houses, called the *isbas*, freezing and starving; they opened a door with guns drawn in case there were any Russians inside. To their surprise, there they were sitting at the table eating and staring strangely at the young intruders. The Russian women had their hair in braids and one of the men made a gesture of invitation and they all started eating together. In the morning the Russian men left, letting the soldiers sleep. Some Italians remained forever. Many changed their names and blended into the countryside. These short, dark-skinned boys fell in love with these tall, very beautiful, Russian women.

Pino, the Italian telling me these stories, had a ten day pass to return to Italy on the day before the Russian attack on the River Don. He had a Russian girlfriend and did not know if he would ever see her again. When he learned during the night that there was going to be a Russian attack, he decided then and there not to take his leave. After the war ended, he decided to stay in Russia—probably in Italy he had another family and he didn't have the courage to return there. He later married his Russian girlfriend, who had, by now, already passed away. He recalled that when he had known her during the war, she had clear eyes and auburn hair with pigtails. We parted with the promise to meet again the next day, but he died during the night.

Boris had a rickety and grungy old car in a small garage close to the house which I repaired and then rented from him. With Boris as a guide, I began to venture out beyond the village. First we went fishing on Lake Baikal. Later the whole family would come and once also Irina met us near Baikal with some friends. At first I did not see her. She was so bundled up that you could only see her blue eyes and a lock of blond hair that poked out from under her headgear.

I could not see the lake, but instead just an immense ice rink on which people walked and a few trucks drove. Using a regular chain saw Boris cut a hole in the ice and then threw a hook down into it to snag a few fish. Baikal is the largest and deepest lake on the earth and is populated by many seals of unknown origin. Some couples who had set up their tents on the ice even had sleeping bags with them. Siberians sometimes go sunbathing on the ice because, in that infinite space they call home, with the icy wind slashing your face, the sun is one of the most precious things to them, infusing a bit of warmth and encouraging their joy of living.

I was beginning to feel part of the family and yet whenever I saw something nice I thought about my wife and my son and I imagined sharing the things that I was seeing with them. In the daydreams that developed at such times I saw my son running on the snow, all decked out in winter gear and my wife, appearing beautiful as always, completely wrapped up like a bunny rabbit with sexy sunglasses. Then I pondered the fact that I had been unable to make her happy, but that, if she were here at this moment, she would see a different, unrecognizable me, and we could start afresh, right from this spot and at this moment, on this vast expanse of ice.

One evening while a little drunk I confided in Boris, telling him my whole story. I described my wife, who had become a complete stranger to me and the death that had taken both her and an insoluble enigma away forever. He responded to my saga by telling me that I was in the right place and that if I could wait patiently a solution would present itself when I least expected it. He told me with passion about the very popular sorcerers, called shamans, who enjoy great respect and favour in Siberia. They communicate with the spirits and divinities, they can cure people and call upon powers that go beyond the earthly or ephemeral. Siberia was the home of many visionaries and shamans, who were persecuted by the communist regime because they abhorred and banned all forms of spiritualism.

Boris was very religious and said that all my problems were a result of the lack of God in my life. There is a boundary beyond which the mind can lose its limitations, where fears dissolve and the world is eternal and absolute. There is a sense today that God has disappeared. In the 20th century God was shut out by communism but now He was being killed by capitalism. Yet we cannot stop looking for Him, for no man can really live without God since there appears to be nothing more meaningless than a world without Him. People today have lost faith and no longer communicate with the supernatural. But without the supernatural, life has no answers.

I've always been personally sceptical about the supernatural or someone credited with supernatural abilities. But Boris seemed so convinced of their reality and powers that he stimulated my curiosity and I promised myself to visit one of them sooner or later. There are many shamans in Siberia. As survivors of both the religious and communist persecutions, they perhaps most represent the character of this land. They reflect the soul of the Siberians, being both intuitive and rebellious.

Now that I had a car I could even venture out alone, often returning to Lake Baikal at the point where the Angara River leaves the lake. Alone I challenged northernmost Siberia which is less easily travelled because of the lack of public transport facilities. The area begins some 250 km. north of Irkutsk. Saying that you are out of this world is not an exaggeration here, since there are no roads but only directions and the cars and their drivers actually cut the path themselves. Occasionally there are footsteps in the snow that intrude on the void and disappear into nothingness. Because you have no reference points, you become much more alert, attentive to various sounds or noises. The first and overwhelming feeling here is that of loneliness, surrounded by a dimension too large to comprehend. Sounds are lost in the silence and one feels a sense of panic, the fear of something never tried before.

One of the first things they teach you here is not to stray too far beyond the perimeter of a city. Death from frostbite can occur without warning or even without you realizing it is happening. You may feel a slight shock, the body stiffens suddenly like a manikin, and you will shut down in silence, without even a cry. Once Boris told me, "here you cannot carve out the customary world designed for human life, as you do in Europe. Siberian nature is more powerful than any of us, and the price you pay by underestimating that truth could be your life." Even in the summer it's dangerous. The melting ice forms swamps full of mosquitoes where it is easy to sink. There are those who ventured out and never returned—maybe some poacher in search of deer or bears. Outside the town it is easy to get lost and never find the way back. During snow storms, when the darkness seems endless or when the environment seems overly hostile, there is a great danger of succumbing to the desire to wrap yourself around a bottle of vodka and just get lost. I don't know what I was looking for while I was traipsing around amongst the ice but maybe my premature death was the solution of which Boris had spoken?

Then in that desert of ice I suddenly saw an apparition in the form of a restaurant, and I heard a woman burst out laughing. The door of the restaurant opened suddenly and a young girl, still laughing, appeared to be trying to escape while an elderly woman grabbed her by the arm and dragged her inside. I felt compelled to stop at that restaurant to get some refreshment—some *pelmeni* maybe, a kind of dumpling—and also to satisfy my curiosity at what I had seen and to savour a little breath of life. The young girl I had seen at the door continually stared at me and, although nothing was said, she had disturbingly expressive eyes. The older woman, who turned out to be the girl's mother, watched us constantly and gave non-verbal indications that I should converse with her little girl. Perhaps she wanted a better future for her daughter and saw me as a likely path to that future. And I had, evidently, the credentials to be the right type; presumably well-off, a man of the world, a bringer of news, life, exotic places.

The girl had a beautiful face, black hair and green eyes. I couldn't believe that such a striking creature could be in the middle of nowhere, waiting for the rare and unlikely appearance of customers or someone to care for her. I had the sudden desire to take her away from this desolation, and help her to discover a little of the real, civilized world. Maybe in Irkutsk she could visit a theater, try some exotic coffees, go strolling among the shops or buy some clothes. When I finally recovered from my fantasy, I saw that she was making some strange signs and pulling out her tongue. The realization struck me that she was not quite right or maybe even retarded. The mother told me that she had never been out of that place.

When I eventually left the restaurant, the girl followed me to the doorway apparently to say good bye and then she just stood there motionless until I left. Maybe the harsh conditions of life and the isolation of the villages creates mental problems for some of its inhabitants. I had already noticed some strange behaviour in people but there are also people who have special sensitivities. Maybe the Siberians differ from other Russians because they are more instinctive and creative, and in some cases also visionary.

They can surprise you at any time, because there is a thin line that divides the normal from the mad.

By now we were enjoying the New Year's holidays. On December 31st, I drove my car to a small village, Bolshoe Goloustnoe, situated on the shore of Lake Baikal, to celebrate the New Year with some friends. Boris was already there waiting for me. I was being careful not to divert right or left in order to avoid sliding into the snow. Like all Siberians I had a shovel in the car, because it's not unusual to have to stop and shovel snow to clear the road.

I didn't arrive at my destination because I had taken a wrong turn. The temperature was minus twenty eight. In addition I had forgotten to refuel and I was already low. It was night and there were no cars or anybody within sight! If my gasoline ran out then I would not even be able to turn on the heater. It was already dark, so I tried to get as close as possible to something looking like a village. I drove very slowly to save petrol and even though I had a mobile phone with me it had no signal. Getting out of the car, I started running madly in the direction of a village, but there were no lights in the windows of the houses and I could not see anyone around. By this time I was shivering from the unbearable cold, when I finally saw a tiny light in one of the windows. Somewhat relieved, I rushed up to the house and opened the door without hesitating, which was strangely unlocked. In front of me was a frightened little girl accompanied by a woman who mysteriously appeared beside her. Unfortunately she didn't understand any English and looked as terrified as the little girl. I discovered there was nobody else in that house, aside from her and the baby, so I tried to explain the situation with what little Russian I had learned.

This was an actual inhabited village but was strictly a summer residence where people usually spent only that season of the year. She could not let me die in the cold, so she had to welcome me into her home. Was there another choice for either of us? So I found myself spending New Year's Eve with this woman, huddled close to the fire while her television aired special year end programs of seasonal songs and dances. She was wearing a tracksuit and sneakers while was in my evening dress, and I tried to put together a few words to communicate with her, with the help of a little dictionary. A few days earlier she had deserted her drunken husband and had taken refuge in this summer house. Until just minutes before we were both lonely and distressed.

Now through some strange coincidence we were spending the New Year together. Despite the difficulty of dialogue, the long silences and elusive glances we exchanged, I felt myself well and at peace there. She also seemed at ease, despite the presence of this stranger in her house.

A few minutes before midnight, she got up suddenly without saying anything, and opened the door to leave. I ran after her. I thought she was crazed, but nearby there was a *banya*, so she took off her clothes in the locker room and went in. After having consumed vodka, entering a *banya* can be dangerous, as this has triggered numerous heart attacks. Since many Russians still do so without consequences I hoped that would be the case with me. At that point, I removed my own clothes, entered the *banya* and sat down beside her. There we were, sitting side by side, feigning indifference like strangers on a train, nervously glancing at the clock on the wall while awaiting the stroke of midnight.

For a brief moment in that *banya* I suffered a strange hallucination that caused a shiver down my spine. Looking at this woman sitting beside me I clearly saw my wife. The profile was the same but how could this be possible? What was happening to me? Was the tension of the last few months finally getting to me? She really did seem like my wife.

At midnight, completely naked, she left the *banya* and took a dip in the snow. I stood paralyzed like a dead man but then I closed my eyes and throwing caution to the wind—it was, after all, minus 28 outside—I also darted outside and threw myself naked into the snow. The feeling that followed was indescribable and certainly unforgettable! The drastic change of temperature seems to give you a tremendous boost of energy, almost akin to a rebirth!

I woke up with a strange twinkle in my eyes caused by a ray of sunlight piercing the curtain. I consciously felt that this was a different day for me. The sun appeared opaque, flooding the valley and our room with a sweet soft light. I stood mesmerized at the window for fear that the effect would disappear at any moment. Later upon exiting the house I heard the sound of a car. It was a UAZ, the famous Russian jeep—frankly it was one of the few vehicles that could help me in the snow. The driver had seen my car and was stopping by to offer help as if he had been called to do so. I appreciated his kindness, although the gasoline that he poured into my car was less than the best.

After fixing the car, I returned to the house to say goodbye to Kira, my hostess. Thinking back I would have stayed, because for the first time thoughts of my wife were not haunting me. I got the impression that she wanted me to stay too, but neither of us said a word. Boris and my other new friends were waiting for me to spend the first of the New Year with them, so I prepared to leave. Just when I was starting up the engine, Kira broke the silence and asked me if I wanted to stay a few more days. She didn't have to ask twice. It was then January 1st, 2001.

Her house had two floors and was furnished with taste and quality. I surmised that she belonged to an upper class social circle, not only because of the cultured way that she carried herself but also because her cottage, being only a summerhouse, was usually built by and for well-off families who resided in the city. Siberians love to spend time in their dachas, which are rarely very far from the cities where they live. They come for holidays or weekends, going out to a *banya* with friends to drink beer or vodka.

With Kira I re-entered the life of a couple enjoying the pleasure of sharing a home together. She is a nice lady, with striking gray eyes and jet black hair. She displays some particularly interesting expressions, sometimes very serious and a little melancholic. Yet she also is very sensitive, despite her outward appearance, because there are moments when she explodes with joie de vivre. One night some of her friends came over to have a good time, bringing the usual abundant supply of vodka along with them. She cooked some *shashlyk*—lamb—but as the evening progressed I felt myself becoming uneasy. I was impatient for her friends to leave, without realizing at the time that I was falling back into my old familiar attitude. I was returning to my default state of being fearful, possessive and needful of defending my house, by erecting a barrier between myself, mine and the world. It was not a good mode for me or for us.

After about a month I left Boris and moved in with her. For both of us a new life had started but it wasn't the life of a standard couple, because she turned out to be a dynamic, sporty woman. Her loves were those of men—she loved to go fishing and it became our passion. Getting up early during Baikal's thawed period we fished at night or before dawn, because the lake is very deep and the fish take refuge at the bottom during daylight time. We caught and cooked fresh on the grill the famous omul, which lives only in this lake. This delicacy is very expensive in restaurants because of the difficulty of catching it. If you put an omul in any water tank it will die almost immediately, because it can only live in Lake Baikal, where the water is so clean as to be drinkable and which has a perfectly balanced ecosystem of anti-polluting microorganisms.

For shamans, the Baikal hides many mysteries, including the disappearances of many people and other stories bordering on legend. I have personally witnessed unpredictable storms just like on the ocean and I've seen a procession of boats head out to appease the spirits of the lake with traditional songs. Most shamans consider Baikal inhabited by spirits possessing occult powers, so the nearer the lake they live the greater a shaman's powers are focused. Sooner or later I thought that I would have to consult one, so great was my need to know the truth of my past. I felt that there was something to be discovered, yet at the same time, out of fear, I was reluctant. Maybe a shaman was the last remaining hope for me to try to connect spiritually with my wife.

The time of Maslenitsa was at hand—this is a Russian traditional festival that takes place during the week before Lent, which lasts one week and more or less resembles a carnival. It's characterized by incredible joy, unbridled revelry and uproar with which the population greets the end of a long and dreary winter. They were welcoming the spring, at a temperature of minus 15, with funny shows in the streets as well as sled rides, sing-alongs, ice-mountain building and much dancing. They prepare a pancake called *bliny*, which is round and symbolic of the sun, and is served with lots of sweets, honey, caviar and salmon. On the last day of Maslenitsa, they burn a straw puppet, representing the dark symbol of winter.

Among Kira's many hobbies was the collection of *sagaan dailya*, an herb much used in Siberia, which grows in Buryatia, on the slopes of Mount Sayany. This plant seems to grow spontaneously anywhere, so this herb is present in many houses in Siberia despite the fact that it grows naturally only in Buryatia. Locals believe that it should be picked only at certain times of the day and practice an actual picking ritual. Used mostly in tea or other hot beverages, it has the effect of giving one more energy and reducing fatigue. To pick this herb we traveled by foot, because most of the places where it grows can be reached only this way or by horseback, or, for the well-to-do, by helicopter.

Helicopters, while expensive, can be very useful for movement within Siberia, and so we also used them sometimes ourselves. She even involved me in this experience, although I was quite hesitant.

One evening we landed by helicopter on the island of Olkhon, which is right in the middle of Lake Baikal and is considered the heart of shamanism. Boris also came with us, because he knew the island well. It was a place of surreal landscapes, supporting a few people who live there in primitive conditions, without even electricity!

Some of the local inhabitants organized a party with dancing, singing and plenty of vodka. Toward evening a very strong wind arose and everyone remained transfixed, listening to sound of the wind. Then I heard a faint drum beat, which gradually became stronger. An old, long haired, wild-looking woman started writhing around, drawing everybody's attention. Her eyes were bloodshot and fearsome and while I stared at her, I noticed some attitudes and poses familiar to me. I saw my son doing a familiar stretching of his arms while he crossed his fingers, which he did commonly as he left the dinner table at night. And then I saw another sign that I knew very well, a tic of the lips that my wife often displayed when she was nervous. The old woman was writhing as if she wanted to remove something from her body. It seemed that there was another presence within her. Could it be the spirit of my wife coming to see me?

The shaman was tormented because, as I was then told, she had incorporated my very soul into her and she was trying to liberate my mind. My fears, torments, mental contortions, all my obsessions had become an intricate tangle that was stirring in her brain and reflected through her eyes. Then she approached me and started talking to me in a strange language sounding like both Russian and Italian at the same time.

It was absurd I know, but I now seemed to understand everything and I felt my energy increase, as if something heavy inside me was melting away. Some may believe that it was only the power of suggestion, but I lived it in the flesh. It seemed to me that I was seeing my wife for the first time and I actually understood her now, even though she was no more. Over many years we had hidden from each other. My whole personality had been constructed as a defense from the world. I had taken our whole relationship for granted because I was afraid of having to question or challenge any part of it. The end result was that I was not attentive to her moods, her silences or her states of mind. She had become a bundle of emotions and feelings, eager to erupt and be expressed, but I was neither interested in hearing about them or dealing with them.

She loved me but ended up betraying me. She wanted to open her heart to me, but I was like a wall through which she couldn't penetrate. In my defensive cloister I was unable or unwilling to understand her. And surely in my mental state I would never have accepted her moments of weakness or psychological crisis. She was helpless to find a way out, but then came the car crash. So perhaps the escape that she couldn't construct herself and that I wouldn't help her with was provided by mere circumstance. Such is the tragic irony of life.

In some ways I have finally made peace with my wife and with myself, opening up the way for a truly new beginning.

A Psychological Perspective

Can the immersion in a life of extreme conditions, bordering on the limits of endurance, help the mind to escape obsessions? Can a total removal from one's native environment, into a distant and alien world, help one forget an acute and unbearable pain?

The answer to these questions may be found in this story. Leaving his old life behind, he still struggles to rid himself of the memory of his loved ones. But his unbearable pain unlocks his fears, his timid and methodical personality. He becomes a new man with nothing to lose; he can finally take risks. In his earlier life, he was unable to take chances or to accept the crisis in his marriage. Now that he understands his wife, he can begin to live a new relationship with greater awareness.

About the Author

DR. ROBERTO DI MARCO holds qualifications in psychiatry, psychology and clinical criminology. He has specialized in the psychology of human relationships within couples, families and society, and lectured in the Department of Neurological Science, the Italian University in Rome, from 1982 to 1989. He has also long studied and consulted on the psychological impact of the expatriate experience.

In addition to the current work, and his other professional writings, including the acclaimed *Il gioco delle coppie* [The Games Couples Play], Roberto Di Marco is also the author of novels and theatre plays, such as *Occhi indiscreti* [Prying Eyes], performed at Rome's prestigious Belli Theatre. He has contributed articles on various subjects to magazines such as *L'Espresso, Penthouse, Cosmopolitan* and *Playboy*. Dr. Di Marco was the author of a monthly column on sexology for the Italian edition of *Playboy* magazine, from 1999 to 2001.

www.ingramcontent.com/pod-product-compliance
Lightning Source LLC
Chambersburg PA
CBHW032125160426
43197CB00008B/526